Managing International Business in China

With the rise of China in the world economy, investors from all over the world are moving to explore business opportunities in this market. Managing international business in a transition economy such as China is a daunting challenge. Tian presents a practical guide to major managerial issues faced by foreign investors in the Chinese market, including the strategic management of *guanxi*, entry mode selection, alliance management, negotiating with Chinese partners, productions operations management, human resource management, marketing management, the protection of intellectual property rights, and corporate financial management. These issues are analysed in the light of relevant theoretical models of international business, with reference to the current management practices of transnational corporations operating in China. With up-to-date case studies, questions for discussion and recommended reading lists at the end of each chapter, this book can be used as a textbook for postgraduate programmes in international business or other management disciplines, and as a textbook for executive training programmes.

XIAOWEN TIAN is Associate Professor in International Business and Chinese Management at Nottingham University, and Associate Professor in International Business at Bond University Business School, Queensland, Australia.

Managing International Business in China

Xiaowen Tian

CAMBRIDGE
UNIVERSITY PRESS

CAMBRIDGE UNIVERSITY PRESS
Cambridge, New York, Melbourne, Madrid, Cape Town, Singapore, São Paulo

Cambridge University Press
The Edinburgh Building, Cambridge CB2 8RU, UK

Published in the United States of America by Cambridge University Press, New York

www.cambridge.org
Information on this title: www.cambridge.org/9780521679930

© Xiaowen Tian 2007

First published 2007

Printed in the United Kingdom at the University Press, Cambridge

A catalogue record for this publication is available from the British Library

Library of Congress Cataloguing in Publication data
Tian, Xiaowen, 1956–
Managing international business in China / Xiaowen Tian. – 1st ed.
  p. cm.
Includes bibliographical references and index.
ISBN-13: 978 0 521 86188 5 (hardback : alk. paper)
ISBN-13: 978 0 521 67993 0 (pbk. : alk. paper)
1. International business enterprises – China – Management – Case studies.   2. Investments, Foreign –
China – Case studies.   3. Joint ventures – China – Management – Case studies.   I. Title.
HD62.4.T53   2007
658′.0490951 – dc22   2006036014

ISBN 978-0-521-86188-5 hardback
ISBN 978-0-521-67993-0 paperback

Contents

Figures

Tables

Boxes

Preface

China is the most populous country in the world. Following rapid economic growth and impressive improvement in people's living standards in recent years, China is now widely accepted as a market with enormous potential. The Chinese market is still limited in per capita terms, but it is precisely this low income per capita that enables China to enjoy a pronounced advantage in cheap labour. Attracted by the huge market potential and the low-cost labour force, investors from all over the world are currently pouring into China to do business.

Doing business in China is not an easy task, however. For some years China has been in the process of transitioning gradually from a command economy to a market economy. This gradual transition has resulted in a complicated and uncertain business regime, which puzzles even the most knowledgeable experts on China. In addition, Chinese culture is different from those in other parts of the world, which can often frustrate foreign investors. For foreign investors, therefore, the main challenge is to learn how to manage business in the uncertain, unfamiliar and complicated Chinese environment. Unfortunately, there is no textbook that comprehensively addresses the managerial issues faced by foreign investors in the Chinese business environment. The aim of this book is to fill this vacuum.

The idea of writing the book occurred to me when I was a research fellow at the Centre for International Business at the University of Leeds in 2003, working on a project on transnational corporations in China. Several months later I took up a position as a lecturer at Nottingham University Business School. I decided to design a module on managing transnational corporations in China for postgraduate students in the management sciences. In preparing the module I went through numerous books, journals, newspapers and online sources, and identified a number of key managerial issues faced by almost all transnational corporations doing business in China. These issues involve a wide range of business activities, including entry mode selection, international business alliances, negotiation, production operations management, marketing management, human resource management, the protection of intellectual property rights, corporate finance management and cross-cultural management. I addressed these issues in eleven lectures, which form the framework of this book.

In delivering the lectures, my thinking was that these managerial issues needed to be discussed in the light of the relevant theoretical frameworks and models of international business and management, with reference to the current business and management practices of transnational corporations operating in China. It was also my belief that these issues should, moreover, be discussed in the context of China's general business environment and specific international business regimes. In consideration of the fact that international business theories and models have already been investigated in detail in many international business textbooks, I deliberately paid great attention to the experiences of transnational corporations in managing business in the business environment as it actually exists in China. As a result, I used a large number of real-world cases to illustrate the points I wanted to make throughout the lectures. I found it very rewarding to move along this line of thinking: the number of students registered in the module increased from forty-one in 2003 to 124 in 2006! I would like to take this opportunity to thank all the students who participated in the lectures and seminar discussions and made helpful comments and suggestions.

Encouraged by positive feedback from the students, I decided to draft book chapters and contact publishers. The responses from several publishers were very encouraging, in particular from Cambridge University Press, where editors Chris Harrison, Katy Plowright, Lynn Dunlop and Paula Parish showed great interest in the book, and sent three sample chapters to experts in the field for review. The review reports were very helpful; without the encouragement from the Cambridge University Press editors and the constructive comments from the anonymous referees the book would not exist in its current form. I would like to take this opportunity to thank Chris Harrison, Katy Plowright, Lynn Dunlop and Paula Parish for their excellent editorial guidance, and the three anonymous referees for their helpful comments. I would also like to thank Mike Richardson, Phyllis van Reenen and Alison Powell for their brilliant work in copy-editing, indexing and producing the book. Finally, I would like to express my gratitude to Michael Barbalas, president of the American Chamber of Commerce in China, who kindly read through the manuscript and made valuable comments and helpful suggestions.

This book can be used as a textbook for postgraduate students in international business or any management disciplines with an area focus on

Asia-Pacific business, and as a textbook for the short training programmes that are offered to executives who are assigned to China operations. In addition, this book can serve as a major reference book for any foreigners doing business in China, or any university academics doing research into transnational corporations there. I will feel greatly rewarded if this book is of assistance to its readers.

Xiaowen Tian

1 Introduction

Let China sleep, for when she wakes she will shake the world.

Napoleon Bonaparte

Some 200 years after Napoleon Bonaparte, the brilliant general who became emperor of France, made the above statement, China has indeed begun to wake up and shake the world. In the past twenty-five years China has been the fastest-growing economy in the world, with an average annual gross domestic product (GDP) growth rate of 9 per cent. The rapid economic growth in a country with a population of 1.3 billion implies, among other things, enormous business opportunities, which attract millions of business people to China from all over the world. Doing business with China has now become a fashion, or, rather, a necessity for survival.

In this opening chapter we first discuss China's rise in the world economy in recent decades from a historical perspective, the driving forces behind the rise and the significance of China's rise to international businesses. We then move on to illustrate the rapid pace of developments with regard to international businesses in China, with a focus on the massive inflows of foreign direct investment (FDI). Finally, we analyse the prime challenge faced by transnational corporations (TNCs) operating in China using a four-choice model, and set out the structure of the book.

The rise of China in the world economy

When Napoleon made the above statement about two centuries ago China was a great economic power in the world, as shown in figure 1.1, accounting for just over 30 per cent of world GDP. Afterwards, however, China – as described by Napoleon – 'fell asleep', and the Chinese economy weakened significantly. Up to the middle of the twentieth century China accounted for just 5 per cent

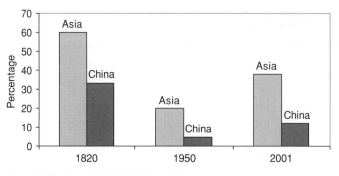

Figure 1.1   Share of China in world GDP (1820–2001)
Source: Maddison website at http://www.eco.rug.nl/~Maddison.

of world GDP, only one-sixth of what it had about one and a half centuries earlier.

Backward and outdated political, economic and social systems were the main cause of China's decline. While Western countries had done away with the long-standing feudal system and begun to move towards democracy and industrialization, Chinese rulers still cherished their outdated social system and resisted reforms and innovations. Their closed minds allowed China to fall prey to foreign commercial and political powers, which, armed as they were with up-to-date knowledge and technology, found that China was too weak to offer any resistance. From the 1840s onwards China was repeatedly defeated by expansionist foreign powers in wars of aggression, including the Opium War (1839–1842) and the War against the Allied Forces (1900). The invasions of foreign powers further weakened the country, accelerating the decline of the Chinese economy.

These wretched experiences taught the Chinese a lesson: the backward come under attack. After the Opium War generations of Chinese undertook the long, hard struggle for a resurgent, modern China. Under the leadership of Dr Sun Yat-Sen the Chinese people overthrew the country's last feudal dynasty, the Qing dynasty, and established the Republic of China in 1911. Soon afterwards, however, China suffered a series of calamitous events: large-scale fighting between warlords, invasion and brutal occupation by imperial Japan, and then civil war between the Nationalists and the Communists. Headed by Mao Zedong, the Communist Party defeated the Nationalist Party and established the People's Republic of China (PRC) in 1949.

Following the establishment of the PRC China enjoyed a relatively long period of peace (except for short-lived involvement in the Korean War, 1950–1953), and managed to rebuild the economy from the ruins left by the protracted wars and political turmoil. Not for long, however; fierce political conflicts broke out among the top leaders of the Communist Party, leading to a series of nationwide mass campaigns, including the One Hundred Flowers Movement (1956), the Anti-Rightist Campaign (1957), the Great Leap Forward (1958) and the Great Proletarian Cultural Revolution (1966–1976). The Communist idealists, headed by Mao Zedong (the Party chairman), gained the upper hand in these struggles, and led China in the direction of an orthodox Marxist-Leninist ideology and a rigid economic planning system aimed at de-linking from the global market system (Tian, 1996, 1998). Realistic Party leaders, such as Liu Shaoqi (the chairman of the PRC) and Deng Xiaoping (the Party general secretary), were purged during the Cultural Revolution, and the economy again suffered tremendously. By the 1970s China was lagging far behind not only the advanced market economies of the West but also the four emerging 'Asian Dragons' of East Asia: South Korea, Taiwan, Hong Kong and Singapore.

After the death of Mao Zedong in 1976 Deng Xiaoping began to emerge as the paramount Party leader, and he initiated policy changes in 1978 that have fundamentally transformed China ever since. Deng's slogan 'White or black, it is a good cat so long as it catches mice' has served as a justification for introducing Western-style market systems to China. The core of Deng's policy initiatives is to make full use of market mechanisms, or, in other words, re-link with the global market system, domestically as well as internationally (Tian, 1996). To re-link with the global market system, China is trying to move from a plan-based economy to a market-based economy, and open up to capital, goods and services from the advanced market economies. The re-linking strategy is proving to be a success, and it has been the main driving force behind China's rapid economic growth for the last few decades. As shown in figure 1.2, the Chinese economy has taken off like a rocket since 1978. Even though the outcome of the rapid economic growth has not been distributed evenly among social groups, the living standard of all Chinese people has undeniably improved enormously. Very few, if any, Chinese would like to go back to the old days of orthodox socialism, and the momentum for reform and opening up remains strong and irresistible. It is expected that China will move further in the direction of re-linking with the global market system, and the Chinese economic boom is far from over.

The rise of China in the global economy has far-reaching implications for the world as a whole, because it generates growth momentum for other countries by increasing demand for their goods, services and capital. By common consent, China has been the powerhouse of the world economy for the last

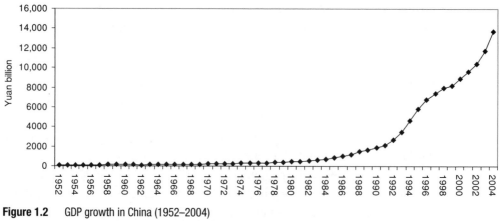

Figure 1.2   GDP growth in China (1952–2004)
Source: *China Statistical Yearbook 2005.*

two decades. In particular, China's rise carries enormous significance for the international business community. China accounts for nearly one-fifth of the world's population, and the majority of Chinese are in poor rural areas. The size of the market, the low cost of labour and China's growth potential together offer unprecedented business opportunities for foreign investors, with the result that the landscape of international business will be transformed in the decades to come.

Development of international business in China

In the pre-reform period China maintained only minimal economic contacts with the outside world, primarily in the area of foreign trade. After the reforms China became increasingly integrated with other parts of the world, and opened up to a whole range of cross-border economic activities. International businesses have developed very rapidly in China since then.

As shown in figure 1.3, China's foreign trade grew rapidly after 1978. The total value of China's foreign trade reached $1154 billion in 2004, about twenty-one times more than that in 1980. Moreover, there was a noticeable change in the composition of foreign trade during this period, with a significant rise in the share of manufactured goods. From 1980 to 2004, as shown in figure 1.4, the share of manufactures in exports increased from around 50 per cent to over 90 per cent, and the share of manufactures in imports increased from 66 per cent to 85 per cent. This change in the composition of foreign trade is a reflection of the progress that China has made in industrialization

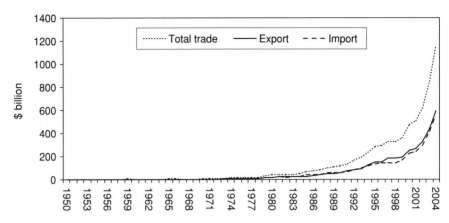

Figure 1.3   Foreign trade with China (1950–2004)
Source: *China Statistical Yearbook 2005*.

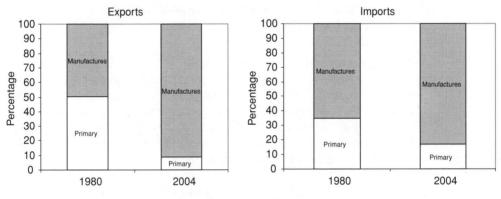

Figure 1.4   Composition of foreign trade with China (1980–2004)
Source: *China Statistical Yearbook 2005*.

over this period. China now has trading relations with almost all countries and regions in the world, with Asian countries being the largest trading partners, followed immediately by Europe and North America (figure 1.5).

The most distinctive feature of the development of international business with China in recent years, however, has been the massive influx of transnational corporations and the boom in foreign direct investment. A clear definition of foreign direct investment and transnational corporation can be found in box 1.1, but suffice it to say that the two terms are used interchangeably in this book to indicate the bulk of international businesses in China today, as they involve direct investment made by a foreign entity in enterprises operating

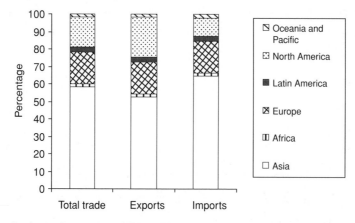

Figure 1.5   Foreign trading partners of China (2004)
Source: *China Statistical Yearbook 2005.*

Box 1.1 Definitions of transnational corporations and foreign direct investment[1]

1. Transnational corporations

TNCs are incorporated or unincorporated enterprises comprising parent enterprises and their foreign affiliates. A parent enterprise is defined as an enterprise that controls assets of other entities in countries other than its home country, usually by owning a certain equity capital stake. An equity capital stake of 10 per cent or more of the ordinary shares or voting power for an incorporated enterprise, or its equivalent for an unincorporated enterprise, is normally considered as the threshold for the control of assets.[2] A foreign affiliate is an incorporated or unincorporated enterprise in which an investor, who is a resident in another economy, owns a stake that permits a lasting interest in the management of that enterprise (an equity stake of 10 per cent for an incorporated enterprise, or its equivalent for an unincorporated enterprise). In the *World Investment Report*, subsidiary enterprises, associate enterprises and branches – defined below – are all referred to as foreign affiliates or affiliates.

- A subsidiary is an incorporated enterprise in the host country in which another entity directly owns more than a half of the shareholders' voting power, and has the right to appoint or remove a majority of the members of the administrative, management or supervisory body.
- An associate is an incorporated enterprise in the host country in which an investor owns a total of at least 10 per cent, but not more than half, of the shareholders' voting power.
- A branch is a wholly or jointly owned unincorporated enterprise in the host country which is one of the following: (i) a permanent establishment or office of the foreign investor; (ii) an unincorporated partnership or joint venture between the foreign direct investor and one or more third parties; (iii) land, structures (except structures owned by government entities) and /or immovable equipment and objects directly owned by a foreign resident;

or (iv) mobile equipment (such as ships, aircraft, gas- or oil-drilling rigs) operating within a country, other than that of the foreign investor, for at least one year.

2. Foreign direct investment
FDI is defined as an investment involving a long-term relationship and reflecting a lasting interest and control by a resident entity in one economy (foreign direct investor or parent enterprise) in an enterprise resident in an economy other than that of the foreign direct investor (FDI enterprise or affiliate enterprise or foreign affiliate). FDI implies that the investor exerts a significant degree of influence on the management of the enterprise resident in the other economy. Such investment involves both the initial transaction between the two entities and all subsequent transactions between them and among foreign affiliates, both incorporated and unincorporated. FDI may be undertaken by individuals as well as business entities. Flows of FDI comprise capital provided (either directly or through other related enterprises) by a foreign direct investor to an FDI enterprise, or capital received from an FDI enterprise by a foreign direct investor. FDI has three components: equity capital, reinvested earnings and intra-company loans.
- Equity capital is the foreign direct investor's purchase of shares of an enterprise in a country other than its own.
- Reinvested earnings comprise the direct investor's share (in proportion to direct equity participation) of earnings not distributed as dividends by affiliates, or earnings not remitted to the direct investor. Such retained profits by affiliates are reinvested.
- Intra-company loans or intra-company debt transactions refer to the short- or long-term borrowing and lending of funds between direct investors (parent enterprises) and affiliate enterprises.

within China in order to acquire a lasting interest. This kind of international business is the focus of analysis for this book, so it warrants closer attention here.

Foreign direct investment started to move into China in 1979, when the Equity Joint Venture Law was issued. In the 1980s, as shown in figure 1.6, FDI grew gradually in China, with an annual inflow of about $1.6 billion. FDI inflows began to slow down again in the immediate aftermath of the Tiananmen Incident in 1989, but soared after Deng Xiaoping called for accelerating economic reforms and further opening up in his much-publicized tour of China's southern provinces in early 1992. Consequently, most of the inflows of FDI in China have occurred after 1992. In 2004 China received $60.6 billion worth of FDI, accounting for more than one-third of total FDI inflows in developing countries and about 15 per cent of FDI inflows worldwide. China has been the largest FDI recipient in the developing world and has consistently been among the top FDI recipients in the world since the mid-1990s.

Today there are about half a million foreign investment enterprises in China, with parent enterprises in more than 170 countries. The foreign investors come

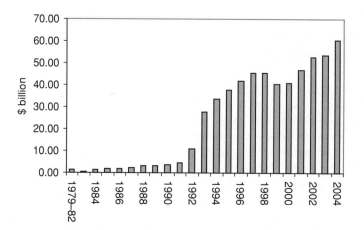

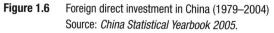

Figure 1.6   Foreign direct investment in China (1979–2004)
Source: *China Statistical Yearbook 2005.*

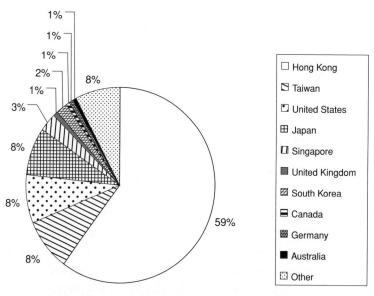

Figure 1.7   Country of origin of FDI in China (1979–2004)
Source: *China Statistical Yearbook 2005.*

mainly from the industrialized or newly industrialized economies in the Asia-Pacific region. In the post-1978 period as a whole, as shown in figure 1.7, Hong Kong was the largest investor, accounting for more than 50 per cent of the total FDI in China, followed by Taiwan, the United States, Japan, Singapore, the United Kingdom, South Korea, Canada and Germany. In recent years the share of FDI from overseas Chinese in Hong Kong, Macau and Taiwan has been declining, while the share of FDI from other parts of the world has increased, indicating that the sources of inward FDI are becoming increasingly diversified over time. Most of the foreign investors were, to varying degrees, more advanced than their Chinese counterparts in terms of production technology and management know-how. Western investors were, for instance, more advanced in high-tech areas, whereas East Asian investors were more advanced in labour-intensive technology. Arguably, China's greatest benefit has been from the technology transfer associated with the massive inflow of FDI (see, for instance, Li, Liu and Parker, 2001; Liu, Parker, Vaidya and Wei, 2001, Buckley, Clegg and Wang, 2002; Tian, Lin and Lo, 2004).

As discussed in chapter 4, foreign direct investments take different forms or entry modes in China. There are three main entry modes of foreign direct investments in China: equity joint ventures (EJVs), cooperative joint ventures (CJVs) and wholly foreign-owned enterprises (WFOEs). In order to maintain control over the pillar industries and to benefit from FDI technology transfer, the Chinese government encourages foreign investors to take the form of joint ventures. In the period from 1979 to 2004 as a whole 44 per cent of FDI was in the form of equity joint ventures, 20 per cent in the form of cooperative joint ventures and 34 per cent in the form of wholly foreign-owned enterprises. Nonetheless, in recent years, with the removal of policy restrictions, FDI in the form of wholly foreign-owned enterprises has increased steadily, while FDI in the form of equity and cooperative joint ventures has declined (figure 1.8). In 2004 wholly foreign owned enterprises accounted for 67 per cent of total FDI. In addition, as shown in chapter 4, some new entry modes of FDI are emerging.

In terms of industry distribution, FDI was first permitted only in oil exploration projects and in a small number of industries. After 1986, and particularly after Deng Xiaoping's southern tour in 1992, foreign investors began to gain access to a wide range of industries, including manufacturing, retailing, real estate, transportation, and banking. Up to 2004 most FDI was made in the secondary sector (60 per cent), with most of the remainder in the tertiary sector (38 per cent) and just 2 per cent in the primary sector. In particular, as shown in table 1.1, the majority of FDI went into manufacturing. There are two reasons for this pattern of industry distribution of FDI. First, China has been very cautious about opening up such service industries as banking, telecommunications and transportation to foreign direct investments, and has set strict restrictions on FDI in these sectors. Secondly, foreign investors are particularly keen to move into manufacturing industry so as to take full advantage of the low labour costs in China.

Table 1.1 Industry distribution of FDI in China (1979–2004)

Specific sector	Percentage share
Manufacturing	63.14
Property and utilities	21.66
Wholesale, retailing and catering	3.33
Construction	2.89
Transport	2.32
Agriculture, forestry, animal husbandry and fishery	1.89
Health care	0.66
Scientific research	0.37
Education	0.29

Source: *China Statistical Yearbook 2005.*

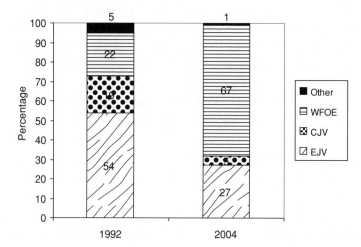

Figure 1.8   Change in entry modes of FDI in China (1992–2004)
Source: *China Statistical Yearbook 2005.*

The geographical distribution of FDI in China has been quite uneven. It is customary to divide China into three regions: eastern, central and western. The eastern region, as shown in map 1.1, consists of twelve provinces located along the coast, and therefore it is also known as the coastal region. The central region consists of nine provinces and the western region consists of ten; together they are called the interior region. As shown in table 1.2, FDI has been primarily concentrated in the coastal region, particularly in Guangdong province. The coastal region enjoys geographical advantages over the interior in terms of the infrastructure, particularly transportation infrastructure. In

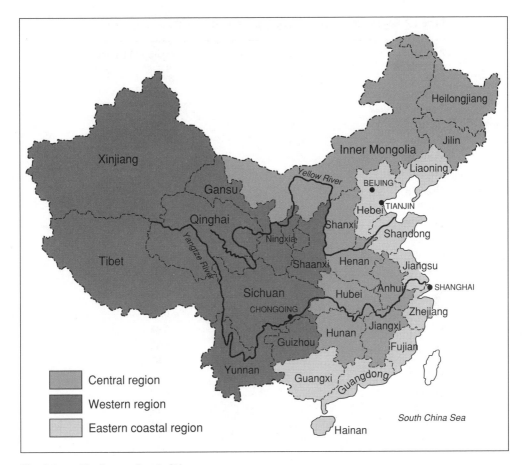

Map 1.1   The three regions in China

addition, as shown in chapter 2, the Chinese government has encouraged FDI to locate in the coastal region from the very beginning of China's opening up. In consideration of the widening gap between the coast and the interior, the Chinese government is now trying to change the uneven regional distribution of FDI in the country, encouraging FDI to move into the interior region.

With China's recent accession to the World Trade Organization (WTO), a new wave of FDI looms large. In particular, three characteristics of the new FDI inflow deserve close attention. First, an increasing number of large-scale transnational corporations will invest in China. Second, an increasing amount of FDI will be in the high-tech areas and capital-intensive projects, such as petroleum, automobile, and large-scale integrated circuits. Third, an increasing amount of FDI will be in the tertiary sector, including securities, banking, telecommunications, transportation and tourism.

Table 1.2 Regional distribution of pledged and realized FDI in China (1979–2004)

Region	Pledged FDI (%)	Realized FDI (%)
East	**88.28**	**87.81**
Beijing	4.49	4.09
Tianjin	3.99	3.90
Hebei	2.00	1.89
Liaoning	5.61	4.39
Shanghai	9.68	8.26
Jiangsu	13.41	12.81
Zhejiang	3.92	3.39
Fujian	9.27	9.47
Shandong	6.49	6.23
Guangdong	24.56	27.86
Hainan	1.62	1.69
Guangxi	1.88	1.85
Central	**7.84**	**8.97**
Inner Mongolia	0.26	0.19
Shanxi	0.52	0.45
Jilin	0.83	0.82
Heilongjiang	0.84	1.01
Anhui	0.83	0.85
Jiangxi	0.70	0.79
Henan	1.20	1.21
Hubei	1.43	1.93
Hunan	1.12	1.53
West	**4.06**	**3.22**
Chongqing	0.60	0.63
Sichuan	1.18	0.95
Guizhou	0.23	0.11
Yunnan	0.42	0.26
Tibet	0.00	0.00
Shaanxi	0.88	0.86
Gansu	0.16	0.13
Qinghai	0.08	0.01
Ningxia	0.07	0.04
Xinjiang	0.16	0.10
Total	**100.00**	**100.00**

Sources: *Almanac of Foreign Economic Relations and Trade of China 1984 to 2005, China Statistical Yearbook 1984 to 2005.*

The challenge faced by transnational corporations in China

Managing international business is a daunting task for TNCs, particularly for those operating in a transition economy such as China. In the international business literature, the argument is put forward that there are a variety of motivations for transnational corporations to move overseas, such as market seeking, technology seeking, resource seeking, diversification seeking and strategic asset seeking (Dunning, 1993). It is argued that different types of TNCs may face different sets of challenges in the overseas markets they enter. In this section, we do not intend to discuss all the challenges faced by the different types of TNCs but, rather, address the prime challenge faced by them all. In so doing, we need to analyse the basic pressures on transnational corporations and the basic strategic options for them to deal with these pressures, using a simplified framework.

We commence our analysis of the pressures and the basic strategic options with a simple assumption: that the primary goal of a company is to make a profit. When every company wants to make profits, there is competition: companies compete with each other to make profits. To an extent, therefore, it is the fierce competition that drives companies to expand overseas. In this competition, a company comes under two major kinds of pressure. The first is differentiation: a company has to differentiate the products it makes from those produced by its competitors in order to make its products competitive in quality and attributes. The second pressure is cost reduction: a company has to keep its costs of production low in order to make its products competitive in price. The ability to deal with these two pressures is, to a large extent, dependent on the core competencies that a company has – that is, the skills, assets and routines that are hard for competitors to imitate. The core competencies can be in any functional area, and could be in the form of production technology, management know-how, brand name, marketing networks, research and development (R&D) facilities or talented managers and workers.

Once a company establishes affiliates in countries other than its home country it becomes a transnational corporation. Overseas expansion can help the TNC deal with the two pressures in three ways. First, it provides new opportunities for the full play and development of core competencies: overseas expansion enables a TNC to exploit its established core competencies in a market where they cannot be easily matched. This is particularly true when a TNC based in an advanced country moves into a developing country such as China, where it can find few competitors to its core competencies in proprietary technology and brand names. Overseas expansion also enables a TNC to develop new core competencies – for instance, in marketing networks and human resources in a new environment. Second, overseas expansion provides new opportunities for differentiation. In particular, a TNC needs to customize its products to the local needs in overseas markets, a process that is known as local differentiation; the localized products differentiate themselves from the products provided by competing companies operating at home. Third, overseas expansion provides new opportunities for cost reduction: overseas expansion enables a TNC to reduce its costs through experience curve economies and location economies (see box 1.2).

Box 1.2 Cost reduction through experience curve economies and location economies

The prime way that overseas expansion can help a transnational corporation reduce costs is through so-called 'experience curve economies'. The concept of experience curve economies is rather involved, but it is very important for an understanding of the rationales for TNC overseas expansion. Put simply, experience curve economies refer to the reduction in costs associated with an increase in output. Experience curve economies occur when there are learning effects or economies of scale. In practice, learning effects and economies of scale are closely linked together; for illustrative purposes, however, they are explained here separately.

'Learning effects' refer to the fact that the unit costs of output are reduced for technological and organizational reasons following an expansion of production scale. Learning effects often come from learning by doing. Through the repetition of the same activities, for instance, workers can learn how to do a job more efficiently, while managers can learn how to carry out a task or run an organization more effectively. That is to say, repetition allows workers and managers to discover improvements and short cuts that increase efficiency and effectiveness. Typically, learning effects tend to be more significant when a technologically complex activity is repeated.

'Economies of scale' refer to the fact that an increase in inputs in production causes output to rise by more than the percentage change in inputs as a result of producing a large volume of output rather than a small one. Economies of scale have many sources, but one of the most important sources is the reduction in unit costs achieved by spreading fixed costs over a larger quantity of the product in question. Suppose that a TNC produces 1000 units of a product, and the fixed costs (the costs that will not increase with the scale of production – e.g. the plant building, the workshop, land and machinery) are estimated to be £1500 while other costs are estimated to be £500. The total costs are, therefore, £2000. The unit costs, which are equal to the total costs divided by the number of units, are £2. Now suppose that the TNC changes to producing 2000 units of the product. The fixed costs remain the same while other costs double. What are the total costs and the unit costs then? The total costs increase to £2500, but the unit costs decrease to only £1.25, much less than before. If human resources are considered as inputs then it is clear that the learning effects discussed earlier could be another source of economies of scale.

The reduction of the unit costs through experience curve economies can make the goods or services that a TNC produces more competitive in price, enabling the TNC to make more profits and beat its competitors in the marketplace. The realization of experience curve economies depends on the demand for the goods or services that a TNC produces. The more overseas markets a TNC enters the larger the demand, and the greater the experience curve economies the TNC can realize.

Overseas expansion can also help a TNC reduce its costs through location economies. As compared to experience curve economies, the concept of location economies is relatively easy to understand. 'Location economies' refer to the economies that arise from locating business activities in the optimal location – the place where the factor endowments that are needed for the business activities are available, abundant and cheap. Due to differences in factor endowments (labour, natural resources, technology, etc.), as illustrated in standard textbooks of international trade, certain countries have a cost advantage in the production of certain products. China, for example, has surplus labour, and therefore excels in the production of labour-intensive goods or services. Clearly, relocating its labour-intensive business activities in China enables a TNC to cut its costs.

The next question is: what are the basic strategic choices for a TNC to reap the benefits from overseas expansion? Generally speaking, there are four basic strategies that a TNC can adopt to reap these benefits. The first is a competency-oriented strategy – that is, a strategy that focuses on increasing profitability by exploiting core competencies. This strategy makes sense for a TNC that has distinctive core competencies, such as Boeing or Microsoft. TNCs pursuing this strategy normally enjoy a monopolistic position in the marketplace and are under little pressure in terms of either cost reduction or local differentiation.

The second is a cost-oriented strategy – that is, a strategy that focuses on increasing profitability by cost reduction through experience curve economies and location economies. TNCs pursuing this strategy tend, for instance, to produce and sell standardized products on a large scale, localize sourcing and localize their staff in order to reduce costs. This strategy makes sense for TNCs that are under relatively high pressure for cost reduction and relatively low pressure for local differentiation, such as those producing semiconductors and mobile components.

The third is a differentiation-oriented strategy – that is, a strategy that focuses on increasing profitability through local differentiation. TNCs pursuing this strategy tend to focus on customizing products and marketing to local needs and, therefore, have a high cost structure. This strategy makes sense

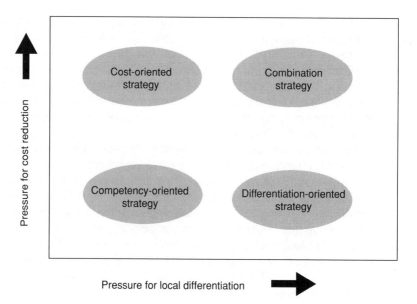

Figure 1.9   The four-choice model

for TNCs that are under relatively high pressure for local differentiation and relatively low pressure for cost reduction, such as those in the spice industry.

The fourth is a combination strategy – that is, a strategy of increasing profitability through core competencies, cost reduction and local differentiation simultaneously. This strategy makes sense for TNCs that are under high pressure for both local differentiation and cost reduction. In reality, most TNCs adopt the combination strategy. Pursuing this strategy is not easy, as cost reduction and local differentiation are sometimes conflicting and contradictory aims; as a result, a balance has to be found on the basis of the particular circumstances a TNC faces.

An illustration of the four-choice model can be found in figure 1.9. The choice of these basic strategies depends largely on the extent to which a TNC is subject to the pressure for cost reduction, or the pressure for local differentiation, or both. The four-choice model provides TNCs with a simple framework for strategic thinking. Whatever the specific area, business strategies ultimately serve the broad strategic objectives of cost reduction, local differentiation, or a strengthening of core competence. A negotiation strategy should, for instance, enable TNCs to reach business deals that help with cost reduction, local differentiation and the strengthening of core competencies to enable the TNCs to make profits.

The prime challenge faced by transnational corporations in China is how they achieve their broad strategic objectives in specific functional areas and business activities in the particular context of China, which is different from those in other parts of the world in many ways. The majority of the chapters in this book are designed to discuss how to deal with this challenge in specific functional areas and business activities, including production operations, marketing, human resource management (HRM), corporate finance, negotiation, entry mode selection, alliance management, the protection of intellectual property rights (IPR) and the practice of *guanxi*. In so doing, we focus on the specific management issues in these areas and activities, and the specific business strategies to address these issues in the particular Chinese context. These management issues and business strategies are all related, directly or indirectly, to the broad strategic objectives analysed in the four-choice model. While reading through the various chapters of this book, we need to locate these management issues and business strategies in the context of the broad strategic objectives analysed in this section, so that we do not lose sight of the whole picture.

The structure of the book

Before moving on to these issues, we first, in chapter 2, discuss the policy environment for international business in China, with a focus on the foreign trade regime, the foreign direct investment regime and the foreign exchange regime. There are considerable restrictions on international business in China, which are being removed only gradually as the process of re-linking with the global market system slowly moves forward. To do business in China, transnational corporations need to understand the rationales, if there are any, for the progressive, rather than 'big bang', removal of these restrictions, and the policy uncertainties as well as the business opportunities associated with China's gradualist approach to liberalization.

Apart from the uncertain policy environment, TNCs need to understand and deal with the Chinese business culture, which is almost certainly something they are not familiar with. *Guanxi* has been identified, for instance, as an important, if not unique, feature of the Chinese business culture that puzzles foreign investors, particularly those from the West. In consideration of the importance of *guanxi*, we devote an entire chapter – chapter 3 – to a discussion of how to make use of the practice of *guanxi* strategically in order to achieve business objectives in China. First we introduce the concept of *guanxi*, and then we present a framework for the strategic management of *guanxi* in the Chinese context. The framework covers environment scanning for *guanxi*, the formulation and implementation of *guanxi*-based strategies and the evaluation and control of *guanxi*-based strategies.

To enter a new country market, TNCs need to know what market entry modes are available in the country in question, and choose carefully between the different modes. The selection of market entry modes is of vital importance, because often it is this that determines the success or failure of an international business. In chapter 4 we turn to the topic of how to select entry modes in China. We first introduce the literature, and propose a hierarchical approach to entry mode selection. Then we examine the modes available for TNCs in China, and changes in the entry modes utilized by TNCs in recent decades. After that we discuss the key factors that TNCs need to take into consideration in selecting their entry modes. Finally, we discuss the possibility of TNCs adopting different market entry modes simultaneously.

When entering a new country market there is often a need for TNCs to form an alliance with a local business partner in order to gain easy access to local market, resources and personal networks. Local firms also need a foreign partner to facilitate their access to foreign capital, advanced technologies and global market networks. In addition, host-country governments often pre-fer alliances to wholly foreign-owned subsidiaries, for a variety of reasons; the Chinese government, for instance, does not allow TNCs to enter certain pillar industries unless they form an alliance with a local Chinese firm. As a result, international alliances are very popular in many countries in the world, including China. In chapter 5 we discuss key issues relating to the formation and managing of an international alliance in China, such as the typology of international business alliances in China, the advantages and disadvantages of different types of international alliance, partner selection, control over an alliance, and conflict management within an alliance.

To do business in China TNCs need to negotiate with Chinese business partners at all the times. Following on from the acknowledged differences in culture, people in different countries may also have different negotiation styles. It is well known that the differences in negotiation style are most striking between Chinese and Westerners, and that negotiating with Chinese is one of the most challenging tasks for Western investors in the country. In chapter 6 we look at negotiation in the Chinese context. We focus on the characteristics of the Chinese negotiation style, the cultural roots of the style, and the strategies that foreign business people may adopt in negotiating with their Chinese business partners.

Given the huge size of China, TNCs may find it difficult to manage production operations in the country. Production operations are one of the most controversial concepts in the management science, but we define them, in this book, as the 'processes that produce goods and services' or the 'processes that transform inputs into products and services'. Production operations management involves many complicated issues, some of which are very technical. In chapter 7 we address those issues that are most commonly faced by TNCs in managing production operations in China, including the centralization or decentralization of production facilities, the location of production sites, the localization of sourcing and the localization of R&D activities.

Marketing management primarily involves making decisions on the so-called 'four Ps': product, price, promotion and place (distribution). In chapter 8 we discuss the key issues that need to be taken into account in making these decisions. First we introduce the debate initiated by Theodore Levitt on the globalization of markets, and study the implications of the debate for marketing in China. We then move on to discuss making decisions on products in China, with a focus on product localization, and making decisions on the price, with a focus on shifts in pricing strategies. Subsequently we look at promotion in China, concentrating on the conservative tendencies of Chinese consumers, the need for local heroes in promotion campaigns and the importance of the corporate image for promotion. Finally, we analyse the main difficulties faced by TNCs in distribution in China, and the strategies that they can adopt to overcome them.

All business activities, no matter whether they are negotiation, production or marketing, have to be carried out by people in a business organization. It is now widely acknowledged that these people are valuable assets or human resources, and should be properly managed. Human resource management in a foreign country differs from human resource management at home in many ways. In chapter 9 we investigate the major issues faced by TNCs in human resource management in China, including the moves towards staff localization, practical approaches to the retention of local Chinese talents, and expatriate management.

Owing to shortcomings in the current regulatory and enforcement regimes, the violation of intellectual property rights is pervasive in China, which frustrates almost all TNCs operating in the country. In chapter 10 we discuss how to protect IPR in the Chinese context. We first examine the roots of the rampant infringement of intellectual property rights, China's laws and regulations on the protection of IPR, and the enforcement of these laws and regulations. Then we analyse the shortcomings in the current Chinese IPR protection regime, and discuss the practical measures that TNCs can adopt to protect their intellectual property rights in the Chinese context.

The Chinese economic system is still in the process of transition to a market system, so are the Chinese financial system and Chinese corporate finance management practices. Many transnational corporations find that managing corporate finance in China is quite different from what they do at home, and they have tried very hard to cope with the differences. In chapter 11 we look into corporate finance management, concentrating on the major taxation, financing and accounting issues that TNCs need to take into consideration in the country.

Summary

Just as Napoleon said at the beginning of the nineteenth century, when he described China as a sleeping giant and warned that the country would shake the world if she woke up, some 200 years later China is indeed beginning to wake up, and emerging as an economic giant in East Asia. China has now become the powerhouse of the world economy, and has attracted millions of investors and entrepreneurs from all over the world.

The development of international business in China has been characterised most strikingly by a massive and sustained inflow of transnational corporations and an astonishing boom, unmatched by any other developing country, in inward foreign direct investment. Following China's entry into the WTO in 2001, more and more large-scale TNCs have begun to move into the country, particularly in the high-tech, capital-intensive and service industries – to such an extent that China is expected to become the most attractive country in the world for doing international business in the years to come.

Managing international business in China is not, however, an easy task for TNCs. The prime challenge they face is achieving their strategic objectives of cost reduction, local differentiation and the strengthening of core competencies in their specific functional areas and business activities in the particular context of China. As this is different from those in other parts of the world in a variety of ways, this book aims to give guidance in how to deal with this challenge in a range of functional areas and business activities.

FURTHER READING

Dunning, J. 1993. *Multinational Enterprises and the Global Economy*. Boston: Addison-Wesley.

Tian, X. 1996. 'China's open door policy in development perspective'. *Canadian Journal of Development Studies* 17 (1): 75–95.

1998. *Dynamics of Development in an Opening Economy: China since 1978*. New York: Nova Sciences.

Questions for discussion

1. What implications does China's rise have for international business?
2. What are the most noticeable patterns with regard to the country of origin, entry mode, industrial distribution and regional distribution of inward foreign direct investment in China?
3. Why have transnational corporations rushed to China to do business?
4. Using the four-choice model, analyse the prime challenge faced by transnational corporations in China.

NOTES

1. For details of the definitions, please see the *World Investment Report 2004*, published by the United Nations Conference on Trade and Development (UNCTAD) in 2005, pp. 345–6.
2. In some countries an equity stake of other than 10 per cent is still used. In the United Kingdom, for example, a stake of 20 per cent or more was the threshold used until 1997.

2 Look before you leap

Search for stones to cross the river.

Deng Xiaoping

When transnational corporations move to China, they need to understand the policy environment for international business in the country. Gradualism is the key to understanding China's policy environment. As indicated in the above statement by Deng Xiaoping, China has pursued its economic reform and opening up in a gradual way as compared to Russia and other eastern European transition economies, where a big bang approach prevailed. In this chapter we first discuss how China has gradually liberalized its foreign trade, foreign direct investment and foreign exchange regimes, and the current restrictions on international business in China. Then we evaluate China's steady approach to opening up in the light of the benefits and costs of liberalization, and look at the implications of the gradual approach for TNCs doing business in China.

China's foreign trade regime

Before 1978 China's foreign trade was under strict state control. Many restrictions were imposed on foreign trade, including a state monopoly of the right to trade, a high tariff rate and numerous non-tariff barriers. In that year China began to liberalize its foreign trade regime, by reducing the tariff and non-tariff trade barriers and by offering the right to trade to more enterprises, state-owned and non-state-owned alike. Particularly after the WTO accession in 2001 (box 2.1), China promised to remove more restrictions on foreign trade in a gradual manner. The gradual removal of restrictions on foreign trade is most clearly illustrated in the agreement that China reached regarding its accession to the WTO, which will be discussed in detail here.

Box 2.1 China's accession to the World Trade Organization

The WTO, formerly called the General Agreement on Tariffs and Trade (GATT), has been the only international organization dealing with the global rules of trade between nations since the end of the Second World War. Its main function is to establish a multilateral trading system to ensure that trade flows as smoothly, predictably and freely as possible. At the heart of the multilateral trading system are the WTO's agreements, which provide the legal ground rules for international commerce. Although the agreements are negotiated and signed by the governments of the WTO member countries, the purpose of the agreements is to help producers of goods and services, exporters and importers to conduct their business internationally. Currently, the WTO has 144 member countries.

China was one of the twenty-three original signatories of the General Agreement on Tariffs and Trade in 1948. After China's revolution in 1949 the government in Taiwan announced that China would leave the GATT system. Although the government in Beijing never recognized this withdrawal decision, nearly forty years later, in 1986, Beijing notified the GATT of its wish to resume its status as a GATT contracting party. Following that announcement China embarked on the tough process of negotiating with the GATT (later the WTO) and its member countries about its entry to this multilateral trading system.

To enter, according to the WTO regulations, China had to implement economic reforms to transform its economy, then based on the centrally planned system, into one based on market mechanisms. The process of China's accession to the WTO was guided by a working party, the membership of which consisted of all interested WTO member governments. Initially the working party was established under the GATT and was concerned exclusively with China's trade in goods. In 1995 it was converted to a WTO working party and its scope was broadened to include trade in services, new rules on non-tariff measures and new rules on intellectual property rights.

A substantial part of China's accession process involved bilateral negotiations between China and individual WTO member countries. These were usually conducted privately, either at WTO headquarters in Geneva or in the countries concerned. The process also involved meetings, either informal or formal, of the WTO working party. While several areas of China's trade policies, such as schedules of market-access commitments on goods and services, were the focus of bilateral negotiations, it was the responsibility of the working party to maintain an overview of how the negotiations were progressing and to ensure that all aspects of China's trade policies were addressed.

By the end of 1999 China had finally completed negotiations with most WTO member countries, and was trying hard to strike deals with the United States, the European Union and Mexico, all of which were vital for China's accession to take effect. China signed the agreement on WTO accession with the United States on 15 November 1999, with the European Union on 19 May 2000 and with Mexico on 13 September 2001, thus completing its negotiations with all WTO member countries. On 11 November 2001 the Protocol on the Accession of the People's Republic of China was passed at the WTO ministerial conference in Doha, Qatar, and China formally became a member of the WTO.

Originally, it was trade in goods that was the only concern in the negotiations under the GATT, which concentrated primarily on lower tariff rates and non-tariff trade barriers. Trade in goods has remained the most fundamental issue in the WTO system to the present day, and, as such, was a key subject of negotiation between China and the WTO on China's accession. Easily the largest part of the Protocol on the Accession of the People's Republic of China is related to China's commitments to freer trade in goods, including the right to trade, tariff and non-tariff barriers, tariff rate quotas, technical barriers to trade, and designated trading.

The right to trade

The right to trade refers to the right to export and the right to import. China agreed to liberalize the right to trade progressively so that, within three years of accession, all enterprises in the country would have the right to trade in all goods throughout the customs territory of China, except for those goods that are subject to state trading, as specified by the Protocol on the Accession of the People's Republic of China.[1] All foreign individuals and enterprises, including those who had not invested or were not registered in China, would be accorded treatment no less favourable than that accorded to enterprises in China with respect to the right to trade.

During the phase-in period, for Chinese enterprises, China would reduce the minimum registered capital requirement for obtaining the right to trade to yuan or renminbi (RMB) 5 million in the first year after accession, RMB 3 million in the second year and RMB 1 million in the third year. In addition, China would eliminate the examination and approval system for obtaining the right to trade at the end of the phase-in period. For foreign affiliates, China would grant the full right to trade to joint ventures with minority foreign shares one year after accession, and would grant the full right to trade to joint ventures with majority foreign shares two years after accession.

According to the Protocol, furthermore, immediately after the entry into the WTO China would eliminate, for both Chinese enterprises and foreign affiliates, any requirements for export performance, trade balance, foreign exchange balance and prior experience in importing and exporting as criteria for obtaining or maintaining the right to import and export.

Tariffs

According to the Protocol, the average tariff rate level would be cut from the then current 14 per cent to 10 per cent in 2008 (see table 2.1). Specifically,

Table 2.1 Reduction in the average tariff rate level (2000–2008)

Year	Average level for all products	Average level for industrial products	Average level for agricultural products
2000	15.6	14.7	21.3
2001	14.0	13.0	19.9
2002	12.7	11.7	18.5
2003	11.5	10.6	17.4
2004	10.6	9.8	15.8
2005	10.1	9.3	15.5
2006	10.1	9.3	15.5
2007	10.1	9.3	15.5
2008	10.0	9.2	15.1

Source: Annex 8 of the Protocol on the Accession of the People's Republic of China.

the average level for agricultural products would be cut from 19.9 per cent to 15.1 per cent in 2008, while the average level for industrial products would be cut from 13 per cent to 9.2 per cent. However, the average level of tariff rate for automobiles and parts and components of automobiles would be cut from 80–100 per cent to 25 per cent and 10 per cent in 2007, respectively. In 2005 all tariffs for information technology (IT) products were to be abolished.[2]

Non-tariff barriers

China promised to abolish all non-tariff trade barriers, including import quotas, import licences and import tendering, for more than 400 tariff lines no later than 1 January 2005. These tariff lines covered mainly automobiles, key parts and components of automobiles, electromechanical products and chemical products. During the phase-in period China would progressively increase the import quotas for these products each year (see table 2.2).

Tariff rate quotas

According to the WTO Agreement on Agriculture, WTO member nations should provide minimum market entry for agricultural products – that is, establish the so-called tariff rate quotas system. Tariff rate quotas imply market entry opportunities rather than an import obligation. After WTO entry China would use the tariff rate quotas system to manage the import of key agricultural products and, to a much lesser extent, some chemical fertilizers. The

Table 2.2 Non-tariff barriers subject to phased elimination

Quota category	Unit	Initial quota volume/ value	Annual growth rate	Phasing-in period
1 Processed oil	Million metric tons	16.58	15%	2004
2 Sodium cyanide	million metric tons	0.018	15%	2002
3 Chemical fertilizer	million metric tons	8.9	15%	2002 (some upon accession)
4 Natural rubber	million metric tons	0.429	15%	2004
5 Rubber tyres used on automobiles	million metric tons	0.81	15%	2002 (some upon accession or 2004)
6 Motorcycles and key parts	Million pieces	286	15%	Motorcycles 2004; key parts of motorcycles 2003
7 Automobiles and key parts	$ million	6000	15%	Cars 2005; other vehicles 2004; key parts of vehicles upon accession or 2003
8 Air conditioners and compressors	$ million	286	15%	Upon accession or 2002
9 Recording apparatus and key parts	$ million	293	15%	2002
10 Magnetic sound and video recording apparatus	$ million	38	15%	Upon accession or 2002
11 Recorders and transport mechanisms	$ million	387	15%	2002
12 Colour TV set and TV tuners	$ million	325	15%	Upon accession or 2002
13 Crane lorries and chassis	$ million	88	15%	2004
14 Cameras	$ million	14	15%	2003
15 Wristwatches	$ million	33	15%	2003

Source: Annex 3 of the Protocol on the Accession of the People's Republic of China.

tariffs for imports of these products within the quotas system are much lower than those outside the system. The implementation date for the final quota quantities would be no later than six years after accession. During the phase-in period the quantities covered by the quotas would progressively increase (see table 2.3).

Technical barriers to trade

Upon accession, in accordance with the terms of the Protocol, China was required to publish in official journals all the criteria that, whether formal or informal, are the basis for technical regulations, standards or conformity

Table 2.3 Products subject to tariff rate quotas

Product	Tariff quota	Share of state trading	In-quota tariff rate	Out-of-quota tariff rate	Date of implementation	Phase-in period tariff quotas
Wheat	9.636 mmt[a]	90%	1–10%	Down from 71% to 65%	2004	2002: 8.468 mmt 2003: 9052 mmt
Corn	7.2 mmt	Down from 68% to 60%	1–10%	Down from 71% to 65%	2004	2002: 5.85 mmt 2003: 6.525 mmt
Rice	5.32 mmt	50%	1–9%	Down from 71% to 65%	2004	2002: 3.99 mm 2003: 4.655 mmt
Soybean oil	3.5671 mmt	Down from 34% to 10%, and to Nil in 2006	9%	Down from 52.4% to 19.9%, and to 9% in 2006	2005	2002: 2.518 mmt 2003: 2.818 mmt 2004: 3.118 mmt
Palm oil	3.168 mmt	Down from 34% to 10%, and to Nil in 2006	9%	Down from 52.4% to 19.9%, and to 9% in 2006	2005	2002: 2.4 mmt 2003: 2.6 mmt 2004: 2.7 mmt
Rapeseed oil	1.24 mmt	Down from 34% to 10%, and to Nil in 2006	9%	Down from 52.4% to 19.9%, and to 9% in 2006	2005	2002: 0.87 mmt 2003: 1.0186 mmt 2004: 1.1243 mmt
Sugar	1.945 mmt	70%	Down from 20% to 15%	Down from 60.4% to 50%	2004	2002: 1.764 mmt 2003: 1.852 mmt
Cotton	0.894 mmt	33%	1%	Down from 54.4% to 40%	2004	2002: 0.8185 mmt 2003: 0.8563 mmt
Wool	0.287 mmt	Nil[b]	1%	38%	2004	2002: 0.2645 mmt 2003: 0.2758 mmt
Wool tops	0.08 mmt	Nil[b]	3%	38%	2004	2002: 0.0725 mmt 2003: 0.0763 mmt
Chemical fertilizers[c]	13.8183 mmt	Down from 90% to 50–51%	4%	50%	6th year after accession	Initial year: 9.40 mmt

[a] mmt = million metric tonnes.

[b] Wool and wool tops are not subject to state trading but to designated trading; designated trading of wool and wool tops abolished three years after accession.

[c] Chemical fertilizers include diammonium hydrogenorthophosphate (diammonium phosphate), UREA and NPK.

Source: Annex 8 of the Protocol on the Accession of the People's Republic of China.

assessment procedures. All the technical regulations, standards and conformity assessment procedures had to be in line with the Agreement on Technical Barriers to Trade (TBTs) immediately after accession.

China was obliged to apply the conformity assessment procedures to imported products only to determine their compliance with the technical regulations and standards as stated in the WTO regulations and the Protocol. Conformity assessment bodies were to determine the conformity of imported products with commercial terms of contracts only if authorized by the parties to such contracts. China had to ensure that the inspection of products for compliance with the commercial terms of contracts did not affect customs clearance or the granting of import licences for the products.

Upon accession, China was required to ensure that the same technical regulations, standards and conformity assessment procedures were applied to both imported and domestically manufactured products. In order to achieve a smooth transition from the previous system, China had to ensure that all the certification, safety licensing and quality licensing bodies and agencies were authorized to undertake these activities for both imported and domestically manufactured products, and that, one year after accession, all the conformity assessment bodies and agencies were authorized to undertake conformity assessment for both imported and domestically manufactured products. The choice of these bodies or agencies is at the discretion of the applicant. For imported and domestically manufactured products, all bodies and agencies should issue the same mark and charge the same fee; they should also follow the same procedures. Imported products should not be subject to more than one conformity assessment. China was obliged to publish and make readily available to other WTO members, individuals, and enterprises full information regarding the respective responsibilities of the conformity assessment bodies and agencies.

No later than eighteen months after accession China had to assign the respective responsibilities to the conformity assessment bodies solely on the basis of the scope of the work and the types of products without any consideration of the origin of a product. The respective responsibilities assigned to China's conformity assessment bodies were to be notified to the WTO's TBT Committee no later than twelve months after accession.

Designated trading and state trading

The term 'designated trading' refers to the government designating some enterprises to act on its behalf in the import and export of certain products, while 'state trading' refers to the state monopoly of trading in certain products. According to the Accession Protocol, state trading of certain products was allowed to remain, while designated trading was to be abolished within three years of accession.[3] At the end of that period all enterprises in China and all foreign enterprises and individuals were to be permitted to import and export the goods previously reserved for designated trading throughout the customs territory of China.

As we can see, the removal of restrictions on foreign trade was designed to proceed gradually after the WTO accession, with considerable phase-in periods. Since accession, in 2001, China has adhered these promises and removed the restrictions on foreign trade as scheduled. Currently, therefore, the right to trade is open to all enterprises; tariffs have been substantially reduced; and non-tariff trade barriers have been removed. Like all other members, China now complies with all the rules on foreign trade set by the WTO. However, foreign traders should pay attention to the goods that, in accordance with the agreement that China reached with the WTO, remain subject to state trading.

China's foreign direct investment regime

After 1979, as mentioned in chapter 1, China started to allow foreigners to invest directly in China, and introduced many regulations on foreign direct investment. Generally speaking, China's policy towards FDI is to encourage foreign investors, through preferential tax treatment and other measures, to use the desired entry modes, to move into preferred locations and to invest in selected industries. Here in this chapter we focus on China's FDI policy with regard to entry modes, location entry and industry entry; the preferential tax policies offered to different kinds of FDI are discussed in detail in chapter 11.

Entry mode

At the start of the opening-up process China allowed foreign investors to enter the Chinese market mainly in the form of equity joint ventures. In 1979 China issued the Law of the People's Republic of China on Sino-Foreign Equity Joint Ventures, in which it was clearly stated that EJVs were encouraged. A few years later, along with the issue of the Law of the People's Republic of China on Wholly Foreign-Owned Enterprises (1986) and the Law of the

People's Republic of China on Sino-Foreign Cooperative Joint Ventures (1988), foreign investors were allowed to enter China in the form of WFOEs and CJVs. Right up to the present, as mentioned in the previous chapter, these three forms remain far and away the main entry modes adopted by foreign investors, accounting for nearly 98 per cent of the total foreign direct investment in China.[4] As far as the three entry modes are concerned, generally speaking, the Chinese government prefers joint ventures (whether equity joint venture or cooperative joint venture) to wholly foreign-owned enterprises.

There are two main reasons for the preference for joint ventures on the part of the Chinese authorities. First, one of the main objectives that China wants to achieve through FDI is gaining access to the advanced technology of the industrialized countries, and joint ventures are (as shown by the analysis in chapter 4) more convenient vehicles for the transfer of foreign technology to local firms than WFOEs. Second, one of the main concerns that China has about the inflow of FDI is the danger of losing control over the national economy. Through restrictions on the distribution of equity shares within a joint venture, China can maintain considerable control over foreign investment in the so-called 'pillar' industries, and thus retain some control over the economy as a whole.

For these two reasons, therefore, the Chinese government has encouraged joint ventures and used to set restrictions on wholly foreign-owned enterprises, through its policy on industry entry (as shown below) and its policy on preferential tax treatment (as shown in chapter 11). The restrictions on WFOEs have been removed only gradually. In recent years China has further relaxed its policy on entry modes, and begun to allow foreign investors to adopt methods that had previously been highly restricted, such as merger and acquisition (M&A).

Location entry

To start with China opened only the coastal region to foreign direct investment, and did not allow foreign investors to move into the interior region. In the last twenty-five years, as mentioned in the previous chapter, nearly 90 per cent of FDI went into the coastal region. The rationale behind this location entry policy was that China wanted to choose a location where the new FDI policy might succeed with relative ease. The coastal region was selected for two reasons. First, it is most attractive region to foreign investors because it has the best infrastructure in the country – essential for the success of foreign-invested projects. Second, the coastal region is adjacent to the overseas Chinese in Hong Kong, Macao and Taiwan, who are the most likely to invest in mainland China due to their historic and ethnic linkages. Indeed immediately after the opening up overseas Chinese investors poured into China to do business, which contributed significantly to the success of the new FDI policy.

A key move that China took to encourage foreign investors to move into the coastal region was the establishment of various special zones along the coastline. In 1979 China established four Special Economic Zones in two coastal provinces: three zones in Guangdong province (Shenzhen, Zhuhai and Shantou) and one zone in Fujian province (Xiamen). In the 1980s various special zones and open areas were established in the coastal region. Not until the 1990s did China began to establish special zones in the interior provinces. Up to 2005 there were many types of special zone at both the national and the local level in China, and most of them were located in the coastal region. The national-level special zones include, for instance, Special Economic Zones (six), Economic and Technological Development Zones (fifty-four), Free-Trade Zones (fifteen), High-Technology Industrial Development Zones (fifty-three), Border and Economic Cooperation Zones (fourteen) and Export-Processing Zones (thirty-eight). The local-level special zones have become so numerous and diversified that the central government recently began to set restrictions on the establishment of new local special zones and dismantle some established local special zones that were considered to be of low standard. In all these special zones, various types of special policy treatment have been granted to foreign investors, including preferential taxes, less red tape and better services and infrastructure.

With the success of the new policy towards foreign direct investment in the coastal region, China gradually removed the restrictions on location entry and allowed foreign investors to move into the interior region. In recent years in particular, with the gap between the coastal and the interior regions widening, China launched the grand plan for developing the western region and turned to encouraging foreign investors to move into the interior of China, especially the western region (Lo and Tian, 2005). In fact, China is now trying to turn the whole interior region into a large 'special zone', and offers foreign investors in this region preferential policy treatment that is more favourable than that offered to foreign investors in the coastal region. Given the poor geography and infrastructure of the western region, however, it is too early to say whether China's new policy on location entry is sufficient to attract foreign investors there.

Industry entry

To avoid losing control over the national economy, China set restrictions on the entry of FDI into certain 'pillar' industries. In 1995 the Chinese government issued the Regulations on Guiding the Direction of Foreign Investment and the Guidance Catalog of Industries with Foreign Investment, which together provide a general guideline for the industry entry of FDI. According to the two documents, foreign investment projects and Chinese industries are classified into three basic categories: 'encouraged', 'restricted' and 'prohibited'. Those foreign investment projects and Chinese industries that are not included in the three categories fall in the category of 'permitted'.

Categorization of industry entry

In the Regulations on Guiding the Direction of Foreign Investment, the Chinese government clearly defines the three categories of foreign investment projects. A foreign investment project is 'encouraged' under any of the following circumstances: (1) if it involves new agricultural technologies, comprehensive agricultural development, or energy, communications and important raw materials; (2) if it involves high and new technologies or advanced application technologies that can improve the performance and increase the technological and economic efficiency of enterprises, or technologies that can help to manufacture new equipments and new materials that domestic production capacity is insufficient to produce; (3) if it is able to meet market demand, raise product grades, develop new markets or increase the international competitiveness of products; (4) if it involves new technologies and new equipments that can save energy and raw materials, comprehensively use and regenerate resources and prevent environmental pollution; (5) if the full manpower and resource benefits of the investment go to either the central region or the western region and it is in conformity with the state's industrial policies; and (6) if it is in accordance with other criteria as provided for by laws and administrative regulations.

All these encouraged projects enjoy the preferential tax treatment given by the relevant laws and administrative regulations. In addition, encouraged projects in energy, communications and municipal infrastructure (coal, oil, natural gas, electricity, railways, highways, ports, airports, city roads, sewage disposal, rubbish disposal, etc.) that require large amounts of investment and have a long period of capital return may expand their related business scope with approval. Permitted projects producing output that is all directly exported will be regarded as encouraged projects.

On the other hand, a foreign investment project is 'restricted' under any of the following circumstances: (1) if it involves technologies that are not updated; (2) if it does not help to save resources and improve the ecological environment; (3) if it involves the prospecting and exploitation of mineral resources that are under state protection; (4) if it is in the industries that are opening up to foreign direct investors in a gradual matter; and (5) if it conflicts with other criteria as provided for by laws and administrative regulations.

These projects are restricted in many ways. The most important restrictions include: the project must take the form of equity or cooperative joint ventures, or must have 'the Chinese party as the controlling shareholder' or 'the Chinese party as the relatively controlling shareholder'. The phrase the Chinese party as the controlling shareholder' denotes that the investment ratio of the Chinese party (parties) in the project must be at least 51 per cent. The phrase 'the Chinese party as the relatively controlling shareholder' means that the investment ratio of the Chinese party (parties) in the project has to be higher than that of any foreign party.

However, restricted projects in which export sales account for 70 per cent or more of their total sales may be regarded as permitted projects provided that they get the approval of the governments of the provinces, autonomous regions or municipalities directly under the central government, separately planned cities, or the relevant ministries, departments and committees under the State Council.

Finally, a foreign investment project is 'prohibited' under any of the following circumstances: (1) if it jeopardizes the state's security or harms public interests; (2) if it pollutes the environment, destroys natural resources or impairs human health; (3) if it takes up too much farmland and is thus unfavourable to the protection and development of land resources; (4) if it jeopardizes the security and usage of military facilities; (5) if it uses special Chinese crafts or technologies to manufacture products; and (6) if it conflicts with other criteria as provided for by laws and administrative regulations.

On the basis of the categories of foreign investment projects defined in the Regulations on Guiding the Direction of Foreign Investment, the Chinese government further divides industries seeking foreign investment, in the Guidance Catalog of Industries with Foreign Investment, into 'encouraged' industries, in which FDI is promoted, 'restricted' industries, in which FDI is limited, and 'prohibited' industries, in which FDI is forbidden. The Catalog is too long to be listed here, but some examples are illustrated in box 2.2.

Box 2.2 Excerpts from the Guidance Catalog of Industries with Foreign Investments[5]

Industries in which FDI is encouraged
1. Agriculture, forestry, animal husbandry and fishery:
   • production of flowers, and construction and operation of flower gardens;
   • growing or breeding of Chinese traditional medical materials;
   • timber (bamboo) afforestation and fine species breeding; and
   • growing natural rubber, sisal hemp and coffee.
2. Mining:
   • prospecting and development of oil and natural gas;
   • prospecting and development of coal and associated resources;
   • prospecting and development of coal gas; and
   • prospecting, mining and separation of iron and manganese reserves.
3. Manufacturing:
   • storage and processing of grains, vegetables, fruits, livestock and poultry products;
   • processing of aquatic products, cleaning and processing of shell products, and development of algae-based functional food;
   • development and production of fruit and vegetable beverage, protein beverages, tea beverages and coffee beverages;
   • production of special textile products for engineering applications;
   • production of high-grade paper products, excluding news printing paper; and
   • production of engineering plastics and plastic alloy.
4. Utilities production and supply:
   • construction and operation of thermal power stations with individual unit capacity reaching 300,000 kW or above;
   • construction and operation of power stations with clean burning technologies;
   • construction and operation of co-generation power stations for both electricity and heat; and
   • construction and operation of natural-gas-burning power stations.

Industries in which FDI is restricted
1. Agriculture, forestry, animal husbandry and fishery:
   • development and production of grains (including potato), cotton and edible oil seeds; and
   • processing of rare species timbers.
2. Mining:
   • prospecting and mining of tungsten, tin, stibium, platinum, barite and fluorite;
   • prospecting and mining of precious metals (gold, silver and platinum);
   • prospecting and mining of diamond and other precious metalloid ores; and
   • prospecting and mining of special and rare coals.
3. Manufacturing:
   • production of rice wine and famous Chinese liquors;
   • production of foreign brand carbonate beverages;
   • oil and fat processing;

- production of cigarettes and filter tips;
- wool and cotton textiles;
- silk;
- publication printing;
- construction and operation of oil refineries; and
- production of blood products.
4. Utilities production and supply:
   - construction and operation of conventional coal-burning power plants with single unit capacity under 300,000 kW, designed mainly for power generation (excluding small power grids).

Industries in which FDI is prohibited
1. Agriculture, forestry, animal husbandry and fishery:
   - breeding and growing of China's rare and precious species; and
   - production and development of genetically modified plant seeds.
2. Mining:
   - prospecting, mining and dressing of radioactive ores; and
   - prospecting, mining and separation of rare earth.
3. Manufacturing:
   - green tea and special teas such as famous tea and black tea processed with Chinese tradition techniques;
   - processing of Chinese traditional medical herbs listed under the state resources protection (muskiness, licorice, jute, etc.);
   - melting and processing of radioactive ores;
   - ivory carving;
   - tiger bone processing; and
   - production of enamel products.
4. Utilities production and supply:
   - construction and operation of power grids.
5. Transportation, storage and post and telecommunication:
   - air traffic control companies; and
   - post and telecommunication companies.

The two documents have been revised several times since 1995. In these revisions, the restrictions on the industry entry of FDI are being removed step by step. More and more industries previously in the 'prohibited' category have been moved into the 'restricted' category, and more and more industries previously in the 'restricted' category have been moved into the 'encouraged' or 'permitted' categories. In all these revisions, however, the service industries remained under the strictest restrictions, and the 'pillar' service industries were not opened up until China entered the WTO in 2001.

Opening up of service industries after WTO accession

In the protracted negotiations on China's accession to the WTO, it was the opening up of the service industries to foreign investors that was the main focus of dispute. In the agreement that was finally reached, China promised to open up its service industries step by step. As China's current restrictions on FDI are mainly in these service industries, let us now discuss in greater detail the gradual removal of these restrictions as mandated by the Protocol on the Accession of the People's Republic of China. China's commitments involve the major service industries, but we focus on the most important of them.

Telecommunications

China's commitments to opening up the telecommunication sector involve both the value-added services and the basic telecommunication services.[6] For value-added services, foreign service providers are allowed to establish only joint ventures. The foreign shares should account for no more than 30 per cent of total shares upon accession, no more than 49 per cent of total shares in the first year after accession and no more than 50 per cent in the second year after accession. The joint ventures were to be limited to Shanghai, Guangzhou and Beijing on accession, and to an additional fourteen cities in the first year after accession. The joint ventures were not to be limited geographically at all in the second year after accession.[7]

With regard to basic telecommunication services, foreign service suppliers are also allowed to establish only joint ventures. For paging services, upon accession the joint ventures were to be limited to Shanghai, Guangzhou and Beijing, with foreign shares accounting for no more than 30 per cent of total shares. Within one year of accession joint ventures could be established in an additional fourteen cities, with foreign shares accounting for no more than 49 per cent of total shares.[8] Within two years of accession joint ventures could be established all over China's territory, with foreign shares accounting for no more than 50 per cent. For mobile voice and data services, upon accession the joint ventures would be limited to Shanghai, Guangzhou and Beijing, with foreign shares accounting for no more than 25 per cent of total shares. One year after accession joint ventures could be established in the same additional fourteen cities, with foreign shares accounting for no more than 35 per cent. Three years after accession joint ventures could have a foreign share total of no more than 49 per cent. Five years after accession joint ventures could be established anywhere in China. For basic domestic and international services, three years after accession joint ventures would be limited to Shanghai, Guangzhou and Beijing, with foreign shares accounting for no more than 25 per cent of total shares. Five years after accession joint ventures could be established in the same fourteen cities, the foreign share amounting to no more than 35 per cent. Six years after accession joint ventures could be established anywhere in

China, with foreign shares accounting for no more than 49 per cent of total shares.

Banking and other financial services

Banking services included in the agreement on China's WTO accession refer to: (1) the acceptance of deposits and other repayable funds from the public; (2) lending of all types, such as consumer credit, mortgage credit, factoring and financing commercial transactions; (3) financial leasing; (4) all kinds of payment and money transmission services, such as credit, charge and debit cards, travellers' cheques and bankers' drafts (including those for import and export settlement); (5) guarantees and commitments; and (6) the trading of foreign exchange, either on own account or on customers' accounts. For banking services in foreign currency, foreign financial institutions would be permitted to provide services in China without any restrictions in terms of types of clients or geographical operations.

For banking services in Chinese currency, however, foreign financial institutions would be permitted to provide services to Chinese enterprises two years after accession, and to all types of Chinese clients five years after accession. In addition, there were geographical restrictions on foreign financial services, to be phased out as follows: upon accession, Shanghai, Shenzhen, Tianjin and Dalian; one year after accession, Guangzhou, Zhuhai, Qingdao, Nanjing and Wuhan; two years after accession, Jinan, Fuzhou, Chengdu and Chongqing; three years after accession, Kunming, Beijing and Xiamen; and four years after accession, Shantou, Ningbo, Shenyang and Xi'an. Five years after accession, all geographical restrictions were to be removed.

Upon accession, furthermore, there would be no restrictions on motor vehicle financing by non-bank foreign financial institutions, and no restrictions on such financial services provided by foreign financial institutions as the transfer of financial information, financial data processing and software related to financial services.

Insurance

Upon accession, foreign providers of life insurance would be permitted to establish joint ventures, with foreign shares accounting for no more than 50 per cent of total shares, and would be allowed to provide individual insurance to foreigners and Chinese citizens in Shanghai, Guangzhou, Dalian, Shenzhen and Foshan. Two years after accession they could extend their services to Beijing, Chendu, Chongqing, Fuzhou, Suzhou, Xiamen, Ningpo, Shenyang, Wuhan and Tianjin. Three years after accession they could provide health insurance, group insurance and pension/annuities insurance to foreigners and Chinese alike, and there would be no geographical restrictions on their services.

Upon accession, foreign providers of non-life insurance would be permitted, in the form of either a branch or a joint venture with 51 per cent foreign ownership, in Shanghai, Guangzhou, Dalian, Shenzhen and Foshan. Two years after accession they could extend their services to Beijing, Chendu, Chongqing, Fuzhou, Suzhou, Xiamen, Ningpo, Shenyang, Wuhan and Tianjin. Three years after accession there would be no geographical restrictions on them.

Upon accession, foreign providers of brokerage services for the insurance of large-scale commercial risks, reinsurance and international marine, aviation, and transport insurance and reinsurance would be permitted, in the form of joint ventures, with foreign shares accounting for no more than 50 per cent of total shares, in Shanghai, Guangzhou, Dalian, Shenzhen and Foshan. Two years after accession they could extend their services to Beijing, Chendu, Chongqing, Fuzhou, Suzhou, Xiamen, Ningpo, Shenyang, Wuhan and Tianjin. Three years after accession there would be no geographical restrictions on them, and the foreign share could be increased to 51 per cent. Five years after accession wholly foreign-owned subsidiaries would be permitted.

Securities

Upon accession, foreign securities institutions would be allowed to engage directly (without a Chinese intermediary) in the B share business, and representative offices of foreign securities institutions in China would be able to become special members of all Chinese stock exchanges.[9]

Three years after accession foreign securities institutions would be permitted to establish joint ventures, with foreign shares accounting for no more than one-third of total shares, and directly engage (without a Chinese intermediary) in underwriting A shares, underwriting and trading B shares, H shares, government bonds and corporate bonds, and launching funds.[10]

Upon accession, foreign services suppliers would be permitted to establish joint ventures, with foreign shares accounting for no more than 33 per cent of total shares, to engage in the management of domestic securities investments. Three years after accession foreign shares could be increased to 49 per cent of total shares.

Distribution

For commission agency services and wholesale trade services (excluding salt and tobacco), foreign service suppliers were to be allowed to establish joint ventures to engage in the distribution of all imported and domestically produced products upon accession, except for books, newspapers, magazines, pharmaceutical products, pesticides and mulching films, which would be permitted three years after accession, and chemical fertilizers, processed oil and crude oil, which would be permitted five years after accession. They would be permitted to have foreign majority ownership in joint ventures two years after accession.

For retail services (excluding tobacco), foreign service suppliers would be permitted to establish joint ventures in five special economic zones (Shenzhen, Zhuhai, Shantou, Xiamen and Hainan) and eight cities (Beijing, Shanghai, Tianjin, Guangzhou, Dalian, Qingdao, Zhengzhou and Wuhan) to engage in the retailing of all products upon accession, except for books, newspapers and magazines, which would be permitted one year after accession, pharmaceutical products, pesticides, mulching films and processed oil, which would be permitted three years after accession, and chemical fertilizers, which would be permitted five years after accession. Foreign service suppliers would be permitted to establish retailing joint ventures in all provincial capitals as well as Chongqing and Ningpo two years after accession, and anywhere in China three years after accession. They would be permitted to have foreign majority ownership in joint ventures two years after accession. However, for chain stores with more than thirty outlets that sell grain, cotton, vegetable oil, sugar, motor vehicles, books, newspapers, magazines, pharmaceutical products, pesticides, mulching films, processed oil and chemical fertilizers, joint ventures with foreign majority ownership would not be permitted. Five years after accession the equity restriction would be removed for chain stores with more than thirty outlets that sell motor vehicles.

For franchising and wholesale or retail trade services away from a fixed location, there would be no restrictions three years after accession. Upon accession, furthermore, foreign investors would be allowed to distribute the products that they manufacture in China, and provide subordinate services including after-sales services.

Tourism

Upon accession, foreign service suppliers would be allowed to construct, renovate and operate hotels and restaurants in China in the form of joint ventures with foreign majority ownership. Four years after accession wholly foreign-owned hotels and restaurants would be permitted, and foreign managers and specialists would be allowed to work in the wholly foreign-owned hotels and restaurants as well as in joint-venture hotels and restaurants.

For travel agencies and tour operators, upon accession, foreign service suppliers would be permitted in the form of joint ventures in the holiday resorts designated by the Chinese government and in the cities of Beijing, Shanghai, Guangzhou and Xi'an under the following conditions: the travel agencies and tour operators should engage mainly in travel business with an annual worldwide turnover of more than $40 million and a registered capital of no less than RMB 4 million in China. Three years after accession the registered capital requirement would be cut down to RMB 2.5 million, and foreign majority ownership would be permitted. Six years after accession wholly foreign-owned subsidiaries would be permitted, and the geographical restriction would be removed. Joint ventures or wholly foreign-owned travel agencies and tour operators would not, however, be permitted to work for Chinese travelling to foreign countries, including Chinese travelling to China's Special Administrative Regions – Hong Kong and Macao – and Chinese Taipei (Taiwan).

Education

For educational services, joint-venture schools with foreign majority ownership would be permitted upon accession. These joint-venture schools may provide primary and secondary education services (excluding national compulsory education), higher education services, adult education services and other education services such as English-language training, but may not provide special education services such as military, police, political and party education.

Foreign individual education service suppliers would be allowed to enter China to provide education services when invited or employed by Chinese schools and other education institutions under the following conditions: (1) they should possess a Bachelor's degree or above; (2) they should have an appropriate professional title or certificate; and (3) they should have at least two years' professional experience.

Transportation

For international transportation in freight and passengers, foreign service suppliers would be permitted to establish shipping companies in the form of joint ventures upon accession under the following conditions: (1) foreign shares should not exceed 49 per cent of the total registered capital of the joint venture; (2) the chairman of the board of directors and the general manager of the joint venture should be appointed by the Chinese side; and (3) the companies should operate a fleet under the national flag of the People's Republic of China.

For international maritime freight-handling services customs clearance services and container station and depot services, foreign service suppliers would be permitted to establish joint ventures with foreign majority ownership upon accession. However, for international maritime agency services, foreign service suppliers would be permitted to establish joint ventures with foreign shares accounting for no more than 49 per cent of the total shares.

For domestic waterway transportation, foreign service suppliers would not be allowed to establish any kind of companies to conduct domestic waterway transportation, but would be allowed to provide international shipping services in ports open to foreign vessels. For domestic freight transportation by road (trucks or cars), foreign service suppliers would be permitted to establish joint ventures, with foreign shares accounting for no more than 49 per cent of total shares one year after accession; three years after accession majority foreign ownership would be permitted; and six years after accession wholly foreign-owned subsidiaries would be permitted. For domestic freight transportation by rail, foreign service suppliers would be permitted to establish joint ventures, with foreign shares accounting for no more than 49 per cent upon accession; three years after accession foreign majority ownership would be permitted; and six years after accession wholly foreign-owned subsidiaries would be permitted.

For storage and warehouse services, foreign service suppliers would be permitted to establish joint ventures, with foreign shares accounting for no more than 40 per cent of total shares upon accession; one year after accession foreign majority ownership would be permitted; and three years after accession wholly foreign-owned subsidiaries would be permitted. For freight forwarding agency services, foreign freight forwarding agencies with at least three consecutive years' experience would be permitted to set up joint ventures, with foreign shares accounting for no more than 50 per cent upon accession; one year after accession foreign majority ownership would be permitted; and four years after accession wholly foreign-owned subsidiaries would be permitted. For aircraft repair and maintenance services, foreign service suppliers would be permitted to establish join ventures upon accession, but the Chinese side should hold controlling shares or should be in a dominant position in the joint ventures.

Professional services

For legal services, one year after accession foreign law firms would be allowed to provide legal services in the form of representative offices, and engage in profit-making activities anywhere in China. However, they would not be allowed to employ lawyers licensed in China.

For accounting, auditing and bookkeeping services, upon accession only certified public accountants (CPAs) licensed by the Chinese authorities would be allowed to establish partnership or limited liability accounting firms in China. Foreign accounting firms would be permitted to affiliate with Chinese firms and enter into contractual agreements with firms from other WTO member countries. The licences issued to foreigners who have passed the Chinese national CPA examination were to be treated the same way as those issued to nationals .

For medical and dental services, upon accession foreign service suppliers would be allowed to establish joint-venture hospitals or clinics with Chinese partners, with foreign majority ownership permitted. The majority of the doctors and medical personnel of the hospitals or clinics should, however, be of Chinese nationality. Foreign doctors with professional certificates issued by their home country would be permitted to provide short-term (six- to twelve-month) medical services in China after obtaining licences from the Ministry of Public Health.

For taxation services, foreign service providers would be allowed to establish joint ventures upon accession, with foreign majority ownership permitted. Six years after accession wholly foreign-owned subsidiaries would be permitted. For architectural services, engineering services, integrated engineering services and urban planning services, foreign service suppliers would be allowed to establish joint ventures upon accession, with majority foreign ownership permitted. Five years after accession they would be allowed to establish wholly foreign-owned subsidiaries.

As shown above, the liberalization of China's FDI regime proceeded in a gradual way, and the restrictions on entry modes, location and industries were removed step by step. After WTO accession China became more and more open to foreign direct investment. The remaining restrictions on FDI are mainly in the area of industry entry. Some industries, particularly those in the service sector, are opened up only to joint ventures, while a small number of highly sensitive industries remain closed to any kind of foreign direct investment. In the process of accelerated globalization, however, these restrictions are expected to be removed in the future, albeit probably still in a gradualist way.

China's foreign exchange regime

Compared to the foreign trade regime and the foreign direct investment regime, the foreign exchange regime is less liberalized. For any country, there are two key issues in the foreign exchange regime: (1) how the foreign exchange

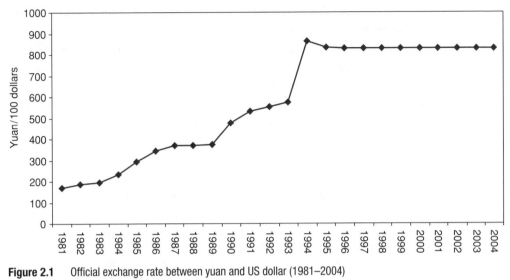

Figure 2.1   Official exchange rate between yuan and US dollar (1981–2004)
Source: *China Statistical Yearbook 2005.*

rate is managed; and (2) to what extent the local currency can be freely converted to foreign currencies. The Chinese government continues to adopt a very restrictive foreign exchange regime right up to the present day, as reflected in a controlled foreign exchange rate and only limited convertibility for the Chinese currency.

Look first at the foreign exchange rate. China has not adopted the free floating system that prevails in mature market economies. In the earlier years of opening up the authorities maintained an exchange rate system in which the Chinese currency was overvalued by a very large margin. The government depreciated the currency moderately in the 1980s and the early 1990s, and then depreciated it more sharply in 1994. Since then the policy that has been pursued has been the so-called 'managed floating exchange rate' system. This policy has, in practice, resulted in a fixed foreign exchange rate, in which the Chinese currency is strictly pegged to the US dollar. The exchange rate between the yuan and the dollar remained virtually unchanged in the following ten years, as shown in figure 2.1.

During the East Asian financial crisis of the late 1990s China came under huge pressure to remove the controls on the exchange rate and adopt a free floating system, which would have allowed the yuan to depreciate in the way that other East Asian countries had depreciated their currencies. However, China managed to survive the crisis without relinquishing the fixed exchange rate system. The opposite happened in more recent years: when the dollar weakened considerably in the international foreign exchange markets. China came under pressure to remove the controls and allow the currency to appreciate. It was in China's interests to appreciate the yuan in order to offset the negative effect of the devalued US dollar, and to allow the Chinese currency to peg to a basket of major world currencies rather than to the dollar alone, so as to minimize the risk from unexpected fluctuations in the value of the dollar. In July 2005, as shown in box 2.3, China initiated an exchange rate reform along these lines.

Box 2.3 China's foreign exchange rate reform of 2005

As a result of the very substantial depreciation of the US dollar in recent years at the same time as rapid economic growth continued unabated in China, the authorities in Beijing came under pressure from the international community to remove their controls over the exchange rate and appreciate the currency. China's major trading partners complained persistently that the yuan was undervalued by a large margin, making Chinese exports artificially cheap.

In particular, the United States attributed its steadily widening trade deficits of recent years to the undervalued Chinese currency and the fixed exchange rate system by which the yuan was pegged to the dollar. US politicians worked together to force China to revalue the yuan and liberalize the exchange rate system. In early 2005, for instance, some US politicians threatened to impose punitive duties of 27.5 per cent on Chinese imports to the United States if China refused to reform the foreign exchange regime.

On 21 July 2005 the People's Bank of China (PBOC) announced that it had decided to reform the exchange rate system. The yuan's value would be strengthened by 2.1 per cent, changing the exchange rate of the dollar to the Chinese currency from the long-standing 8.27 to 8.11. Moreover, the yuan would no longer be pegged to the US dollar alone, as it had been for ten years, but would float daily within a 0.3 per cent band against a basket of major foreign currencies. It was reported later that these currencies included the US dollar, the euro, the Japanese yen, the Korean won, the Singapore dollar, the British pound, the Malaysian ringgit, the Russian rouble, the Australian dollar, the Thai baht and the Canadian dollar. The PBOC did not disclose the weighting given to each of the foreign currencies, which enables the PBOC to intervene in the exchange rate to ensure that the exchange rate does not stray far from RMB 8.11 to the US dollar.

China's major trading partners welcomed the reform China's exchange rate system, but insisted that the currency is still undervalued by 20 to 35 per cent, and accordingly called for a more substantial revaluation and a more radical reform initiative. It is unlikely that China will pursue any kind of one-step revaluation and reform, however, as this would not be consistent with the gradualist approach to opening up that has been adopted over the last twenty-five years. Given the lessons that Beijing has learnt from the East Asian financial crisis, furthermore, it is very unlikely that China will adopt a free floating rate in the foreseeable future.

Turn now to the question of convertibility. In the 1980s and early 1990s the Chinese currency was not convertible on either the current account or the capital account.[11] With the rapid growth of foreign trade and investment, however the shortcomings of the currency's inconvertibility became increasingly apparent, and in 1994 China initiated a programme to resolve these problems by moving away from inconvertibility. By 1996 full convertibility of the yuan on the current account had been achieved, and the plan was to achieve full convertibility on the capital account in the next few years. With the outbreak of the East Asian financial crisis, however, the Chinese government became very cautious about moving in the direction of full capital account convertibility for fear that international speculators could as a result speculate on the yuan and destabilize the Chinese economy, as they had with some East Asian economies in 1997. Reflecting this caution, therefore, the Chinese currency remains largely inconvertible on the capital account.

Nevertheless, some moves towards capital account convertibility have been made in recent years, particularly after accession to the WTO. For example, foreign investors were not allowed to invest in China's stock markets in the Chinese currency until 2002, when the so-called QFII (Qualified Foreign Institutional Investor scheme) was introduced. Under the QFII scheme, as shown in chapter 11, foreign institutional investors can become QFIIs and apply for foreign exchange quotas to invest in China's stock markets in yuan upon approval from the Chinese government. The authorities continue to set very strict limits on the amount of foreign currencies that can be converted into yuan by each FQII, however, so as to avoid the adverse effect on local capital markets of a sudden withdrawal of foreign investments.

In sum, China still maintains tight control over the foreign exchange rate and the convertibility of the Chinese currency, and has a long way to go to achieve the full liberalization of the foreign exchange regime. Foreign investors need to learn how to deal with foreign exchange issues when doing business in China; this topic is discussed in detail in chapter 11.

A comment on gradualism

China has made significant progress in its gradual opening up to the outside world since 1978. Given that there are still some restrictions on foreign trade, foreign direct investment and foreign exchange, we are entitled to ask some questions. Why was it that China did not fully liberalize the foreign trade, foreign direct investment and foreign exchange regimes overnight? What are the possible risks – and opportunities – that foreign investors may encounter in the policy environment of gradual liberalization? A comment on China's gradualist approach to opening up is in order.

In the early period of reform and opening China was criticized for going too slowly, and was urged to adopt radical policies and rapid liberalization. When the disastrous consequences of the big bang approach, and the so-called 'shock therapy' adopted by Russia and some other East European transition countries, became apparent, however, more and more people began to appreciate the merits of the gradual approach of the Chinese. Especially after the East Asian financial crisis, China's steady and progressive way with reform was widely acknowledged as a wise choice for a developing and transition economy in its efforts to deal with the challenges posed by globalization and to minimize the adverse effects of opening up the economy.

The free market forces unleashed by the globalization process are like a double-edged sword. On the one hand, they can undoubtedly bring benefits, as evidenced by China's rapid economic growth over the past two decades, and the successful integration of other developing and transition economies into the global market system; at the same time, however, these forces may also do damage to such economies. Massive inflows of foreign capital, for instance, can destroy indigenous industries (the infant industry argument), deprive the recipient countries of control over their economies (the dependency theory) and cause economic destabilization if the foreign capital were to be suddenly withdrawn from recipient countries (as shown in the East Asian financial crisis). These adverse effects may be avoided or minimized if the recipient countries adopt a gradualist approach to opening up and maintain a moderate degree of government intervention. As Joseph Stiglitz, the Nobel Prize Laureate in economics in 2001, has pointed out, some government intervention is desirable, because it can correct market failure and improve economic efficiency (Stiglitz, 2002). He partly attributes the economic success that China has achieved in recent years to its gradual approach to opening up, which has enabled China to minimize the costs of integration with the global market system.

Moreover, the gradualist approach may generate business opportunities to foreign investors in China that would not otherwise have been available. As restrictions on international businesses are removed step by step there are always opportunities for foreign investors to pursue, and benefit from, the so-called 'first-mover' strategy. As laid out in standard textbooks of international business, a first-mover firm can potentially benefit in at least three ways: (1) it can pre-empt the market and establish a strong brand name before its rivals;

(2) it can build up sales volume, explore economies of scale and cut its unit costs ahead of its rivals; and (3) it can create switching costs that tie customers to its products or services. Over the past two decades many foreign investors, including such giant retailers as Wal-Mart and Carrefour, have made full use of the business opportunities arising from the gradual opening up of China industrial sectors, adopting the first-mover strategy and reaping the benefits from doing so.

It is also the case, however, that the gradualist approach can increase risks for foreign investors in China. In the process of opening up gradually there is a great degree of uncertainty about what is and what is not permitted in the policy settings at any one time. It is very difficult for foreign investors to decide whether or not to venture into these policy 'grey zones'. When such giant direct sellers as Amway, Mary Kay and Avon moved to China to do business in the mid-1990s, there was no clear policy message as to whether direct selling was permitted or not. The foreign direct sellers did very well for three years until 1998, when the Chinese government suddenly issued a ban on the practice (see chapter 8). All the foreign direct sellers suffered huge losses, and had to change their business operations drastically to meet the new requirements. Foreign investors need to understand the risks as well as the opportunities they may face in China in the policy environment of gradualism.

Summary

Transnational corporations have to understand the policy environment in which they are doing business in China, particularly the foreign trade regime, the foreign direct investment regime and the foreign exchange regime. Unlike the transition economies in East Europe, China has adopted a gradual approach to reform and opening up. Consequently, gradualism is key to understanding the country's policy environment.

China launched its policy of reforming the foreign trade regime in 1978, starting with the gradual reduction of tariff and non-tariff trade barriers and the gradual removal of restrictions on trading rights. After WTO entry in 2001 China further liberalized its foreign trade regime with regard to trading rights, tariff and non-tariff trade barriers, tariff rate quotas, technical barriers to trade, designated trading and state trading As demonstrated by the agreement reached between China and the WTO on China's accession, the liberalization of the foreign trade regime was scheduled to proceed in a step-by-step manner.

China's early policy towards foreign direct investment was to encourage foreign investors, through preferential tax treatment and other measures, to use the desired entry modes, to move into the desired locations and to invest in the desired industries. The liberalization of the FDI regime was mainly reflected in the gradual removal of these restrictions. After WTO accession, China promised to remove the restrictions on foreign entry into key service industries progressively. To date, the main restrictions on foreign direct investment are in the area of industry entry: some industries have been opened up to FDI only in the form of joint ventures, while a small number of highly sensitive industries remain completely closed to foreign investors.

Of the three regimes, it is the foreign exchange regime that is the least liberalized in China. Although the authorities have made efforts to move away from a fixed foreign exchange rate system and to resolve the problem of the yuan's inconvertibility, China to this day maintains a tightly controlled exchange rate and allows only very limited currency convertibility on the capital account. Given the lessons that the government has learnt from the East Asian financial crisis, it is highly unlikely that China will fully liberalize its foreign exchange regime anytime soon.

The free market forces unleashed by globalization cut both ways, causing economic dislocation as well as rewards to developing and transition economies that are being integrated into the global market system. A gradualist approach to liberalization may help, and adopting such an approach has won the support of Nobel-Prize-winning economist Joseph Stiglitz, on the grounds that it minimizes the adverse effects of economic integration. Moreover the gradual approach generates business opportunities for firms prepared to pursue the first-mover strategy, although at the same time the risks arising from policy uncertainties need to be borne in mind. Transnational corporations should be fully aware of both the opportunities and the risks that they may face in China in the policy environment of gradualism.

FURTHER READING

Lo, V., and Tian, X. 2005. *Law and Investment in China: The Legal and Business Environments after the WTO* Accession. London: Routledge.

Stiglitz, J. E. 2002. *Globalization and its Discontent*. London: Allen Lane.

World Bank. 1997. *World Development Report 1996: From Plan to Market*. Washington, DC: World Bank.

World Trade Organization. 2001. Protocol on the Accession of the People's Republic of China. Available at http://www.wto.org.

Questions for discussion

1. Is gradualism key to understanding the policy environment for international business in China? Why?
2. Illustrate China's gradual approach to opening up using as an example the liberalization of either the foreign trade regime, the foreign direct investment regime or the foreign exchange regime.
3. Highlight the major restrictions that exist at present on foreign trade, foreign direct investment and foreign exchange in China.
4. Is there any rationale for China's adoption of the gradual approach to opening up? Relate your argument to the debate on the benefits and costs of globalization.
5. What are the business opportunities and risks associated with the gradual approach to opening up?

NOTES

1. See annex 2A of the Protocol on the Accession of the People's Republic of China for a list of the goods under state trading; available online at http://www.wto.org.
2. See annex 8 of the Protocol for details of China's commitment to reductions in the tariff rate for agricultural and industrial goods.
3. See annex 2A of the Protocol for a list of the goods under state trading. See annex 2B for details of the specified goods for which designated trading was to be phased out.
4. For other investment-related entry modes, see chapter 4.
5. The industries listed in the three categories are only some examples. For details of all the industries in these categories, see the full text of the latest Guidance Catalog of Industries with Foreign Investment at the website http://www.chinacouculatesf.org/eng/kj/zyxx/t43951.htm.
6. Value-added services include electronic mail, voicemail, on-line information and database retrieval, electronic data interchange, enhanced/value-added facsimile services, code and protocol conversion, and on-line information and/or data processing (including transaction processing).
7. The fourteen cities are Chendu, Chongqing, Dalian, Fuzhou, Hangzhou, Nanjing, Ningpo, Qingdao, Shenyang, Shenzhen, Xiamen, Xi'an, Taiyuan and Wuhan.
8. The fourteen cities are the same as before.
9. See chapter 11 for a detailed discussion of B shares.
10. See chapter 11 for a detailed discussion of China's stock market.
11. The current account records trade in goods and services, as well as transfer payments. The capital account records purchases and sales of assets, such as stocks, bonds and land.

3 Manage *guanxi* strategically

The key to get anything important accomplished in China lies not in the formal order, but rather in who you know, and in how that person views his or her obligations to you. The Chinese call this concept *guanxi*. The term literally means 'relationships', but in this context it translates far better as 'connections'. Of course, it is by no means unique to China: Western society is hardly without its own concept of 'pull'. It is just that the Chinese have raised *guanxi* to an art. It pervades the social order, and nowhere more than in today's PRC. If you have *guanxi*, there is little you can't accomplish. But if you don't, your life is likely to be a series of long lines and tightly closed doors, and a maze of administrative and bureaucratic hassles (Scott D. Seligman (1999, p. 34)).

In addition to the uncertain policy environments discussed in the previous chapter, transnational corporations need to understand and deal with a business culture in China that they are not familiar with. *Guanxi* is often identified as the most prominent feature of Chinese business culture, and it puzzles TNCs, particularly those from the West. In this chapter we first introduce the concept of *guanxi*, and then discuss how to manage *guanxi* in China from a strategic management perspective.

Introduction

Translated literally, the Chinese term '*guanxi*' refers to relationships with neither a positive nor a negative connotation, as shown in the neutral expression of, say, the relationship between a Mr Smith and a Mr Clegg, the relationship between company A and company B or the relationship between the Earth and the Sun. Language is, however, rooted in, and influenced by, social and cultural settings, and the meanings of words and terms in a language may alter to have certain special connotations in a particular social and cultural context – as has occurred to the term *guanxi* in the Chinese language. In the current

Chinese social and cultural context, as has been widely noted, the term 'guanxi' has begun to carry some special connotations, to the extent that it is now defined by scholars as, for instance, 'tight, close-knit networks' (Yeung and Tung, 1996), 'interpersonal connections' (Xin and Pearce, 1996), the 'existence of direct particularistic ties between two or more individuals' (Tsui and Farh, 1997), 'drawing on connections in order to secure favors in personal relations' (Luo, 2000), 'relationships between or among individuals creating obligations for the continued exchange of favors' (Dunfee and Warren, 2001), 'friendship with implications of continued exchange of favors' (Pye, 1992) and 'something more than a pure interpersonal relationship – it is a reciprocal obligation to respond to requests for assistance' (Tsang, 1998). No matter how differently they define it, almost all scholars agree that the term now has a pragmatistic connotation, referring to interpersonal relationships or connections through which the persons involved may achieve their goal, be it political, economic, educational or whatever. In a sense, guanxi has now become a term describing a certain kind of favour-seeking pragmatistic social practice, which we may call Guanxi practice.

It is unclear when exactly this change happened, but it would appear that, although the guanxi practice is rooted in traditional Chinese culture and history, it became all-pervasive only after China had embarked on its economic reform programme in the late 1970s (Arias, 1998; Seligman, 1999). It is debatable whether guanxi practice is unique in China, but suffice it to say that the Chinese have developed it in such a vigorous and distinctive way that they have raised it to an art form (Seligman, 1999).[1] There is disagreement over why the practice of guanxi is so pervasive in China today, but it is clear that, apart from the Confucian influence, Mao's bureaucratic heritage, the absence of the rule of law and the lack of free market forces in the process of China's transition to a market system are all in part responsible (Wall, 1990; Luo, 2000; Tang, 2003). It is questionable whether guanxi practice can directly benefit investors, but it is fair to say that it has certainly helped investors resolve many practical problems that possibly would not have been handled effectively otherwise (Seligman, 1999; Luo, 2000). Despite the obvious practical benefits of guanxi practice, however, scholars are now deeply divided on whether it is ethical. As shown in box 3.1, some consider guanxi practice to be ethically acceptable in China, while others tend to believe that it is unethical and virtually equal to corruption (Yang, 1988; Lovett, Simmons and Kali, 1999; Donaldson and Dunfee, 1999; Chan, Cheng and Szeto, 2002; Su and Littlefield, 2001; Fan, 2002).

Box 3.1 The debate on the ethics of *guanxi*

In the current debate over *guanxi*, the most controversial issue is, probably, whether or not *guanxi* practice is ethically acceptable. The challenge to the ethics of the practice of *guanxi* comes from different lines of reasoning. It is, for instance, argued that it discriminates against people outside the *guanxi* network, which runs contrary to the principle of fair competition in a free-market economy. People within a *guanxi* network have the privilege of receiving favours from one another, and thus obtain an unspoken advantage over outsiders. In a society based on the rule of law and fair competition, people should have the right to be treated equitably and impartially, and should not be discriminated against simply because they happen to be outside a *guanxi* network.

The most serious accusation is, however, that *guanxi* practice is equivalent to corruption, or inevitably leads to corruption. It is argued that the exchange of favours invariably leads to corruption if it involves, as it does in most cases, government officials in a *guanxi* network. In this context, the exchange is actually a kind of exchange between money and power (*qianquan jiaoyi*). Corruption is most likely to occur in the so-called 'B2G *guanxi*' in the business world, in which business solutions are found through personal connections with government officials. Ying Fan (2002, p. 377) claims: 'It is safe to say that there is no business *guanxi* network that is not tinted by corruption and no corruption without using *guanxi*. Inside China, *guanxi* is the synonym for corruption and other wrongdoings such as nepotism, bribery and fraud.' This accusation echoes arguments made by other scholars, such as Mayfair Yang (1988) and Steve Lovett, Lee Simmons and Raja Kali (1999).

The challenge to the morality of *guanxi* practice indeed puts many in a dilemma: if they do not practise *guanxi* they are unlikely to succeed in China; but if they do practise *guanxi* they may be doing something ethically wrong. To overcome this dilemma, some scholars try to find ethical grounds for *guanxi* practice, arguing, for instance, that it cannot be evaluated on the basis of such Western values as the rule of law, fair competition and free markets because '*guanxi* is based on Eastern principles, and can be as ethical as any Western system' (Lovett, Simmons and Kali, 1999, p. 234). One of the most important developments in business ethics is the growing emphasis on the context of behaviour and on local value systems, or the 'authentic norms of local communities' (Donaldson and Dunfee, 1999, p. 199). This line of argument takes the cultural roots of *guanxi* in the Confucian tradition as a justification for *guanxi* practice in contemporary China: as Confucianism emphasizes social relationships, *guanxi* practice should therefore be deemed ethically acceptable in the Chinese cultural context.

Furthermore, it is argued that *guanxi* practice is fundamentally different from corruption, and does not necessarily lead to corruption. *Guanxi* is based on emotion and long-term considerations, whereas bribery is based on pure gain and loss considerations and is for immediate and specific purposes. As some claim, therefore, '*guanxi* is not corruption, but an ethical system designed to deal with a different perspective on society' (Lovett, Simmons and Kali, 1999, p. 236).

The defence of *guanxi* practice purely on the basis of the unique nature of Chinese culture is not sufficient to convince the opponents, just as the challenge to *guanxi* practice purely on the grounds of Western-style universalistic value systems is not convincing either. Probably a more appropriate approach to understanding the ethics of *guanxi* practice is to look at the issue from a global and comparative perspective, and examine *guanxi* in the context of a Chinese society that is undergoing a socio-economic transformation as it engages in the globalization process. This approach requires taking into account not only the cultural roots of *guanxi* but also the socio-economic background against which *guanxi* practice became so prevalent in the course of transition. In doing so, it is inevitably necessary to distinguish between different kinds of *guanxi* practices, to look into the different driving forces behind each of them and to analyse the different contexts in which *guanxi* is practised. In particular, it is crucial to distinguish ethically acceptable *guanxi* practice from ethically unacceptable *guanxi* practice that does involve corruption and other wrongdoing. There is a need to make a major effort in this direction.

Debate is debate, and yet transnational corporations have to face and deal with *guanxi* practice in the real business world of China today. Being aware of the central role of *guanxi* in current Chinese business culture and the importance of *guanxi* practice to business success in the emerging Chinese market, more and more TNCs tend to take it seriously and consider cultivating *guanxi* as a strategy for doing business in China. That is, TNCs are in practice developing *guanxi*-based strategies, making use of *guanxi* practice to achieve business objectives. Although the current literature has touched upon the practical issue of how to use *guanxi* practice in the business world, the analysis is ad hoc or *ad hominem* and, therefore, can provide little strategic guidance for TNCs in the real Chinese business world.

In this chapter we propose a practical analytical framework for making strategic decisions on managing *guanxi* practice in the real Chinese business world. It is argued that *guanxi* practice, no matter how controversial it may be, has to be treated strategically by all transnational corporations in China, and would more appropriately be analysed within a strategic management framework. The established models and concepts in the field of strategic management, such as environment scanning (including PEST analysis and SWOT analysis[2]), strategy formulation, strategy implementation, and strategy evaluation and control, could be used as convenient tools for the analysis of strategic management of *guanxi* in China. Section 2 discusses how to use such basic concepts as PEST analysis and SWOT analysis to conduct environment scanning specifically for *guanxi* practice in China. Section 3 analyses the key issues that TNCs need to take into consideration when they decide to formulate and implement *guanxi*-based strategies. Section 4 highlights the importance of strategy evaluation and control in managing *guanxi* practice in China. Section 5 summarizes.

Environment scanning for *guanxi*

In strategic management, the purpose of environment scanning is to examine the external and internal strategic factors that influence the operation of a firm. External factors include general factors and industry-specific factors. General factors refer to political, economic, social and technological factors, and the scanning of these factors is called PEST analysis. Industry-specific factors refer to the characteristics of suppliers, customers and competitors in a specific industry that have to be taken into account strategically. Internal factors include organization-specific variables, such as the corporate structure, the corporate culture and the available resources of a firm. Specifically, the purpose of scanning the external factors is to identify the external opportunities and threats that a firm faces, while the scanning of internal factors is to identify the internal strengths and weaknesses that a firm has in responding to the external opportunities and threats. Therefore, environment scanning is often referred to as SWOT analysis. Obviously, SWOT analysis is the starting point for a firm in making any strategic decisions.

For a firm that needs to make a strategic move to practise *guanxi*, therefore, environment scanning specifically in relation to *guanxi* practice is essential. The environment scanning has to focus on the external and internal factors that are closely and directly related to *guanxi* practice, including the general factors that determine the scope, the potential and the limits of the practice in China, the industry-specific factors that determine the extent to which *guanxi* practice matters in a specific industry, and the organization-specific factors that determine the capacity of an organization to exercise *guanxi* practice. Environment scanning of this type not only covers the general issues discussed in the literature on *guanxi* but also touches upon specific issues related to a particular industry and a particular organization.

General factors

For general factors, environment scanning is virtually a PEST analysis of the political, economic, social and technological variables that influence *guanxi* practice in China. The PEST analysis helps to assess the extent to which a firm needs to exercise *guanxi* practice, highlight the opportunities for the firm to make use of the practice, and identify the threats associated with it, particularly the risks the firm may face if it refuses to practise *guanxi* in China. In other words, the PEST analysis is supposed to help a firm understand why *guanxi* practice is pervasive in China and why the firm has to deal with it strategically in doing business in China. The current debate on the causes of the prevalence of the *guanxi* practice in contemporary China provides rich sources for analysis, and the scanners need to study the debate carefully and refer to the arguments that seem most relevant. A *guanxi*-related PEST analysis may go, for instance, as follows.

For political factors, the prevalence of *guanxi* practice is arguably attributable to the absence of the rule of law and the presence of a powerful bureaucracy in China, which increase the personal power of government officials. Without proper legal safeguards, individuals and organizations turn to those in power and rely on personal connections with them for political and legal protection. China has, of course, passed many laws and regulations since the late 1970s. As is well acknowledged, however, what really matters in China is not the laws and regulations but the interpretation of these laws and regulations by those in power. The bureaucratic presence strengthens the personal power of government officials and, therefore, encourages individuals and organizations all the more to rely on personal connections with government officials to get business done. According to Alun Wu (2003), for instance, it required twenty-eight official stamps for Pierre Cardin to open a restaurant in Beijing. To overcome the red tape, a Chinese lady, Song Huaigui, was appointed as the CEO of Pierre Cardin in China, and she used her *guanxi* in Beijing to get business done and became the 'woman behind the glittering success' of Pierre Cardin in the country. There is no doubt that China is trying to establish a society based on the rule of law and to reduce bureaucracy in the government, and that *guanxi* practice may weaken in the long run. So long as the rule of law has not been fully established and bureaucracy is still present and strong, however, *guanxi* practice is needed to overcome the weaknesses in the political and legal system; this situation is likely to continue for the foreseeable future at least.

In terms of economic factors, there is no doubt that the prevalence of *guanxi* practice can be attributed to the lack of free-market mechanisms in resource allocation. Yang (1988, p. 40) provides a clear illustration for this point.

A friend in Beijing described how he was able to buy a sleeper ticket which was usually difficult to purchase: he approached his mother who works in a hospital serving railroad workers; she made a request to someone she knew at the train station office, who then wrote down her son's name on a slip of paper and also made a telephone call to the ticket seller. The son then took the slip to the train ticket station where they actually have a special window booth just to sell tickets to *Guanxi Hu* or people with *Guanxi*, got in line, and bought his ticket.

If the sleeper tickets were sold at the market price – that is, if the sleeper tickets were allocated by free-market mechanisms and their price were allowed to rise and fall with the change in demand and supply – there would be little need for people to get the tickets through *guanxi*. This is, of course, a case that happened in the early years of economic reform, and China has undoubtedly made great strides in introducing market mechanisms in resource allocation since then. Nevertheless, the government's aim is to establish a *socialist* market economy, and not to allow the full play of free-market forces. So long as government intervention in resource allocation persists, *guanxi* practice will remain necessary for the acquisition of scarce resources.

As for social and cultural factors, many agree that *guanxi* is rooted in the Confucianism-dominated Chinese culture, which, as Geert Hofstede (1991) has noted, distinguishes itself from other cultures, particularly those of Western countries, by such characteristics as having a high power distance (i.e. status distinctions are accepted and high-status individuals are expected to exert their power), a collectivist outlook (emphasizing the connectedness of society rather than excessive individualism) and its long-term orientation. In fact, Confucianism has an even stronger influence on Chinese society and culture than Hofstede realized. Insofar as the practice of *guanxi* is concerned, for instance, it is closely related to the Confucian emphasis on the importance of interpersonal relationships in a society, particularly the so-called five cardinal relationships: those between ruler and minister, between father and son, between husband and wife, between elder and younger brothers and between friends. These interpersonal relationships are supposed to be reciprocal, in the sense that the senior cares about the junior while the junior respects the senior; reciprocal relationships form the basis on which a society operates. These Confucian teachings have fundamentally shaped the social behaviour of the Chinese and have become the most influential moral principles in China, as indicated by such proverbs as 'if you honour me a foot, I shall honour you ten feet in return' and 'dealing with a man as he deals with you'. Although Confucianism was criticized during the Cultural Revolution, it has regained its position in Chinese society since the late 1970s, providing the fertile cultural and social soil in which *guanxi* practice flourishes in contemporary China. For as long as Confucianism remains influential in the country, the practice of *guanxi* will continue to fit in well with the Chinese mentality and culture.

Turning now to technological factors, it is evident that the rapid development of information technology has greatly facilitated interpersonal communications and, therefore, the exercise of *guanxi*. *Guanxi* practice is primarily interpersonal and is, in most cases, conducted in private on a person-to-person basis. Developments in IT, such as mobile telephones and the internet, provide convenient vehicles for private interpersonal communications, by which the exchange of personal favours 'under the table' has become very easy and can even be unnoticed.

This PEST analysis of *guanxi* appears to deliver a strong message that *guanxi* practice is based on some fundamental political, economic and cultural factors in contemporary Chinese society, and has been greatly facilitated by the advance in technology in the information era. As a consequence, there is huge potential and opportunity for individuals and organizations to practise *guanxi* in China, and great risk of failure if individuals and organizations refuse to do so to cope with these general factors. To survive and succeed in the emerging Chinese market, a firm has to deal with *guanxi* strategically, and make full use of *guanxi* practice in daily operation to achieve its business objectives.

Industry-specific factors

For industry-specific factors, the main purpose of environment scanning is to analyse the suppliers, customers and competitors in the industry to which a firm belongs in terms of their relevance to *guanxi* practice. The aim is to ascertain the extent to which *guanxi* practice is needed in dealing with the customers, suppliers and competitors in this specific industry, and how likely the firm is to fail if it refuses to practise *guanxi*. In other words, the industry-specific analysis seeks to assess the opportunities for employing *guanxi* in the specific industry, and the extent to which the firm would be under threat if it does not exercise *guanxi* in that specific industry.

If, for instance, there are plenty of suppliers in China for a firm to choose from, there is little need for the firm to practise *guanxi* with these suppliers. In contrast these suppliers may try to exercise *guanxi* with the firm so as to compete for supplying the firm with what it needs. If, on the other hand, there are insufficient suppliers, a firm may feel forced to utilize *guanxi* with the suppliers or relevant government officials in order to ensure supply, and treat the *guanxi* with the suppliers or relevant government officials as being of vital importance. Yadong Luo (2000, p. 18) provides an illustrative example.

A Chinese deputy general manager of a Sino-foreign joint venture once urgently needed certain components in her factory. The components were in short supply but through her *guanxi*, she managed to obtain them from a friend in a factory in another city. Based on mutual trust, a cash-on-delivery price was agreed upon verbally and the components were sent to her factory. However, her factory was experiencing a cash flow problem when the components arrived. In order to uphold her credibility, she paid the bill out of her own savings – an amount roughly equal to her annual salary. She says that if she had not done so, the *guanxi* with her friend would have been tarnished.

This case shows how important *guanxi* practice is when the supply is insufficient in an industry.

By the same token, if there is plenty of demand for the goods or services that a firm produces – i.e. plenty of customers – the firm does not need to exercise *guanxi* very much in order to expand its customer base. If there is little demand, however, the firm is under pressure to promote its products and services and expand its customer base through its *guanxi* networks. In fact, many salespersons in Chinese firms rely on their personal networks with the customers to sell what firms produce.

Finally, if the market structure of an industry is very competitive, a firm in that industry may feel it unnecessary to practise *guanxi*. All the firm needs to do is improve its own competitive capacity to beat its competitors in an environment of free and fair competition. If the market structure of an industry is under the protection of the government, on the other hand, it is often necessary for a firm to exercise *guanxi* in order to enter the protected market. Many transnational corporations have indeed, as shown below, had to exercise *guanxi* to enter such highly protected industries as banking, automobiles and the retail sector in China. Had they not done so they would have risked the market being pre-empted by their competitors. It is clear that a firm is under greater threat in a protected industry than in a competitive industry if it does not utilize *guanxi*.

Organization-specific factors

For organization-specific factors, environment scanning serves mainly to analyse such internal factors as the corporate structure, the corporate culture and the firm's available resources in terms of their relevance to the exercise of *guanxi*. Once the potential and opportunities for *guanxi* practice are judged to be sufficiently great, a firm has to examine those internal factors that determine its capacity to practise *guanxi*.

To begin with, for instance, a firm has to have the right human resources – i.e. the right people, who already have the much-needed *guanxi* in China or who have the ability to establish such *guanxi*. If a firm does not have the right human resources it has no competitive advantage in its employment of *guanxi* practice, and alternative strategic options have to be taken into consideration. If, on the other hand, a firm has staff who have very good *guanxi*, or are able to establish very good *guanxi*, with the targeted persons or organizations in China, the firm has a competitive advantage in the exercise of *guanxi*. This explains why many firms in China tend to recruit employees with relevant *guanxi* networks or with the ability to establish such networks.

A firm also needs to think about how to accommodate *guanxi* practice in its corporate culture. The practice of *guanxi* may look unethical in some cultural settings and, therefore, may be in conflict with the corporate culture of a firm that emphasize ethical values based on other cultural traditions. In that case, the firm needs to assess the extent to which *guanxi* practice can be tolerated in the context of its established corporate culture. This is not a problem for most domestic firms in China, as *guanxi* practice has virtually become a part of their corporate culture, but it does present a problem for many TNCs, particularly those from Western countries, where ethical values developed in the context of the rule of law and fair competition may conflict so violently with *guanxi* practice that it becomes very difficult for these companies to accept a certain type of *guanxi* practice in China. As shown in box 3.2, some Western TNCs are required to report to the legal authorities in their home country if they find that their Chinese subsidiaries are using *guanxi*-based strategies in marketing in a way that clashes with Western rule of law and value systems.

Furthermore, a firm has to take into consideration the structure of corporate governance to see whether it allows and facilitates the exercise of *guanxi*. *Guanxi* practice is interpersonal, and it requires the players in the game to have considerable personal power and autonomy in decision-making. Once again, this is not a problem for most Chinese firms, as personal power is generally strong in these companies, particularly in the family-based private Chinese firms. It may present a problem for many Western TNCs, however, which have a standard structure of corporate governance in which the autonomy of managers is greatly constrained and limited by the board of directors, the board of supervisors and shareholders' meetings.

Environment scanning for these general, industry-specific and organization-specific factors thus allows a firm to identify the *guanxi*-related opportunities, threats, strengths and weaknesses. The basic questions addressed in *guanxi*-related SWOT analysis can be summarized as follows.

- To what extent does *guanxi* practice imply opportunities for a firm doing business in China?
- To what extent does *guanxi* practice imply threats to a firm doing business in China, particularly in the event of a firm refusing to apply *guanxi* practice?

Box 3.2 Diagnostic Products Corporation in China

As a result of the economic reform programme, the income of Chinese employees is now linked to their performance. It has become common practice among Chinese employees to make use of *guanxi* to enhance their performance, and this is especially true in marketing. Salespeople tend to promote and sell goods through personal networks, and try to establish and expand their personal networks whenever possible. It is particularly crucial for these salespersons to establish personal networks with customers or potential customers.

To generate and maintain a customer base, salespeople often give gifts or kickbacks to customers or potential customers, who then make purchases of the goods or services promoted by the salespeople on a regular basis. This has become a common way of doing business in China: everyone knows the trick, but no one reports it. If business people do not follow the practice, they have difficulty in doing business in China. This places Western business people in a dilemma, and when the competition intensifies some of them begin to follow the practice, as shown in the case of salespeople of the Chinese subsidiary of Diagnostic Products Corporation (DPC).

Diagnostic Products Corporation, a US-based transnational corporation manufacturing diagnostic medical instruments, established an affiliate in Tianjin – a city in north-east China. To sell the instruments, salespeople of DPC (Tianjin) established and maintained *guanxi* networks with laboratory personnel, physicians and purchase officers in three hospitals in Tianjin for many years, and gave kickbacks to them. From late 1991 to December 2002 the salespeople allegedly paid a total of approximately $1.6 million in the form of 'commissions' in order to obtain and retain business with these hospitals. The commissions, which ranged from 3 per cent to 10 per cent of the sales, allowed DPC (Tianjin) to earn some $2 million in profits from the sales.

In most cases, the commissions were paid in cash and hand-delivered by DPC (Tianjin) salespeople to those in the hospitals who controlled purchasing decisions. DPC (Tianjin) recorded the payments on its books and records as 'sales expenses'. The general manager approved the budgets for sales expenses including the 'commissions', and regularly prepared and submitted the financial statements including the sales expenses to Diagnostic Products Corporation headquarters in the United States. In 2000 the head office detected the problem in the financial statements submitted by DPC (Tianjin), and reported the case to the US authorities, including the Department of Justice and the Securities and Exchange Commission. The chief financial officer of DPC, Jim Brill, said to the media that DPC has done the right thing in reporting the case; as an American company, DPC could not allow its subsidiaries to do business in that way.

The Department of Justice ruled that the conduct of DPC (Tianjin) violated the Foreign Corrupt Practices Act (FCPA) of 1977, and asked DPC (Tianjin) to pay a fine of $2 million. The Securities and Exchange Commission also requested DPC (Tianjin) to disgorge its ill-gotten gains of approximately $2.8 million, representing its net profit in China for the period of its misconduct plus prejudgement interest. DPC (Tianjin) agreed to pay the penalties.[3]

- To what extent does a firm have the capacity to exercise *guanxi*?
- To what extent does a firm lack the capacity to exercise *guanxi*?

Each of the four basic questions may contain a set of more specific questions to be addressed in detail in the SWOT analysis. The answers to all these questions are crucial for a firm to make strategic decisions on whether or not to use *guanxi* practice in China and, if so, to what extent.

Formulation and implementation of *guanxi*-based strategies

Once a firm has decided to use *guanxi* practice on the basis of the information obtained from environment scanning, the next steps are to formulate appropriate *guanxi*-based strategies and implement them. Strategy formulation and strategy implementation are normally treated as separate stages in the strategic management literature, but they are so closely related to each other in the real strategic management process that they are better discussed together for practical purposes. In the context of *guanxi* practice, strategy formulation refers to the development of long-term strategies and policies for the effective management of the *guanxi*-related opportunities and threats in the light of the *guanxi*-related corporate strengths and weaknesses identified in the above environment scanning process, while strategy implementation refers to the process by which these strategies and policies are put into action. The key issues that need to be addressed in formulating and implementing *guanxi*-based strategies include the level of the strategies, the basic policies, and the detailed programmes, budgets and procedures through which the strategies and policies are put into action.

Guanxi-based strategies can be implemented at three levels: corporate, business and functional. *Guanxi*-based strategies at the corporate level are concerned with how to use *guanxi* practice to serve the firm's overall goals in terms of its general attitude towards growth and management. *Guanxi*-based strategies at the business or unit level are concerned with how to use *guanxi* practice to improve the competitive position of the firm's products or services in a specific industry or a specific market segment served by that business unit. *Guanxi*-based strategies at the functional level are concerned with how to use *guanxi* practice to develop the firm's competitive advantages in a specific functional area, such as human resource management, R&D or marketing. *Guanxi*-based strategies could be used simultaneously at the three levels, and they should complement and support each other. The *guanxi*-based strategies at the functional level may, for instance, support *guanxi*-based strategies at the business level, which, in turn, support *guanxi*-based strategies at the corporate level. Although an understanding of these levels is useful in theory, it is often unnecessary to distinguish between *guanxi*-based strategies at the three levels in practice, as *guanxi* is often used to achieve the objectives of the firm, its business units and its functional divisions at one and the same time. When a marketing manager of a firm exercises *guanxi*, for instance, to promote the goods and services produced by a business unit in the firm, the manager is pursuing a *guanxi*-based strategy to serve the objectives of the functional division, the business unit and the firm all at the same time.

Basic policies can be devised in relation to *guanxi*-based strategies, and these constitute the broad guidelines for decision-making that link the formulation of *guanxi*-based strategies with the implementation of these strategies. These guidelines state clearly what can be done with *guanxi* practice and what should not be done with it, and can therefore serve to regulate *guanxi*-based strategies in a way that fits in with the firm's mission and objectives. A firm may, for instance, set the following policy guidelines: 'the firm will not exercise any *guanxi* practice that would reduce product or service quality in any way'; 'the firm will never utilize *guanxi* to conduct bribery in any circumstances'; and 'the firm will not tolerate the use of *guanxi* practice for personal gains'. The practice of *guanxi* is, as mentioned above, an ethically controversial issue, so these kinds of broad policy guidelines in relation to the use of *guanxi* are necessary to limit it within ethically acceptable boundaries so as to accommodate the *guanxi*-based strategies that a firm formulates and implements in its established corporate culture.

Detailed programmes, budgets and procedures can then be designed to implement *guanxi*-based strategies in the light of the broad guidelines. The term 'programme' refers to a set of activities or steps needed to accomplish a single-use plan – say, establishing a team to work on all kinds of *guanxi* for a specific task. 'Budget' refers to a statement of the programmes in terms of dollars, and it lists the detailed costs of each programme. As can be imagined, it is usually very costly to cultivate *guanxi*. According to a survey conducted by the Hong Kong Independent Commission Against Corruption, the costs 'to establish *guanxi*, or connections, average in the PRC three to five percent of operating costs, or $3 billion to $5 billion of foreign investments that have been made there' (Su and Littlefield, 2001). It is necessary, therefore, to take the *guanxi*-related costs into consideration, and have a budget adequate for *guanxi*-related programmes. 'Procedures' refer to a system of sequential steps or techniques that describe in detail how a *guanxi*-related task or job is to be carried out. To nurture *guanxi* with a particular government department, for instance, a firm may need to find someone who knows the key officials in that department, and establish frequent informal contacts with them – say, dining out with them and organizing various recreational activities for them. Strategies and policies, no matter how impressive they are, have to be put into action through these detailed programmes, budgets and procedures.

In formulating and implementing *guanxi*-based strategies it is essential to understand some of the key characteristics of *guanxi*, which should shed a great deal of light on how to pursue these strategies. It is well acknowledged in the literature, for instance, that *guanxi* is personal (Hackley and Dong, 2001). *Guanxi* between organizations is important, but it is built up and maintained by interpersonal relationships. When the individuals in the *guanxi* network leave, the *guanxi* between organizations is finished unless a new interpersonal *guanxi* nexus is put in place. In any event, therefore, a firm needs to do all it can to establish and nurture interpersonal *guanxi* no matter whether it deals with supplier firms, customer firms or government departments. Thus it is essential for a firm to find the employees within the firm or look for new employees outside the firm who have already had, or can establish, this kind of personal *guanxi* and use it effectively. This explains why many firms in China pay great attention to the ability of employees to cultivate useful personal *guanxi*, and reward those who can use his or her personal *guanxi* to further the aims of the organization. Indeed, the ability to establish personal *guanxi* has actually become a criterion for companies in their choice of new employees, especially at management level, in contemporary China. This personal nature of *guanxi* indicates, therefore, that in pursuing any *guanxi*-based strategy a firm needs to develop programmes or procedures to find and reward employees with the ability to establish and use personal *guanxi* for organizational purposes.

It is widely acknowledged that *guanxi* is transferable (Fan, 2002; Park and Luo, 2001; Luo, 2000). That is, if a Mr Smith has *guanxi* with a Mr Clegg, who happens to be a friend of a Mr Larmour, then Mr Clegg can introduce Mr Smith to Mr Larmour, or vice versa. Business between Mr Smith and Mr Larmour is unlikely to start until direct personal contact between them has been established through Mr Clegg. Whether or not the *guanxi* is transferred successfully depends largely on how satisfactory Mr Clegg feels about his *guanxi* with Mr Smith and Mr Larmour, respectively. When a firm cannot find direct personal *guanxi* with the people in the targeted organizations, therefore, it should try to find indirect personal *guanxi* – i.e. someone who knows the individuals in the targeted organizations and who can introduce the firm to them. This implies that a firm needs to maintain a web of *guanxi* that is as wide as possible, and use intermediaries, go-betweens or 'matchmakers' whenever necessary.

It is well known that *guanxi* is reciprocal (Arias, 1998; Tsang, 1998; Luo, 2000). A person who receives a favour from another person is expected to return the favour to that person in the near future. A person who does not follow the rule of reciprocity and refuses to return a favour is considered to be untrustworthy, and is likely to lose his or her *guanxi* for good. The exchange of favours often works to the advantage of the weaker party in the *guanxi* network, however, who may call for special favours for which he or she does not have to reciprocate equally. This is because the imbalance of personal power between the two parties in a *guanxi* network leads the stronger party to the understanding that he or she cannot expect equal reciprocity from the weaker party, at least for the time being. Whenever a firm uses personal *guanxi* to ask for a favour from another party, therefore, it should always thinks about how to return the favour in the near future, and how to do so with sincerity. Furthermore, it is more beneficial to establish *guanxi* with a stronger party than with a weaker party. In implementing *guanxi*-based strategies, a firm needs to work out favour-returning programmes, budgets and procedures, and to select carefully its *guanxi* partners (*guanxi hu*).

It is also commonly accepted that, although the practice of *guanxi* is essentially pragmatic, it may involve friendship and emotion (Dunfee and Warren, 2001; Pye, 1992; Luo, 2000). *Guanxi* bonds two individuals, mainly through the exchange of favours, and the ultimate purpose of *guanxi* practice is to seek favours from someone so that things can be done. It may be the case that friendship and emotion are involved, but this is not a necessary condition for *guanxi* practice. *Guanxi* that is no longer profitable is easily broken, however, unless it involves friendship and emotion. In other words, *guanxi* that is based on friendship is much stronger, more reliable and more stable than *guanxi* that is based purely on pragmatic motives. Therefore, even if a firm has pragmatic motives in pursuing *guanxi*-based strategies, it should try to establish and nurture *guanxi* not only on the basis of the exchange of favours but also on the basis of friendship and emotion, particularly in situations where the targeted *guanxi* partner has a long-term strategic bearing on the firm. This explains why forging friendships is often taken to be – or, at least, is claimed to be – the number one consideration in *guanxi* practice in China.

Lastly but not exclusively, as has already been mentioned, *guanxi* is controversial ethically, and it tends to be conducted in secrecy (Hackley and Dong, 2001; Lovett, Simmons and Kali, 1999; Chan, Cheng and Szeto, 2002; Su and Littlefield, 2001; Fan, 2002). *Guanxi* practice is needed when things cannot be done through regular official procedures, or cannot be done efficiently through regular official procedures. *Guanxi* practice therefore often involves the exchange of favours with government officials, which may be considered to be unethical, or even equivalent to corruption. As such, it is often conducted in private, not in public. In formulating and implementing *guanxi*-based strategies, therefore, the firm has to design its programmes and procedures carefully, in such a way that the exchange of favours is culturally and legally acceptable and, therefore, is not regarded as corrupt, and the exchange of favours is not carried out in the public gaze. This explains why, in China, business is often conducted at the dinner table, in hotel rooms and at home, not at formal negotiation tables.

Evaluation and control of *guanxi*-based strategies

Once *guanxi*-based strategies have been put in place, the process of implementation should be closely monitored, and, if problems arise, proper corrective measures have to be taken to bring the damage under control. This is what is called strategic evaluation and control in strategic management.

To evaluate *guanxi*-based strategies, a firm needs to compare the actual performance of such strategies with what it was hoping to achieve through them. *Guanxi* strategies are, for instance, often used to overcome the bureaucratic barriers to business operations. As shown in the case of Pierre Cardin in China, the appointment of Song Huaigui was obviously a strategic move by Pierre Cardin to overcome, through *guanxi* practice, various forms of red tape, including the twenty-eight official stamps required to open a restaurant in Beijing. Whether or not, and to what extent, this objective has been achieved should be a key criterion for Pierre Cardin in its evaluation of its *guanxi*-based strategy and of the programmes, budgets and procedures by which the strategy was put into effect, including the appointment of Song Huaigui. If the objective has not been achieved satisfactorily, appropriate corrective action would need be taken. The fact that Song Huaigui appears to have been doing very well in her post indicates that Pierre Cardin's *guanxi*-based strategy has been implemented successfully.

Not every transnational corporation, however, is as lucky as Pierre Cardin. Many TNCs have met problems in pursuing *guanxi*-based strategies in China, and some of them have made huge losses. As determined by the characteristics of *guanxi*, in fact, it could be very risky for a TNC to pursue *guanxi*-based strategies in China. As mentioned above, *guanxi* is ethically controversial, and is likely to lead to corruption on the part of government officials. Once corrupted government officials have been exposed and captured, even though the TNC may not get caught up in criminal charges, the *guanxi* network established by the company has broken down, and the company's business is likely to be affected. It is reported that when Chen Xitong, the Mayor of Beijing, was arrested on corruption charges in 1995, some TNCs that had established *guanxi* with him lost their investments (Tsang, 1998).

Even if the government officials with whom a transnational corporation has established *guanxi* have not become corrupt, the TNC may still suffer if these officials leave their posts. This relates back to the personal nature of *guanxi*, mentioned above, which means that *guanxi*-based strategies are highly vulnerable to personnel changes in the *guanxi* network. Personnel changes on one side of the *guanxi* network may lead to the breakdown of the relationship between business organizations, and the cancellation of previous business deals. It has been reported (Clifford, 2003), for instance, that Newbridge Capital, based in the United States, reached a deal to buy a controlling share in Shenzhen Development Bank (SDB) in 2002. This deal was supported by the then Premier, Zhu Rongji, and other senior government officials in charge of China's banking and securities, with whom Newbridge Capital had established *guanxi*. The deal was going so well that the Chinese side even allowed Newbridge Capital to send its own management team to SDB to assume management control before the final details were ironed out. Soon after Premier Zhu Rongji retired and the Cabinet was reshuffled in March 2003, however, the deal was de facto cancelled and the management team sent by Newbridge Capital was dissolved. Frustrated by the incident, Newbridge Capital filed a lawsuit in a Texas court against SDB on 20 May 2003.[4]

The riskiness of *guanxi*-based strategies may also be increased by a lack of understanding of how *guanxi* works in China, and on inability on the part of transnational corporations to handle *guanxi* practice carefully. In China, for instance, central and local government are both important players in policy-making, and the local governments may have even greater power and influence than the central government in some respects. Therefore, if a TNC works on *guanxi* only with the central government, paying no attention to cultivating *guanxi* with local governments, it may encounter many difficulties and problems. A case in point is the Suzhou Industrial Park, an intergovernmental joint project between China and Singapore. In the beginning, as shown in box 3.3, the Singaporean side did not pay much attention to nurturing *guanxi* with the local Suzhou government, which became one of the major reasons for the frustrations it suffered subsequently.

Box 3.3 Sino-Singaporean Suzhou Industrial Park

In 1992 the Chinese and Singaporean governments announced that they would jointly develop an industrial park in Suzhou, Jiangsu province, China. Two years later China's Vice-Premier, Li Lanqing, and Singapore's Senior Minister, Lee Kuan Yew, signed a formal agreement, and the China–Singapore Suzhou Industrial Park Development (CSSD) was officially set up to build and manage the industrial park. In the Joint Steering Council of the CSSD, Li Lanqing was the co-chair alongside Singapore's Deputy Prime Minister, Lee Hsien Loong. The Singaporean side held 65 per cent of the shares in the industrial park, while the Chinese side held the remaining 35 per cent.

The Suzhou Industrial Park was a government-level joint venture designed to provide superb infrastructure and services to foreign investors in China. In establishing the project, the Singaporean leaders, who believed that they knew Chinese culture very well, focused on nurturing *guanxi* with the highest level of Chinese leaders, including Deng Xiaoping and his son (Deng Pufang), Party Chairman Jiang Zemin and Premier Zhu Rongji. Indeed, the project was supported by top Chinese leaders from the very beginning: Jiang Zeming reportedly said that the project was the 'priorities of all priorities, and it must not be allowed to fail'.[5]

The Singaporean side did not, however, make an effort to cultivate *guanxi* with the Suzhou local government, and even declined an offer made by the local authorities regarding the location of the industrial park. Being 'marginalized', the Suzhou local government felt that it was losing face. As a direct consequence, later on it promoted its own industrial park, the Suzhou New District Park, to compete with the Suzhou Industrial Park in attracting foreign investors. Without support from the local government the Suzhou Industrial Park ran into serious trouble, and made very sizeable losses in the late 1990s.

The Singaporean side was furious. Lee Kuan Yew openly accused the Suzhou New District Park of stealing potential tenants by undercutting industrial unit prices, and accused the Suzhou local government of being more interested in promoting the Suzhou New District Park than the Suzhou Industrial Park. Singapore's leaders then began to lobby the central government in Beijing to act decisively on the problem. It was said that the Singaporean side had instructed Beijing to close the Suzhou New District Park, or at least to bar it from receiving any new foreign investment.

However, the Singaporean side overestimated the power of the Chinese central government and underestimated the autonomy of Suzhou's local authorities. Chen Deming, the Mayor of Suzhou, stressed that the local government had done nothing wrong and that there was fair competition between the two parks. Furthermore, he insisted that it would have been a mistake for the local authorities to give 50–50 treatment to the two parks, as the Suzhou Industrial Park had the backing of two national governments while the Suzhou New District Park had to fend for itself (Pereira, 2004). The local government therefore refused to do anything detrimental to the interests of its own Suzhou New District Park.

Seeing no hope of any improvement in the situation, the Singaporeans decided to renegotiate the terms of the joint venture with the Chinese side. In June 1999 the Singaporean government announced that it would reduce its shareholding from 65 per cent to 35 per cent, and in January 2001 the transfer of the shareholding took place. Thereafter the Suzhou local government began to represent the Chinese side as it now acted as the controlling shareholder, and provided full support to the Suzhou Industrial Park – which has, reportedly, been running well ever since. This case shows, among other things, the importance of cultivating *guanxi* with local governments in China.[6]

Alternatively, if a transnational corporation works on *guanxi* only with local governments, paying little attention to cultivating *guanxi* with the central government, it may also suffer. The experience of Carrefour, a retailer based in France, provides a case in point. Starting from the early 1990s China began to allow foreign investors to enter, in the form of joint ventures, the retail sector in a strictly limited number of coastal cities, and asked them to secure approval from the central government before setting up retail outlets. A number of foreign companies, including retail giants Carrefour and Wal-Mart, moved into China. Some of them, such as Wal-Mart, paid attention to *guanxi* with the central government and managed to get approval from the central government. Others, including Carrefour, focused on cultivating *guanxi* with the local governments, paying little attention to *guanxi* with the central government. They often bypassed the central government, and managed to get approval from the local governments to set up retail business operations in localities under the jurisdiction of the local governments. In February 2001 Carrefour was ordered by the Chinese central government to restructure the business operation of its twenty-eight stores in fourteen cities so as to meet government regulations. Over the following two years Carrefour struggled to carry out the restructuring order, and it was unable to open any new stores until February 2004. By contrast, Wal-Mart managed to gain approval from the central government to open fourteen new stores in China in March 2001, only one month after Carrefour received the restructuring order. Clearly, Carrefour was paying the price for neglecting *guanxi* with the central government (Yong, 2001; Wang, 2001).

No matter what the causes are of the problems in pursuing *guanxi*-based strategies, TNCs have to learn how to deal with these problems when they arise – that is, how to take corrective actions to bring the damage under control. Depending on the situation, a firm may adopt one of a number of approaches to strategy control. In most cases, TNCs may find it more beneficial to repair their *guanxi* networks and adjust their *guanxi*-based strategies than abandoning them completely. In the case of Carrefour, for instance, it began to pay attention to *guanxi* with the central government after receiving the restructuring order, worked with the central government closely to change its business operations to meet the requirements and finally managed to get approval from the central government to open new stores in February 2004. In the case of the Suzhou Industrial Park, as shown in box 3.3, the Singapore side made crucial compromises in order to gain the support of the Suzhou local government, by changing the control structure of the joint venture. The Suzhou local government then had an interest in developing the project, and soon appointed a vice-mayor to head the management team. With strong support from the local government, the Suzhou Industrial Park began to make profits. If all their efforts to repair a *guanxi* network fail, however, TNCs may have to resolve the problems through recourse to the law, as Newbridge Capital did. No matter what approach is taken, the underlying principle of strategy control is the minimization of damage and losses.

Summary

Guanxi practice is so pervasive in China that transnational corporations often have to utilize it themselves as a strategy for doing business – that is, to make use of *guanxi* practice to achieve their business objectives. The current literature on *guanxi*, however, hardly addresses the practical issue of how to exercise *guanxi* practice strategically in the real Chinese business world. To overcome this shortcoming, this chapter presents a framework for the strategic management of *guanxi* in China.

It is proposed that TNCs need to make strategic decisions on *guanxi* on the basis of an environment scanning of the external and internal factors related to the practice of *guanxi* in China, including the general factors and the industry-specific factors that determine the scope, potential and limits of *guanxi* practice in China, and the organization-specific factors that determine the capacity of a TNC to exercise *guanxi*. In so doing, TNCs can obtain a clear idea of the opportunities and threats they face, and the strengths and weaknesses they have in the employment of *guanxi* in China. TNCs are then in a position to make strategic decisions on whether or not, and to what extent, to achieve their business objectives through *guanxi* – i.e. to pursue *guanxi*-based strategies.

In formulating and implementing *guanxi*-based strategies, TNCs need to pay attention to the levels of their strategies, the broad policy guidelines for the strategies, and the detailed programmes, budgets and procedures through which the strategies and policy guidelines are put into effect. It is suggested that, in implementing *guanxi*-based strategies, special attention should be paid to some of the key characteristics of *guanxi* – that it is personal, transferable, reciprocal, pragmatic (with the possible involvement of friendship) and ethically controversial. In particular, the analysis of these characteristics sheds much light on how to design specific programmes and procedures to pursue *guanxi*-based strategies in company's individual circumstances.

Despite all the promise of great benefits that they hold out for TNCs, *guanxi*-based strategies can still be very risky, and they may lead to problems or even failure. The problems may arise from the ethically controversial nature of *guanxi* practice, from changes in the personnel of a *guanxi* network or from a lack of understanding of *guanxi* practice on the part of transnational corporations. No matter what the causes of the problems are, a careful evaluation of *guanxi*-based strategies and the taking of corrective action to bring any damage under control constitute a very important part of the strategic management of *guanxi* in China.

FURTHER READING

Dunfee, T. W., and Warren, D. E. 2001. 'Is *guanxi* ethical? A normative analysis of doing business in China'. *Journal of Business Ethics* 32 (3): 191–204.

Luo, Y. D. 2000. *Guanxi and Business.* Singapore: World Scientific Publishing.

Seligman, S. D. 1999. '*Guanxi*: grease for the wheels of China'. *China Business Review* 26 (5): 34–8.

Tsang, E. W. K. 1998. 'Can *guanxi* be a source of sustained competitive advantage for doing business in China?'. *Academy of Management Executive* 12 (2): 64–74.

Xin, K. R., and Pearce, J. L. 1996. '*Guanxi*: connections as substitutes for formal institutional support'. *Academy Management Journal* 39: 1641–58.

Yeung, I. Y., and Tung, R. L. 1996. 'Achieving business success in Confucian societies: the importance of *guanxi* (connections)'. *Organisational Dynamics* 25 (2): 54–65.

Questions for discussion

1. What is *guanxi*?
2. Is *guanxi* practice unique to China? If not, what are the equivalents in other cultural settings?
3. Why is *guanxi* practice so prevalent in China?
4. Is *guanxi* practice ethical?
5. Should transnational corporations adopt *guanxi*-based strategies to do business in China? How?
6. In your opinion, what should TNCs take into account in formulating, implementing, evaluating and controlling *guanxi*-based strategies?

NOTES

1. The author would like to thank an anonymous referee for making this point. The referee points out: '[p]ersonalized networking and interpersonal connections are universally important in business. Think about the interlocked board membership and well-connected boards in US and Japan's corporations, think about such relational investments as company-paid

golf-club membership, "business" tours, and other type of legal corruptions as presented in *Corporate Governance* by Robert Monks and Nell Minow (2001, 2004). It means that the existence of and demand for *guanxi* (in terms of personalized networking and interpersonal connections) are not China-specific. What are more China-specific include the ways to cultivate, maintain, and develop personalized network and interpersonal connections, and the high sensitivity of Chinese to face (refers to, mainly, an individual's dignity, self-respect, and prestige) and reqing (i.e., humanized obligation).'

2. PEST refers to political, economic, social and technological factors; SWOT refers to strengths, weaknesses, opportunities and threats.

3. See website sources http://www.usdoj.gove/opa/pr/2005/May/05_crm_282.htm and http://business.sohu.com/20050531/ n225770986.shtm.

4. Reports indicate that Newbridge Capital finally managed to secure control of SDB at the end of 2004.

5. http://www.sipac.gov.cn/.

6. The Suzhou Industrial Park case also shows, as discussed in chapter 5, the importance of proper control arrangements in an international business alliance. Case source: Pereira (2004).

4   Select an entry mode

A mode of entry is an institutional arrangement chosen by the firm to operate in the foreign market. This decision is one of the most critical strategic decisions for the firm. It affects all the future decisions and operations of the firm in that country market. Since each mode of entry entails a concomitant level of resource commitment, it is difficult to change from one entry mode to another without considerable loss of time and money (V. Kumar and Velavan Subramanian (1997, p. 53)).

When a transnational corporation plans to move into a new overseas market it has to, first of all, think about how to enter this market. There are many ways or modes by which a TNC can enter a new market, such as exporting, franchising, licensing, joint ventures and wholly owned subsidiaries. Selecting an entry mode is one of the most important strategic decisions that a TNC has to make when it enters the Chinese market, so important that it may determine its success or failure in China. In this chapter we first review the literature on entry mode selection in international business studies, and propose an approach to the classification of market entry modes. Subsequently, in section 2, we illustrate the market entry modes available to TNCs in China, and highlight major changes in the entry modes that have been adopted. We then discuss the main considerations for entry mode selection in China using a hierarchy model in section 3, and explore the possibility of using a combination of different entry modes in section 4. Section 5 summarizes.

Introduction

It is argued, in the international business literature, that market entry mode is closely associated with the degree of resource commitment, risk exposure and management control of a transnational corporation, and that the choice of market entry modes is determined by a variety of factors. Incorporating different theoretical perspectives, John Dunning (1988) proposes an eclectic

OLI paradigm for analysis of the choice of entry modes. According to the paradigm, the choice of market entry modes is affected by three broad categories of factors. The first is related to ownership (O). It is argued that TNCs possess proprietary assets that enable them to compete with both companies in the home market and companies in the overseas market, and that the choice of entry modes depends on the nature of the proprietary assets that TNCs possess. The second is related to location (L). It is proposed that countries have specific location characteristics, and TNCs should choose their entry modes on the basis of the location characteristics of the country it wants to enter. The third is related to internalization (I). It is suggested that different entry modes imply different degrees of internalization and thus different amounts of transaction costs, and TNCs should choose their entry modes on the basis of the transaction costs involved.

In the light of the research on determinants of entry mode selection, scholars tend to agree on the basic categories of factors that a TNC should take into account in selecting an entry mode, but disagree on how to take them into account in making decisions on entry modes. Basically, there are two broad approaches to addressing the 'how' issue. The first is a simultaneous approach, which looks into all entry modes simultaneously as if they are all associated with, and influenced by, a set of factors at the same level in the same time-span. Wojin Chu and Erin Anderson (1992), for instance, consider entry modes as being associated with such factors as resource commitment, risk exposure and control, and take all entry modes as a continuum, from exporting to wholly owned subsidiaries. The position of each entry mode in the continuum is determined by the degree to which the entry mode is subject to the influence of these factors. Furthermore, Sanjeev Agarwal and Sridhar Ramaswami (1992) and Peter Buckley and Mark Casson (1998) set an entry mode as a baseline, against which all other entry modes are compared and assessed in the light of the transaction cost involved. Underlying this approach is an assumption that managers consider all market entry modes simultaneously rather than sequentially, and consider the determinants of all these entry modes at the same time rather than at different stages of the decision process.

The second is a hierarchical approach, which examines market entry modes sequentially as if they are at different levels of a hierarchy. Kumar and Subramaniam (1997) for instance, argue that a natural hierarchy exists among market entry modes. All entry modes can first be classified into equity and non-equity entry modes: equity entry modes include joint ventures, acquisitions and greenfield investments, while non-equity modes include exporting and contractual agreements. At the next level, the equity modes and non-equity modes can be each further divided into groups of entry modes, and so on. There are different groupings of factors that affect the selection of market entry modes at different levels of the hierarchy. Underlying this approach is an assumption that managers consider the choice of entry modes sequentially, and consider only a few of the critical factors at each level of the hierarchy. Following this approach, Yigang Pan and David Tse (2000) test hypotheses about the choice of entry modes using data collected from China. Pan and Tse agree with Kumar and Subramaniam on the classification of entry modes by the equity criterion at the first level of the hierarchy, but disagree with them on the classification of entry modes at subsequent levels.

Theoretically speaking, the two approaches both have strong points and weak points. Practically speaking, however, the simultaneous approach is very demanding in terms of the data needed to gain relevant information and the time consumed to collect the data, because it takes into account all entry modes and all influential factors at the same time. In the real business world, managers often do not have enough resources and time to collect the relevant data on all entry modes and all influential factors, and have to make a decision on entry modes within the constraints. The hierarchical approach obviously offers managers a convenient framework with which to do so, because it takes into consideration only a few entry modes and a selection of key influential factors at any one time. As this book is mainly concerned with strategy making in the real business world, we therefore use the hierarchical approach as a framework for the analysis of the selection of entry modes in China.

We acknowledge, however, that there are shortcomings in both the hierarchical framework proposed by Kumar and Subramaniam in 1997 and the hierarchical framework proposed by Pan and Tse in 2000. In a hierarchical classification of entry modes, for instance, a distinction should be made between exporting (a very traditional form of international business) and investment (a relatively recent form of international business) at the very beginning, so as to reflect a fundamental difference between the two broad categories of market entry modes. In addition, the classification of contractual agreements as non-equity entry modes is confusing if it is applied to the Chinese context because some important contractual agreements in China are actually equivalent to equity entry modes. There is, for example, an important entry mode called cooperative (or contractual) joint venture in China, which is established on the basis of a contractual agreement between a local Chinese company and a foreign company that holds no less than 25 per cent of the total shares of the joint venture. This entry mode cannot be considered as a contractual agreement within the category of non-equity mode, and thus

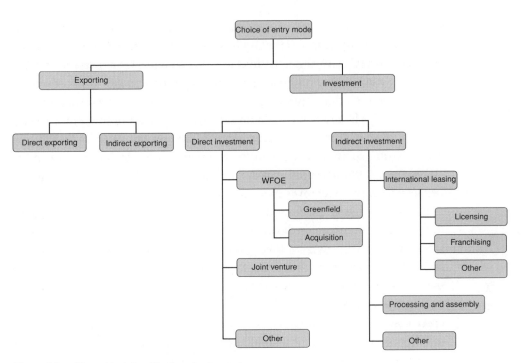

Figure 4.1   Hierarchical classification of entry modes

cannot be analysed in the existing hierarchical frameworks. In the study on entry mode selection in China conducted by Pan and Tse, this entry mode was simply excluded from the hierarchical framework.

To overcome this shortcoming, as illustrated in figure 4.1, we propose a new hierarchical approach to the classification of entry modes. At the first level of the hierarchy is the division between exporting and investment. In economic terms, exporting is related to the output, or the product, that is to be sold once and for all, while investment is related to investing in the production process, and is expected to yield a lasting income. The distinction between the two is so fundamental that it has to be taken into account at the very beginning. The first decision that a transnational corporation needs to make on the selection of entry modes is whether to sell its products to a new market or make an investment in the new market. As the distinction between the two is very clear, there is no need for it to be explained further here.

At subsequent levels, however, some explanations are in order. We begin with the division between foreign direct investment and foreign indirect investment. The term 'foreign direct investment' is well defined and widely used in the international business literature, but, surprisingly, the term 'foreign indirect investment' is not. According to the United Nations Conference on Trade and Development and the Organisation for Economic Co-operation and Development (OECD), foreign direct investment refers to an investment made to acquire a lasting interest in an enterprise operating outside the economy of the investor, including equity capital, reinvested earnings and intra-company loans. UNCTAD and the OECD do not define foreign indirect investment, but acknowledge that non-equity forms of investment, such as franchising and licensing, are not included in their statistics of foreign direct investment (UNCTAD, 2005). It would appear that there is a need for a clear distinction between foreign direct investment and foreign indirect investment.

In the new hierarchical model of entry modes, we argue that the crucial difference between foreign direct investment and foreign indirect investment is whether the foreign investor directly invests in and *owns* either all or an effective share of the production (or service) facilities in an enterprise operating outside the economy of the investor so as to acquire a lasting interest. The threshold for an effective share is considered to be 25 per cent of the total equity stakes of an enterprise in China, although it is normally considered to be 10 per cent or so in other countries (UNCTAD, 2005). All entry modes falling in the category of foreign indirect investment fail to meet this criterion. The investors indirectly invest in the production (or service) facilities, through leasing out technology and management know-how or providing components or equipment, but none of them *owns* an effective share of the production (or service) facilities in order to acquire a lasting interest. In a sense, therefore, the distinction between direct and indirect investment can be considered as a distinction between equity and non-equity investment. The distinction is critical, because it indicates a fundamentally different degree of resource involvement in the recipient country by the foreign investor. Once a decision has been made to invest in a foreign market, a question that immediately follows is whether to invest in directly and own the production facilities in that country so as to acquire a lasting interest, or whether to make an indirect investment in that country in the form of licensing, franchising, processing, compensation trade or others.

In the new hierarchical mode, furthermore, we take licensing and franchising as forms of international leasing, in that they are different from other forms of leasing only in what is leased. In the case of licensing, what is leased is technology, copyright, patent or trademark. In the case of franchising, what is leased is the whole management system. In both cases, the licenser and the franchiser gain a rent in the form of licence fees or royalties. All these kinds of leasing are different from other types of indirect investment, such as processing and assembly, where foreign investors provide components or even equipment for the assembly of the final product while local companies do the job and earn processing fees. With this new hierarchical model clearly defined, we now proceed to discuss the entry modes available in China and the main considerations for entry mode selection. We acknowledge, however, that the detailed classification of entry modes in the hierarchical mode may vary from country to country. As will be seen, this variety needs to be taken into account when we apply this model to China.

Entry modes in China

Exporting is the most traditional entry mode in China. Exporting was permitted even before China opened up, but it grew rapidly after 1978 in line with the gradual liberalization of the foreign trade regime. Insofar as entry modes are concerned, what distinguishes the post-1978 period from previously is not exporting but the opening up to foreign investment. Since 1978, as shown in figure 4.2, the growth of foreign investment has been much faster than the growth of exporting (importing on the part of China). From 1983 to 2004, for instance, the growth of foreign investment was nearly twice as rapid as the growth of exporting. As China does not provide data on direct and indirect exporting, however, it is impossible to ascertain the change in the composition of the entry modes within the category of exporting.

By contrast, China provides relatively detailed data on foreign investment, so we are able to take a close look at the composition of the entry modes within this category. At first China allowed only a very limited number of entry modes in the form of foreign investment, including joint ventures, processing and assembly, and joint developments. Now almost all the investment-related entry modes that are available in mature market economies are permitted in China, albeit to varying degrees. According to China's official statistics, foreign investment is divided into two broad categories. The first is foreign direct investment, including equity joint ventures, cooperative joint ventures, wholly foreign-owned enterprises, foreign companies limited by shares (FCLSs), cooperative developments (CDs) and others. The second is called 'other foreign investment', and includes share trading, international leasing, compensation trade, and processing and assembly, which is equivalent to the category of foreign indirect investment in the hierarchical model illustrated in the previous section. A brief explanation of these investment-related entry modes is provided in table 4.1.

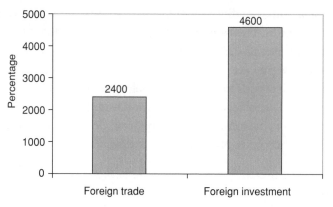

Figure 4.2   Growth of foreign investment and exporting in China (1983–2004)
Source: *China Statistical Yearbook 2005.*

We should be aware that the official classification does not include all the entry modes that involve investment in China. Establishing a representative office, for instance, has proved a very popular method for transnational corporations in China ever since China opened up, but it is not included in the official classification. A representative office is established by a TNC to conduct limited business activities, including the collection of information, the establishment of local contacts, lobbying for licences and negotiation with the Chinese government or potential business partners. According to Chinese regulations, a representative office is not allowed to engage in direct profit-making activities. It has to be sponsored by a Chinese company or organization, and is licensed only for a period of three years. Despite these constraints, TNCs often set up a representative office as the first step to entering the Chinese market.

Nevertheless, the official Chinese classification of entry modes and the official Chinese statistics provide a basis on which we can propose a hierarchical mode of entry modes specifically for China. The model is illustrated in figure 4.3. Given the importance of foreign investment, as explained previously, we focus on the investment category, examining some striking changes in TNCs' investment-related entry modes in China.

First of all, as shown in figure 4.4, foreign direct investment and foreign indirect investment each accounted for roughly a half of total foreign investment in the first four years after China opened up. From the mid-1980s onwards, however, FDI began to gain ground remarkably. Over the twenty years from 1985 to 2004 FDI accounted for about 96 per cent of total foreign investment, with indirect investment accounting for the remaining 4 per cent. Transnational corporations clearly favour foreign direct investment to foreign indirect investment. Apart from the relaxation of the regulatory environment in China,

Table 4.1   Official Chinese classification of foreign investment

Category	Explanation
Foreign direct investment	
Equity joint venture	A foreign company and a local company together establish a new enterprise, and share profits and risks on the basis of their respective equity contribution. The foreign share cannot be less than 25% of the total shares of the joint venture.
Cooperative joint venture	A foreign company and a local company together establish a new enterprise, and share profits and risks on the basis of contractual agreements. The foreign share can be in the form of such intangible assets as patents, trademarks or non-patented technology, but cannot be less than 25% of the total shares of the joint venture.
Wholly foreign-owned enterprise	A foreign company establishes a new enterprise in China and holds the capital of the new enterprise. The foreign company is liable to the new enterprise to the extent of its investment.
Foreign company limited by shares	A foreign company purchases more than 25% of the total shares of a Chinese stock company.
Cooperative development	Foreign companies cooperate with local Chinese companies in projects related to exploring and producing natural resources, such as minerals, gas, and offshore oil, which often require a large amount of up-front foreign capital and have a long payback period.
Other foreign investment	
Share trading	A foreign company trades the shares of companies listed on Chinese stock markets, but does not obtain effective ownership of these listed companies.
International leasing	A foreign company rents its properties out to a local Chinese company to earn a rent. The properties may include technology, management systems, equipment, etc.
Compensation trade	A foreign company provides capital or technology to a domestic company in return for payment in kind instead of cash. The payment is normally a percentage of the profits from the sale of the goods produced by the foreign capital or technology.
Processing and assembly	A foreign company provides components, raw materials, designs or even equipment to a local Chinese company for processing and assembling. The Chinese company then delivers the finished products back to the foreign company in return for a processing fee.

as shown in the next section, the change has much to do with TNCs' assessment of business risks, intellectual property protection and other factors in China.

Within the category of foreign direct investment, the most significant change has been the decline of joint ventures and the rise of wholly foreign-owned enterprises in recent years. In the early 1980s more than 90 per cent of FDI was made in the form of joint ventures; in 1985, for example, they accounted for

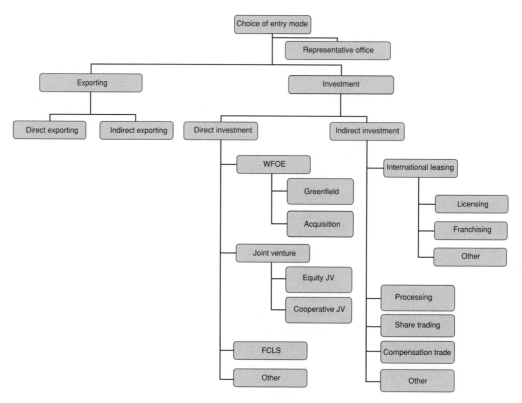

Figure 4.3   Hierarchical classification of entry modes in China

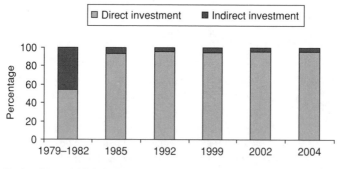

Figure 4.4   Foreign direct and indirect investment in China (1979–2004)
Source: *China Statistical Yearbook 2005.*

93 per cent of total FDI. From the late 1980s onwards, however, and especially from the early 1990s, wholly foreign-owned enterprises grew at a much faster rate than joint ventures. Consequently, the share of WFOEs in total FDI rose rapidly, while the share of joint ventures (EJV$_s$ as well as CJVs) declined. From 2001 onwards, as shown in figure 4.5, WFOEs began to replace joint ventures

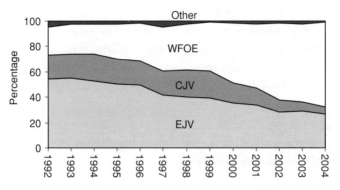

Figure 4.5   Composition of foreign direct investment in China (1992–2004)
Source: *China Statistical Yearbook 2005.*

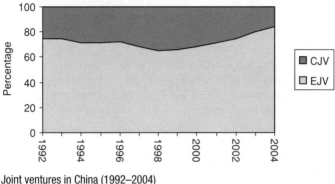

Figure 4.6   Joint ventures in China (1992–2004)
Source: *China Statistical Yearbook 2005.*

as the major form of foreign direct investment; in 2004 they accounted for 67 per cent of total FDI. It is evident that transnational corporations are tending to be increasingly in favour of wholly foreign owned enterprises at the expense of joint ventures. The change is related to the removal of regulatory restrictions, but also to TNCs' consideration of other factors discussed in the next section.

At the next level of foreign direct investment, as shown in figure 4.6, there has been a change in the composition of entry modes within the category of joint ventures in recent years. As an important entry mode in China, cooperative joint ventures gained ground throughout the 1990s, but after 1999 they began to lose out to equity joint ventures. The change seems to indicate, as analysed in chapter 1, that transnational corporations have begun to prefer investment made in the form of tangible assets in China in recent years. As shown in box 4.1, however, the change may be related to the fluctuations in China's regulatory environment as well. Unfortunately, the Chinese government does not publish data on the composition of entry modes within the category of wholly foreign-owned enterprises, so it is impossible to ascertain the changes that may have occurred within this category. As mergers and acquisitions have not been allowed in China until recently, however, anecdotal evidence suggests the majority of WFOEs have been in the form of greenfield investment.

Box 4.1 Cooperative joint ventures in the Chinese telecommunications industry

Telecoms has been one of the industries least open to foreign investors in China. To enter this industry, foreign investors have to bypass the regulatory restrictions by means of some flexible arrangements. In the early 1990s foreign investors began to move into the industry through cooperative joint ventures, one of the most flexible entry modes available in China, and throughout the 1990s CJVs remained the predominant foreign investment structure in the telecoms industry.

A format known as Chinese–Chinese–Foreign (*Zhong–Zhong–Wai*) was particularly popular then. In this format, foreign companies would establish a CJV with Chinese partner companies (Chinese–Foreign) that were usually affiliated with China Unicom Ltd – a large, state-owned Chinese telecoms service provider. Then the foreign companies would lease their equipment and provide consulting services to Unicom through the cooperative joint venture, using a revenue-sharing contract between their Chinese partners and Unicom (Chinese–Chinese).

Although China benefited from advanced foreign telecoms technology through the flexible arrangement, the legal status of this kind of CJV in the telecoms industry remained ambiguous and uncertain throughout the 1990s. At the end of the 1990s China decided to ban CJVs in the telecoms industry, on the grounds that they allowed foreign investors to gain disproportionate returns on, management control over and protection of their technology when they reached their deals with the financially week Unicom. According to the agreement on China's accession to the WTO, equity joint ventures were to be the only form of foreign investment allowed in the basic telecoms industry.

Subsequently, however, Unicom, and other Chinese telecoms companies, were placed under the Ministry of Information Industry, putting them all in a stronger position to negotiate for favourable terms with foreign companies. Therefore, China began to relax the restrictions on cooperative joint ventures in the telecoms industry. In the Guidance Catalog of Industries with Foreign Investment, issued in 2002, telecoms was moved from the prohibited to the restricted category, and foreign investors were allowed to enter the industry through both cooperative and equity joint ventures.

From 2002 onwards foreign telecoms companies, including AT&T and American IDC Corporation, have established a few cooperative joint ventures and equity joint ventures under 'cooperative agreements' with the Chinese telecoms industry, providing internet-related services. As CJVs may offer greater flexibility than EJVs, they are very likely to gain ground in China's sensitive industries in the future.[1]

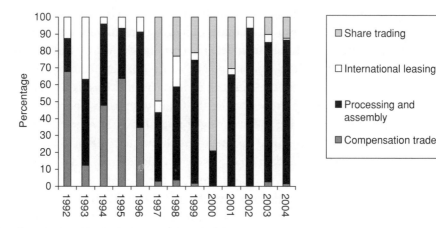

Figure 4.7   Composition of foreign indirect investment in China (1992–2004)
Source: *China Statistical Yearbook 2005.*

There are two other forms of foreign direct investment in China that need to be explained: cooperative developments and foreign companies limited by shares. CDs are joint projects between a foreign company and a local Chinese partner that relate to the exploration and development of natural resources, such as minerals, gas and offshore oil. These projects require a large amount of up-front foreign capital and have a long payback period, so they are not popular with foreign investors. CDs accounted for less than 1 per cent of total FDI in 2004. FCLSs are companies listed on Chinese stock markets with foreign shares accounting for more than 25 per cent of the total shares. If the foreign share increases to more than 50 per cent of the total, this entry mode then becomes acquisition. This entry mode was allowed in China in 1995, but has not grown very much since then owing to the tight control over the stock market and the country's cautious attitude towards mergers and acquisitions. In 2004, for instance, FCLSs accounted for only 1 per cent of total FDI in China. These two entry modes do not feature prominently in our discussion.

Within the category of foreign indirect investment, as shown in figure 4.7, the most significant changes have been the decline of compensation trade and international leasing, and the rise of share trading and processing and assembly, in recent years. Compensation trade accounted for 68 per cent of total foreign indirect investment in 1992, but only 2 per cent in 2004. International leasing accounted for nearly 40 per cent of total foreign indirect investment at its height in 1993, but only 3 per cent in 2004. In contrast, processing and assembly accounted for 20 per cent of the total in 1992, but 81 per cent in 2004. Share trading was negligible in the early 1990s, then grew so rapidly that it accounted for nearly 80 per cent at its height in 2000, though it fell back to 15 per cent in 2004.[2] As the absolute amounts of indirect investment remain very small and volatile, we do not look in detail at entry modes within this category.[3]

At the next level, unfortunately, we do not have data on the composition of entry modes in the category of international leasing. As a matter of fact, we do not really know whether the Chinese statistics on international leasing include franchising and licensing or not. Chinese law and regulations on these entry modes remained opaque throughout the 1990s, and China has still not published official data on the two entry modes even today.[4] Indeed, it is very difficult for China to collect the data because of a particular feature of the two entry modes: the investment is not made in equity form but in the form of intangible assets, which are difficult to calculate and assess. In standard international practice, these entry modes are calculated on the basis of the royalties and licensing fees paid to foreign franchisors or licensors (UNCTAD, 2005). Nevertheless, anecdotal evidence suggests that transnational corporations have been entering the Chinese market in the form of licensing and franchising since the early 1990s, including Pierre Cardin, McDonald's and KFC. As shown in the case of Super 8 Hotels (box 4.2), for instance, franchising has become a popular entry mode among TNCs operating in the Chinese hotel industry in recent years.

Box 4.2 Super 8 Hotels (China)

Super 8 Hotels, the world's largest franchise economy lodging chain by number of hotels, until recently operated only in the United States and Canada. In June 2004, immediately after China issued its Provisional Measures for the Supervision of Foreign Invested Enterprises Engaging in Commercial Franchising Business, Super 8 opened its first Chinese franchise hotel, in Beijing. Super 8 has since developed franchise hotels in five other locations in China, and plans to expand to thirty-eight major cities in the near future.

The parent company of Super 8 is Cendant Hotel Group. Cendant Hotel Group is also the parent company of other franchise hotel chains, including AmeriHost Inn, Days Inn, Howard Johnson, Knights Inn, Ramada, Travelodge and Wingate Inn. Apart from Super 8 hotels, Cendant Hotel Group plans to develop roughly fourteen Days Inn, fifteen Ramada and twenty-one Howard Johnson franchise hotels in China in the next year and a half.

These franchise hotels chains offer lodging at different prices, targeting different groups of customers. With their five-star rating, Howard Johnson hotels target senior executives. Ranging from three and a half to five stars, Ramada hotels are frequented by senior or mid-level executives. Days Inn hotels range from three to three and a half stars and thus house mid-level executives. By contrast, Super 8 hotels range from two and a half to three stars, primarily targeting Chinese business travellers, group tours and budget travellers. In addition, Super 8 hotels house budget travellers and backpackers from Australia, New

Zealand, Japan, South Korea, Singapore and other countries. It is planned that Super 8 hotels will start in Beijing, Shanghai, Guangzhou, Chongqing and other first-tier cities, and then move to Dalian, Chendu, Hangzhou, Harbin, Xiamen and other second-tier cities. In the end, the Super 8 hotel chain will expand to smaller cities and towns in China.

The master franchisee partner of Super 8 in China is Tian Rui Hotel Corporation (TRHC), based in Hong Kong. Under the master franchisee agreement, TRHC acts as franchisor of Super 8 in mainland China on behalf of Cendant Hotel Group, and develops the Super 8 brand and franchise hotel system there. In promoting the Super 8 brand, Cendant Hotel Group encourages the master franchisee to maintain the same high international standards in China as in the United States and Canada, on the one hand, and tailor the Super 8 hotels somewhat to suit Chinese culture and conditions, in terms of hotel layout and design, room size and car park space, on the other hand. Nevertheless, Super 8 has managed to implement basically the same operating process and management style in China as in the United States and Canada, in order to ensure service consistency. Super 8 (China) has been running very well, but now it is facing competition from new foreign entrants such as Green Tree Inn and emerging local hotel brands such as Home Inn, Motel 168 and Jinjiang Inn.[5]

Main considerations for entry mode selection

The changes in the relative utilization of these entry modes in China illustrated above reflect, of course, the changes in China's international business regime. The rise of wholly foreign-owned enterprises within the category of foreign direct investment reflects, for instance, the removal of restrictions on this entry mode in certain industries, as discussed in chapter 2. In addition, the absence of acquisition, licensing and franchising in the official statistics reflects the regulatory restrictions on these entry modes in China. To an extent, however, it can be argued that the changing composition also indicates some significant shifts in TNCs' preferences for certain kinds of entry modes within the policy constraints. As China further liberalizes its foreign investment regime following WTO accession, TNCs will have an increasing degree of freedom in selecting their entry modes. It is crucial, therefore, for transnational corporations to know how to choose between the various entry modes when they have a choice. In this section, we discuss the most important factors that TNCs need to take into consideration in their selection process.

In the discussion, we use the hierarchical model illustrated in figure 4.3 as an analytical framework. We assume that there are different sets of factors determining entry mode selection at different levels of the hierarchy, and that managers should pay attention to the most relevant factor(s) in their selection of entry modes at any given level of the hierarchy. Following this line of thinking, we discuss entry mode selection from the highest to the lowest level of the hierarchy, and focus on only the most crucial factors at each level of the hierarchy. To simplify the issue, in addition, we use Dunning's eclectic model as a main framework of reference in the discussion, and classify all factors into three categories: location, ownership and transaction cost. In selecting entry modes, therefore, TNCs should take into consideration the most important factors in these categories in relation to the crucial differences between the entry modes under comparison at the same level. We should be aware, however, that the three categories of factors are not all relevant at every level of the hierarchy, and we discuss only the most relevant of them at a given level of the hierarchy. Furthermore, we do not intend to discuss all the entry modes available in China, focusing only on the most important of them.

Exporting versus investment

The key difference between exporting and investment is that the former involves the short-term sale of goods produced outside China while the latter involves long-term investment in facilities that produce goods inside China. In choosing between exporting and investment, TNCs should, first of all, take into consideration location-specific factors. China, for instance, has an obvious advantage in its cheap labour force. If it is cheaper to produce goods in China than in the home country, it is in the interest of TNCs to make an investment in China to producing goods there rather than producing goods at home and then exporting them to China. Many, if not all, TNCs from developed countries have moved to China to make use of the country's cheap labour force. TNCs from less developed countries, however, where the labour force is cheaper even than that in China, would find exporting to China more attractive than investing there. Another location-specific factor is country risk. If China is considered to be a country with high risk, investing in China would be less attractive to TNCs than exporting, because it involves a greater degree of resource commitment and, therefore, a greater degree of exposure to risk than exporting. One of the reasons China attracted only a small amount of foreign investment in the 1980s was that it was then considered to be a country with high political risk. After Deng Xiaoping's southern tour in 1992 foreign investment poured into the country, because of the realization that the political environment had improved significantly as a result.

Transaction cost is another key consideration at this level. If China places costly tariff and non-tariff trade barriers in the way of the products that a TNC produces and exports to China, for instance, the transaction cost of exporting would be very high. It is, therefore, in the interest of the TNC to invest in China so as to produce and sell the products there. Alternatively, if the tariff and non-tariff trade barriers are low, the TNC may find it attractive to produce goods at home and export them to China. In a sense, ironically, the high tariff and non-tariff trade barriers that China maintained in the early period of opening up played a key role in 'attracting' foreign investment to the country. Interestingly, however, foreign investment continued to move into China even after the gradual removal of the tariff and non-tariff trade barriers in recent years, which has much to do with the beneficial effect of China's aforementioned location advantage.

Relatively speaking, ownership considerations play a less important role in selecting entry modes at this level than location and transaction cost considerations. Nevertheless, ownership cannot be completely excluded here. If a TNC has very strong core competencies in its marketing network rather than in production, for instance, it may find that exporting is preferable to investment. On the other hand, if a TNC has its core competencies in production as opposed to its marketing network, it may find that investment is a better choice.

Direct versus indirect investment

The crucial difference between foreign direct investment and foreign indirect investment is that the former involves effective foreign equity ownership of the production (or service) facilities in China while the latter does not. In choosing between the two, TNCs should first take country risk into consideration. If the risk of investing in China is high, for instance, direct investment is not attractive to TNCs, because it will be very difficult for them to withdraw the investment they made in the production (or service) facilities in China if unexpected problems arise. In these circumstances indirect investment is preferable, because TNCs can withdraw the investment they have made with relative ease. As the vast majority of foreign investment in China is made in the form of direct investment, this indicates, in a sense, that TNCs do not now consider China a high-risk country.

Transaction cost should also be taken into consideration. If the protection of intellectual property rights is weak in China, for instance, indirect investment in the form of licensing and franchising is not an attractive option, because transnational corporations may find it difficult and costly to protect their technology and management know-how from being infringed by local Chinese companies. TNCs have to spend money, time and energy in protecting their IPR, which increases the transaction cost. In these circumstances, therefore, TNCs may find it beneficial to internalize their business activities by setting up production facilities in China to produce goods using their technology and management know-how themselves. In a sense, therefore, the slow growth of indirect investment reflects the weak protection of intellectual property rights in China – something that is analysed in chapter 10.

Finally, but not exclusively, ownership-specific factors should be taken into consideration. If a TNC has, for instance, core competencies in intangible assets such as patents, trademarks and copyrights rather than in tangible assets, it may find that indirect investment in the form of licensing and franchising is preferable to direct investment. If a TNC has core competencies in tangible assets, on the other hand, it may find that direct investment is more attractive than indirect investment. If a TNC has no core competencies in intangible assets in the form of technology or management know-how at all, furthermore, it is impossible for the TNC to make an investment in the form of licensing and franchising. Given the country risks and transaction costs, most TNCs make decisions on whether to make direct or indirect investment on the basis of ownership considerations.

Joint venture versus wholly foreign-owned enterprise

The key difference between a joint venture and a wholly foreign-owned enterprise is that the former involves a local partner while the latter does not. In choosing between the two entry modes, therefore, it is crucial for TNCs to take transaction cost into consideration first. A Chinese partner normally has local knowledge and a local network that may help TNCs reduce transaction cost when they venture into the Chinese market. On the other hand, however, conflicts between partners may occur, which increases transaction cost. TNCs should think carefully about the advantages and disadvantages of the joint venture option in terms of transaction cost. If the transaction cost of establishing and managing a joint venture is greater than establishing and managing a WFOE, it is in the interest of a TNC to establish a wholly owned enterprise to 'internalize' its business activities. The decline of joint ventures and the rise of WFOEs in China in recent years reflect the trend that the cost of establishing and managing the former is considered to be greater than the cost of establishing and managing the latter. This does not come as a surprise, given that TNCs have now got to know much more about China than before and do not need a Chinese partner as much as they did previously.

Ownership-specific factors should also be taken into consideration. It is very difficult for a TNC to protect its technology from leaking to a local partner in the setting of a joint venture. If a TNC has proprietary technology that could easily be copied by a local partner in a joint venture setting, therefore, it may find it more beneficial to establish a WFOE than a joint venture. In a sense, the popularity of WFOEs reflects a rise in TNCs' concerns over technology leakage in China. Many local Chinese companies have indeed successfully made use of joint ventures to learn about advanced technology and management know-how from transnational corporations. Some of these local companies, such as Haier and TCL, have already managed to establish their own brand names, and begun to compete with their foreign counterparts in international markets. It is, therefore, quite reasonable that TNCs should now have become cautious about technology leaking in the setting of joint ventures.

Moreover, country risk should be taken into consideration as well. In a joint venture, a TNC can share the costs and risks with a local Chinese partner. If the risks of investing in China are high, a TNC may find joint ventures preferable to WFOEs. If the risks are low, on the other hand, a TNC may find joint ventures less attractive, as it does not need a local partner to share the risks. The decline of joint ventures reflects, in a sense, the perception that China is no longer a high-risk country.

Greenfield investment versus acquisition

Greenfield investment refers to starting a new enterprise from scratch while acquisition refers to purchasing an established local enterprise. Given the key difference between the two entry modes, transnational corporations should primarily take into consideration the relative transaction cost in terms of the time consumed and the effort involved in starting a new enterprise or in purchasing an established local enterprise in China.

It is estimated that it takes at least five to ten years for a newly established wholly foreign-owned enterprise to achieve a profitable scale in China (Woodard and Wang 2005, p. 13). By that time, in addition, competition may have become so fierce that it is very difficult for the new enterprise to survive without substantial additional investment. The acquisition of an established local enterprise may achieve a profitable scale quickly, because the purchased local company can bring in an established customer base, an established marketing network and thus a sizeable increase in market share immediately. In China's context, however, acquisition is a highly restricted entry mode, and is subject to approval from the government at different levels. The complexity of the approval process depends on the type of acquisition target, the size of the acquisition transaction and the impact of the acquisition deal on the industry involved. It could be, therefore, very costly for a TNC to acquire a local company in terms of the effort it has to make to nurture *guanxi* to go through the complex bureaucratic procedure. A TNC needs, therefore, to balance the costs and the benefits of acquisition as compared to greenfield investment, and choose the one with the smaller transaction cost.

Cooperative versus equity joint venture

The most important difference between an equity joint venture and a cooperative joint venture is that the foreign and the Chinese partners share profits and risks on the basis of their respective equity contributions in the former, and on the basis of their contractual agreement in the latter. As intangible assets such as trademarks, copyrights and patents are normally included in the contractual agreement, a CJV provides a more flexible platform for a TNC to join forces with a local Chinese company than an EJV. In choosing between the two entry modes, therefore, a TNC should primarily take into account the core competencies it has. If it has core competencies in intangible assets rather than equity resources, for instance, it may find that CJVs are preferable to EJVs. As shown in box 4.1, however, choosing these two entry modes is sometimes subject to regulatory restrictions in China.

Leasing versus processing

The most outstanding difference between leasing and processing is that a TNC leases its technology, management, equipment, etc. out to a local company to earn a rent in the former, and provides a local company with components and other resources for the processing and assembly of the finished articles in the latter. In making a choice between the two entry modes, therefore, a TNC should, first and foremost, take into consideration the core competencies it has. If it has core competencies in a complete 'package' of technology, equipment and management know-how, it may find leasing an attractive option; if, however, it has core competencies in providing components and other resources, it may find processing and assembly an attractive option.

Licensing versus franchising

The key difference between licensing and franchising is that a TNC rents technology out to a local company in the former, whereas in the latter it rents the whole management system out to a local company. In choosing between the two entry modes, obviously, a TNC should primarily take into account the core competencies it has: if these lie in technology alone, it may find licensing attractive, but, if they lie in the whole management system, it may find franchising the more appealing option.

Combination of entry modes: a solution?

Each entry mode has its distinctive advantages, as shown above. More often than not, TNCs find that the adoption of one entry mode alone cannot fully serve their needs in complex business environments, and therefore they frequently find it advantageous to adopt more than one entry mode at the same time. The combination of entry modes enables TNCs to take full advantage of the strengths of several entry modes simultaneously.

When Coca-Cola moved to China in the early 1990s it had to make a decision on whether to enter the Chinese market through joint ventures or through wholly foreign-owned enterprises. On the one hand, Coca-Cola needed to take precautions against the possible infringement of its intellectual property – the ingredients of Coca-Cola drinks. On the other hand, Coca-Cola had to make use of local Chinese partners to achieve product localization and cost reduction. In the end, Coca-Cola came up with an ingenious solution: adopt both entry modes at the same time. To maintain control over its core competencies – the ingredients and formulas of its drinks – Coca-Cola set up one WFOE in Shanghai to produce the concentrates for Coca-Cola drinks. To reap the benefits that local partners can bring to operations in China, in the meantime Coca-Cola established one joint venture to design and produce localized soft drinks and twenty-four joint ventures to engage in bottling. Reportedly, Coca-Cola has been doing very well with this combination of two entry modes.

It needs to be borne in mind, however, that the adoption of several entry modes at the same time is very demanding in resources. In fact, most TNCs that have adopted the combination approach are very large, including McDonald's, KFC and Motorola. It is unclear whether this approach is appropriate for small and medium-sized TNCs. Resources permitting, however, a TNC should consider the possibility of adopting more than one entry mode in China simultaneously.

Summary

To enter the Chinese market, transnational corporations need to choose from among the various entry modes that are available to them in China. Many factors need to be taken into account in entry mode selection, but three broad categories of factors are most important: location, ownership and transaction cost. There is some controversy over how best to take these factors into consideration when choosing an entry mode, but for practical purposes a hierarchical approach to entry mode selection appears to be more useful and feasible than a simultaneous approach. Using a hierarchical model, we have examined the entry modes available to TNCs in China, and discussed how to choose among these entry modes.

There are different sets of factors that should be taken into consideration in selecting entry modes at each level of the hierarchy, and TNCs need to focus on the most applicable factor(s) at a given level of the hierarchy in making decisions on entry modes. It seems that the more they move down the hierarchy the fewer the factors that they need to consider. It should be noted, however, that, if TNCs choose among entry modes at different levels of the hierarchy, they should take into account all the factors that matter at all the levels involved. It should also be noted that the discussion on considerations of entry mode selection in this chapter is not exclusive but illustrative. There are other factors that, though not discussed here, also need to be taken into consideration. Nevertheless, the discussion in the chapter shows that the selection of entry mode has to take into account the most important factor(s) at the relevant level of the hierarchy, with particular reference to the crucial difference between the entry modes under comparison.

Each entry mode has its distinctive advantage, and the adoption of one entry mode alone may not best serve the diversified needs of TNCs operating in China's complex business environment. The simultaneous adoption of different entry modes may help to resolve the problem. The combination approach to entry mode selection is very demanding in resources, however, and may not be feasible for smaller TNCs.

FURTHER READING

Agarwal, S., and Ramaswami, S. N. 1992. 'Choice of foreign market entry mode: impact of ownership, location, and internalization factors'. *Journal of International Business Studies* 23: 1–27.

Buckley, P. J., and Casson, M. C. 1998. 'Analyzing foreign market entry strategies: extending the internalization approach'. *Journal of International Business Studies* 29(3): 539–62.

Chu, W., and Anderson, E. 1992. 'Capturing ordinal properties of categorical dependent variables: a review with application to modes of foreign entry'. *International Journal of Research in Marketing* 9: 149–60.

Kumar, V., and Subramaniam, V. 1997. 'A contingency framework for the mode of entry decision'. *Journal of World Business* 32 (1): 53–72.

Pan, Y., and Tse, D. K. 2000. 'The hierarchical model of market entry modes'. *Journal of International Business Studies* 31 (4): 535–54.

Questions for discussion

1. Apart from factors related to ownership, location and transaction cost, are there any other factors that should be taken into consideration in entry mode selection? If so, what are they?

2. Comparing the simultaneous approach with the hierarchical approach to entry mode selection, illustrate why the latter is more applicable than the former.

3. Why have transnational corporations tended to be in favour of some entry modes rather than others in China in recent years? Explain the major changes in entry modes in China in recent years, assuming that TNCs have the freedom to choose among these entry modes.

4. With reference to Chapter 2, illustrate the constraints of the regulatory environment on entry mode selection in China, using the example of Chinese regulations on joint ventures and wholly foreign-owned enterprises, or on mergers and acquisitions, or on licensing and franchising.

NOTES

1. See Folta (2005).

2. Foreigners were allowed to trade shares of companies listed on Chinese stock markets in the early 1990s, when the B share scheme was initiated (see chapter 11 for details). Unless the purchased shares exceeded 25 per cent of the total shares of a listed company, they were treated as indirect investment.

3. In fact, the quality of the official Chinese data on foreign indirect investment is very poor and inconsistent, as shown in the various *China Statistical Yearbooks*. We should, therefore, take the data with a grain of salt.

4. With regard to franchising, the Interim Measures for the Regulation of Commercial Franchise Operations were issued in 1997, but it was not specified clearly whether these measures applied to foreign franchise. In 2004 China issued Provisional Measures for the Supervision of Foreign Invested Enterprises Engaging in Commercial Franchising Business, which serves as the basic legal framework for foreign franchise. With regard to licensing, the only regulations that can be referred to are those in the Contract Law issued in 1999. It remains the case that China does not have laws and regulations specifically for licensing.

5. See Miller (2005).

5   Form an alliance

While an independent effort may at first appear to be the most attractive option, few companies have the necessary resources, skills and capabilities to become viable go-it-alone competitors in China. An alliance with a Chinese company encompasses a broad range of potential collaboration from supply or marketing agreements to joint ventures. Although China alliances are risky and certainly face significant challenges, if properly designed and managed they are the most effective method for building and profiting from a competitive position in one of the world's toughest and most important markets (Pieter Klasas Jagersma (2002, p. 3)).

In the previous chapter we looked at different entry modes. In some of these entry modes, such as joint ventures, transnational corporations need to form an alliance with a local Chinese partner. In the contemporary world, of course, business alliances cover a wide range of forms and areas, and have now become 'the normal way of doing business' (Lasserre, 2003, p. 97). Given the difficulties in going it alone in China, in particular, it is often in the interests of TNCs to form business alliances with local Chinese partners. In this chapter we first introduce the typology of international business alliances in China, and then discuss the three most important issues of forming and managing an international business alliance in China: partner selection, control over the alliance and conflict management.

International business alliances in China

Business alliances can be defined in different ways. They may be defined, for instance, as 'cooperative agreements between potential or actual competitors' (Hill, 2003, p. 346), or 'the sharing of capabilities between two or more firms with the view of enhancing their competitive advantages and/or creating new business without losing their respective strategic autonomy' (Lasserre, 2003, p. 97). These definitions indicate that a business alliance involves cooperation between companies; these companies may be potential or actual competitors; the cooperation is conditional; and the purpose of the alliance is to enhance the competitive advantage of the participating companies. To put it simply, we may define a business alliance as a cooperative and capacity-sharing arrangement between (potentially or actually) competing companies to help them achieve their respective strategic objectives. An international business alliance refers to the aforementioned arrangement between companies from different countries; in this context, between a TNC based outside China and a local company in China.

Why should companies form international business alliances? In general, such alliances are set up in the first instance because transnational corporations need a local partner in order to ensure easy access to local resources, marketing and personnel networks. In the case of China, where *guanxi* plays a crucial role in business, TNCs have a particular need for a local partner so as to achieve so-called 'soft integration' – 'immediate access to Chinese personnel at all levels of the organization . . . , access to an established supplier base . . . , access to an established distribution system that is inflexible and complex . . . , and access to an established customer base' (Jagersma, 2002, p. 4). In addition, TNCs may need a local Chinese partner to guide them as a teacher, in soft integration and to share their risks in the investment.

Another reason why international business alliances are formed is that local companies need a TNC in order to obtain easy access to foreign capital, advanced technology and global marketing networks. As the level of technology is relatively low in China, local companies are particularly keen on the advanced technology that TNCs may offer through an alliance. Consequently, as Jagersma (2002, pp. 4–5) has pointed out, '[t]he traditional basis for a China alliance has been the foreign company providing new technology or products in exchange for the Chinese company providing market access and soft integration capacities'. Finally, international business alliances are also established because host country governments often prefer alliances to wholly foreign-owned enterprises in order to maximize the beneficial effects and minimize the adverse effects of inward foreign direct investment. With the economy still supposed to be under the control of the socialist state in China, the Chinese government is especially cautious in connection with opening up the so-called pillar industries to WFOEs. From the very beginning of the economic reform process the government encouraged TNCs to enter the Chinese market through alliances such as joint ventures rather than through wholly owned enterprises. Even today, five years after China entered the WTO, such pillar industries as banking, telecommunications, automobiles, insurance

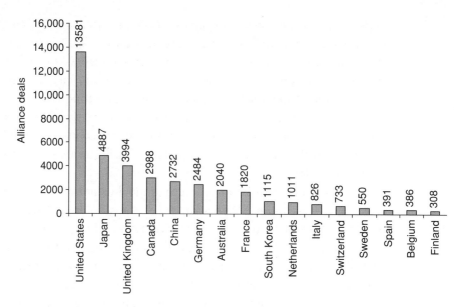

Figure 5.1   International alliances by nationality of participating companies, (1995–2000)
Source: Thomson Financial Database.

and securities remain open only to joint venture collaboration, not to WFOEs.

As a result of these factors, international alliances have become very popular all over in the world in recent years, not least in emerging markets such as China. In the period from 1995 to 2000, for instance, China ranked fifth in the number of alliance deals, exceeded only by the United States, Japan, the United Kingdom and Canada (see figure 5.1). Considering that China began to open up to the outside world only in 1978, the extent to which international business alliances have developed in China is staggering. The figures need to be taken with a grain of salt, however, because they do not explicitly say what kind of international business alliances they refer to. According to the Thomson Financial Database, there were 2732 alliance deals in China in the period from 1995 to 2000. According to the *China Statistical Yearbook*, however, there were 8706 joint ventures established in China in 1999 alone. The figure compiled from the Thomson Financial Database may, therefore, refer to a very narrowly defined form of international business alliances. In fact, as discussed below, international business alliances cover a wide range of forms or types.

In general, international business alliances may take four basic forms, and all of them are now permitted in China. The first is the short-term joint project agreement. This kind of alliance is formed when a TNC wants to conduct a project in conjunction with a host Chinese partner – say, to develop a new product or launch a promotion campaign together with a local company. This type of alliance is common in the areas of R&D and marketing. IBM, for instance, conducted many joint projects with Legend (now Lenova), a Chinese computer company, in R&D and new product development. Many TNCs have held promotion fairs to sell their products in China in collaboration with local partners. This kind of alliance is loose and short-lived, and it is over once the project is completed. It may become a prelude, however, to other kinds of business alliances or business deals.[1]

The second form of international business alliance is the long-term joint functional agreement. This kind of alliance is formed when a TNC wants to cooperate with local Chinese partners in a functional area of daily business operation, and is common between TNCs and local companies that have upstream or downstream business connections, such as between designers and manufacturers, manufacturers and suppliers, and manufacturers and distributors. Wal-Mart and Carrefour, for instance, have formed strategic alliances with many local suppliers in China. These local Chinese companies sign contracts with Wal-Mart and Carrefour, supplying them with goods on a regular and long-term basis. The same alliance relationship can be found in the cases of KFC, McDonald's, Coca-Cola and Volkswagen, and many other TNCs operating in China that have local Chinese partners to act as their suppliers on a regular and long-term basis. As both sides in these alliances are closely connected in their daily business operations, this kind of alliance is more stable than short-term joint project agreements.

The third form of international business alliance is the joint venture. This kind of alliance occurs when a TNC and a Chinese company together establish a new business entity, a joint venture, in which the two parent companies share the profits, risks, costs and losses. In this kind of alliance both sides are closely bonded together by their assets in the joint venture, and yet they enjoy independence within their respective parent companies. This type of alliance is normally formed when a TNC and a local company both want to achieve long-term strategic objectives, such as market entry and technology transfer. In practice, joint venture is the most popular form of international business alliance in China. There are numerous examples of this kind of alliances in China, involving such famous transnational corporations as Coca-Cola, Motorola, Peugeot Citroën, Ford, General Motors (GM), Toyota and Volkswagen. As both sides are closely bonded by assets, this kind of alliance is quite stable and more difficult to break up in comparison with the first two forms of alliance.

The fourth form of international business alliance is equity participation by one partner in the assets of the other. This kind of alliance occurs when a TNC directly holds the equity of a local company, or both the TNC and the Chinese company hold each other's equity. This kind of alliance is similar to a joint venture in the sense that both sides are closely bonded by assets, but different in the sense that the parent companies are not fully independent any more. This type of alliance is very close to merger and acquisition, but is still regarded as an alliance so long as one partner does not hold a majority share in the other. China has been very cautious about this kind of alliance for fear that it would lead to an increase in M&A activity in the country; it was not until 1999 that China began to permit it. In 2003, for instance, only nine such alliances were established in China, including the one set up between Kodak and a Chinese film-maker – Lucky Film (see box 5.1). A more recent case involved Newbridge Capital, a US-based investment company that bought a stake in the Shengzhen Development Bank, a local bank located in the Shenzhen Special Economic Zone. Alliances of this type may serve as a prelude to mergers and acquisitions.

Box 5.1 The alliance between Kodak and Lucky Film

In October 2003 Eastman Kodak, a photographic film-maker based in the United States struck a deal to purchase 20 per cent of the equities of Lucky Film, a Chinese photographic film-maker listed on the Shanghai Stock Market. The formation of the business alliance was a very important strategic move for Kodak, taken so that it could develop in the emerging China market, where competition in the photographic film industry has intensified in recent years.

Kodak is a world leader in imaging products and services, operating in over 150 countries in the world and employing more than 80,000 workers. Kodak began its move into China in the early 1990s, but its advance there was slow until 1993, by which time it had operations in only three cities, with a total of thirty employees. In that year, however, George Fisher, who had previously served as the chairman and chief executive officer (CEO) of Motorola and had successfully led that company into the Chinese market, became the chairman and CEO of Kodak. Under his leadership, Kodak developed very rapidly in China.

Kodak created a Greater China division, opened up a number of new representative offices in the country, sent senior expatriate executives to head the China operations and expanded the retail presence for Kodak products in China. In 1998 Kodak negotiated successfully with the Chinese government for an investment of $1 billion to purchase three loss-making state-owned enterprises in the film industry in Shantou, Xiamen and Wuxi. With these acquisitions Kodak gained control of most of China's imaging industry, leaving Lucky Film as the only remaining local film producer. In addition, the Chinese government promised to bar other foreign film-makers, including such Japanese giants as Fuji and Konica, from setting up film production facilities in China for four years.

When the ban expired in 2002 Fuji and Konica were eager to establish manufacturing bases in China, and they had little choice but to seek an alliance with Lucky Film, which held about 20 per cent of the Chinese film market. In order to consolidate its position in China's film market, Kodak responded with the bold move of proposing a strategic alliance with Lucky Film ahead of its Japanese competitors. Out of the three foreign candidates, Lucky Film, which by then was suffering from a decline in sales, decided to choose Kodak as its alliance partner, on the grounds that Kodak had more advanced technology and a greater market share in China.

The terms of the alliance deal were that Kodak paid $100 million for a 20 per cent share of Lucky Film, $45 million being paid in cash or in the form of an emulsion-making line for colour imaging products, and the remainder being paid in the form of upgrading Lucky Film's triacetate film base production and coating lines. The alliance benefited both sides. It helped Kodak protect its dominant position in the Chinese film market from its Japanese competitors, and it helped Lucky Film gain the advanced technology it needed to improve its own competitive position.

Since the deal Kodak has managed to maintain its control over two-thirds of the Chinese film market. With the rise of digital cameras, however, Kodak is now under pressure to move beyond traditional photographic film to develop digital photography and imaging in China. It is estimated that sales of digital cameras have been growing by about 70 per cent annually in recent years, and Kodak has had to expand its network of processing outlets with digital capabilities. Kodak is now exploring the possibility of extending its alliance with Lucky Film to the area of digital imaging.[2]

The four types of international business alliance can be taken as four different strategies that transnational corporations may adopt to form business alliances in China. A TNC needs to exercise care when choosing from among these options, evaluating not just the aforementioned characteristics of each of them but also the practical needs of the corporation. As it is relatively easy to manage short-term joint project agreements and long-term joint functional agreements, on account of the loose bond between the partners, the following discussion primarily, though not exclusively, focuses on the key issues of managing the last two types of international business alliance in China.

Partner selection

No matter what kind of international business alliances TNCs aim to forge in China, the first step is the selection of a local partner. As alliances often involve partners with different objectives, interests, capacities, organizational attributes and cultural backgrounds, with the clear potential for conflict between them, it is crucial that TNCs choose very carefully from among the candidate Chinese partners so as to minimize the unfitness between the two sides in any alliances that are formed. Otherwise, the alliance may encounter serious difficulties, or even end up in failure. There are many criteria for selecting alliance partners in China, but the three most important are: strategic fit, capacity fit and organization fit. In selecting local partners, TNCs need to assess them against these criteria.

Strategic fit

To evaluate the strategic fit, it is necessary for TNCs to assess the extent to which the strategic objectives of the partners are compatible and complementary. Clearly, a company forms an alliance with another company in order to achieve its strategic objectives, yet, more often than not, partners in an alliance have different strategic objectives, but still want to achieve their respective strategic objectives through the alliance. That is to say, in the words of the Chinese proverb, alliance partners are often 'sleeping in the same bed but having different dreams'. In selecting a partner, a company can hardly expect that partner to have exactly the same strategic objectives as itself, but it can hope that the partner's strategic objectives are different from, but compatible with and complementary to, its own.

As discussed previously, a foreign company will probably need a Chinese partner primarily for easy access to local market and resources, while a Chinese company will probably need a foreign partner primarily for easy access to foreign capital, advanced technology and a global marketing network. With few exceptions, this generalization applies to almost all international business alliances between TNCs and local companies in China. In practice, therefore, it would appear that, although the two sides have different strategic objectives, their judgement is that they should be able to achieve their respective objectives through forming an alliance. Indeed, the strategic objectives of the two sides may be complementary and compatible in general, but in individual cases they may not be. A local company may, for instance, have resources but little marketing network in China, and therefore it would not be a good partner for a TNC looking for an established marketing network in the country. By the same token, a TNC may possess advanced technology but little way of global marketing network, and therefore it would not make a good partner for a Chinese company seeking an established global marketing network.

Although it is unreasonable, if not impossible, to require a partner to 'sleep in the same bed and have the same dream', it is essential to know whether the strategic objectives in the 'dreams' of the partner are compatible and complementary.

To ascertain whether this is the case, it is useful to assess the criticality of the alliance to the partners by asking the questions: how important is the alliance to the partner, and will the partner depend on the alliance in order to achieve its own strategic objectives? Positive answers to these questions demonstrate that the alliance is important for the partner and that the commitment of the partner to the alliance is high, which often indicates a good strategic fit. In selecting a local partner, therefore, a transnational corporation needs to know whether what it has is really what the Chinese partner needs, and whether what the Chinese partner has is really what it needs.

It should be noted that the real needs of a local company and the strategic objectives that a company wishes to achieve through the alliance may be explicit and stated openly in some cases, but in other cases may be implicit and not revealed. It is important, therefore, for TNCs to conduct careful investigations into their potential Chinese partners, so as to identify their real needs and objectives.

Capacity fit

To assess the capacity fit, TNCs need to evaluate the extent to which the partners in the alliance will be capable of meeting each other's needs, and capable of helping each other achieve their respective strategic objectives. Although partners in an alliance may have what each other needs, the alliance may still fail if they do not have the capacity of making use of what they have to meet these needs and help each other achieve their objectives. A Chinese company may, for instance, have an established customer base as required by a transnational corporation needs, but it may not be a good partner if it does not have the capacity to make use of the customer base so as to meet the TNC's needs. The capacity is comprehensive and is related to a wide range of areas, including core competencies, corporate image, personal network (*guanxi*) and financial strength. In selecting a local partner, therefore, it is useful for TNCs to ask themselves whether that partner has the capacity to help them achieve their strategic objectives through the alliance, and assess the capability of the partner in these areas in detail.

In terms of core competencies, attention should be paid to the competencies that the local company has in the key functional areas that will affect the ability of the TNC to achieve its strategic objectives through the alliance. It is essential, for instance, for the Chinese partner to have the qualified human resources to undertake the kind of work required by the alliance, the capability of finding good local suppliers for the alliance, the capacity to promote the goods and services produced by the alliance in China, the ability to provide detailed information for the alliance about the local market, and so on. Any deficiency in competencies in any of these areas could result in difficulties for the international alliance, or even failure. For example, Guangzhou Automotive Manufacturing, the Peugeot's partner in China, did not have the competencies in skilled workers to produce the quality components that Peugeot needed, which became – as shown below – one of the main reasons for the termination of the alliance.

As for the corporate image, attention should be paid to whether the local partner enjoys a good reputation for its products, after-sales service, social responsibilities, etc. One research finding, for example, is that Chinese customers are particularly loyal to the products made by companies that have a good image in China. When an alliance begins to promote the goods or services that it produces in the country, Chinese customers will, therefore, be very sensitive to the corporate image that the Chinese partner had in the past in deciding on whether or not to buy the alliance's products. As pointed out by Luo (2001), for instance, Panda Electronics Group, the local partner of Philips, was very famous in China for producing high-quality products in electronics and for providing good customer service. The good corporate image of the local partner helped greatly to promote the electronics products that the alliance (Huafei Colour Display Systems) manufactured in China.

With regard to personal networks, attention needs to be given to the *guanxi* that the local partner has established in China. As discussed in chapter 3, *guanxi* plays a key role in Chinese society, and it is often used as a strategy to achieve business objectives. As TNCs are usually weak in this respect, it is very important for them to select a Chinese partner that has well-established *guanxi*, not only with people in the business world but also with officials in government at both the central and the local levels. This kind of *guanxi* often paves the way for the success of an international business alliance in China. There are numerous examples in which local partners with established *guanxi* have contributed to the success of international business alliances in China. In the case of Bell Telephone Equipment Manufacturing Company (a joint venture established by Bell and China Postal and Telecommunication Corporation), for instance, the Chinese partner made full use of its superior relationship with such top Chinese leaders as Jiang Zemin and Zhu Rongji to help develop the alliance.

In terms of financial strength, the important area to focus on is whether the local partner has sufficient financial capacity to carry out the work needed by the alliance. Other things being equal, a loss-making and insolvent Chinese company is not a good candidate for alliance partner, as it does not have the financial resources to fulfil its role as partner. If a Chinese partner is supposed to provide the land and infrastructure for the operation of the alliance but does not have the financial resources to do so, for instance, the alliance can hardly be expected to work. In addition, poor financial resources often indicate weaknesses and shortcomings in major areas of the management in a company, which are also detrimental to an alliance. In selecting a local partner, therefore, TNCs should look into the financial strength of the prospective partner in terms of profitability, liquidity, leverage and asset efficiency.

Organization fit

To evaluate the organization fit, TNCs need to assess the extent to which the organizational attributes of the partner in the alliance are conducive to the operation of the alliance. In the context of China, TNCs should pay special attention to such attributes as the organizational leadership, ownership type, learning ability, foreign experience and human resource management skills of local partners. All these organizational attributes affect the partners' capacity to meet the needs of the alliance, and thus have a significant impact on the performance of the alliance. In selecting a Chinese partner, therefore, it is useful for TNCs to ask themselves whether that partner will have organizational attributes that are conducive to the alliance and that can help achieve their strategic objectives through the alliance.

To begin with, as pointed out by David Berlew (1974, p. 22), organizational leadership is 'the process of instilling in others shared vision, creating valued opportunities, and building confidence in the realization of the shared values and opportunities'. As such, leadership is crucial to a business organization. Leadership is particularly important in China, where authoritarian styles of management prevail in most business organizations, state and private alike. Good leadership can provide the foresight and vision that guide the organization in the right business direction well before others, and thus enhance that organization's chances of success. As China is in the process of economic reform and opening up, open-minded and reform-oriented leadership can foresee the future better, cope better with the rapidly changing business environment and fit in better with the organizational context of international business alliances. This kind of leadership can strengthen the capacity of the local Chinese partner company, thereby increasing the opportunities for the success of any alliance that the company forms with a transnational corporation. Examples of this are provided by the alliances formed between Celanese Corporation and Jiangsu Tobacco Company, between Hewlett Packard and Beijing Computer Industry Corporation, between McDonnell Douglas and Shanghai Aviation Industrial Corporation, and between Wang Computer and Shanghai Computer Company (Luo, 2001).

Second, ownership structure has undergone significant changes in China since the economic reform started in 1978, and has diversified subsequently. There are many different forms of ownership in China today, but they can be roughly classified into three basic types: state-owned, collective-owned and privately owned. TNCs need to know the advantages and disadvantages of each of the ownership types, and look for a local partner with the ownership type that helps to achieve their strategic objectives. State-owned enterprises, for instance, have privileged access to infrastructure, distribution channels and financial resources, and have good connections with central government. They are good candidates for partnership if a TNC wants to achieve rapid market penetration through connections with the central government. Based on clearly defined property rights, on the other hand, private enterprises are efficient and, therefore, are good candidates for partnership if a TNC wants to achieve quick financial returns to investment. Collective-owned enterprises have very good connections with local governments, and are good candidates for partnership if a TNC wants to develop business through local connections in China. As ownership structure is extremely diversified in China today, a detailed scrutiny of the ownership structure of potential local partners is essential.

Third, in the context of economic reform and opening up, it is crucial that a local company has the ability to learn how to adapt to the rapidly changing business environment in China. The learning ability of the Chinese company is vital to the success of an international business alliance because it has to be able to learn how to adapt to the new role as a partner that it needs to play in the alliance. In an international business alliance, for instance, a local partner is supposed to acquire knowledge of advanced technology and management know-how from the foreign partner, and use the learnt knowledge in the day-to-day running of the alliance. To make an international business alliance work, therefore, it is crucial that the local partner has the ability to acquire, process, assimilate and integrate new knowledge and skills. In selecting a Chinese partner, a TNC needs to pay attention to the learning ability that the partner has demonstrated.

Fourth, closely related to learning ability, foreign experience is also an important organizational attribute that may affect the performance of a local partner in an international business alliance. TNCs normally bring to the alliance corporate cultures, business concepts and management styles that are different from those prevailing in Chinese companies. If a Chinese partner has experience in doing international business, the learning and adjusting process will be considerably shortened. Moreover, a local company with rich foreign experience can better communicate with the foreign partner in an international business alliance, and thus avoid unnecessary misunderstanding and conflicts within the alliance. Other things being the same, therefore, TNCs should choose a Chinese partner with deep foreign exposure and experience.

Finally, but not exclusively, the success of an international business alliance is heavily dependent on whether the partners have the human resource management skills needed in a cross-cultural setting. As the employees in a China-based international business alliance are mostly local Chinese, the local partner normally plays a greater role in human resources management than the foreign partner. It is crucial for the local partner to have the skills to manage Chinese employees in a cross-cultural setting, and have the skills to collaborate with the foreign partner in managing human resources in the alliance. These skills cover a wide range of areas, such as recruiting and retaining valued employees, training and career development, labour relations and adapting Chinese management culture and style to a cross-cultural setting. In selecting a Chinese partner, TNCs should pay attention to whether the partner has the kind of human resources management skills that are needed for the success of the alliance.

Control over alliances

Partners in an international business alliance often have different strategic objectives, as discussed earlier, so each side tends to seek control over the alliance in order to run the alliance in a way that best serves its own interests. The design of the control structure of an alliance is, therefore, a very important issue for both sides, especially an alliance in the form of a joint venture where the asset contribution share affects directly the degree of control over the alliance. Poorly designed control structures often lead to conflicts between partners in an alliance, disappointing performance or even failure. In addition to selecting a good partner, TNCs need to think carefully about the control structure of an alliance, and negotiate with the Chinese partner to develop a control arrangement that can best promote the development of the alliance and best serve the interests of both sides.

Although control over an alliance is important, it is not always achievable, or even desirable. In theory, whether or not a partner in an alliance should take control depends upon many factors, but two of them are crucial: the host-country government regulations and the relative strength of the partners in the alliance. We illustrate this point in the context of transnational corporations operating in China.

Host-country government regulations

Control over an alliance, particularly an alliance in which equities are involved, is a very sensitive issue in a host country if the alliance happens to be in an industry that is considered to be of vital importance to the country – one of the so-called pillar industries. Governments in host countries, particularly host countries in the developing world, tend to worry about the possible loss of economic independence if foreign companies move in and gain control over these pillar industries in equity terms, and therefore they often set strict restrictions on equity-involved alliances in these industries. As a result alliances controlled by a foreign partner in the form of majority equity constitute one of the most restricted entry modes in international business.

The issue of foreign control over an alliance in equity terms is particularly sensitive in China, where the Communist Party has been in power for many years and is trying to pursue economic reform in such a way that economic development is achieved without jeopardizing the Party's control over the economy. The Chinese government did not allow TNCs to purchase any share, not to mention a controlling share, in local companies until recently, and very few TNCs have actually undertaken the fourth form of alliance in China – purchasing a portion of the equity of a local company. As acquisitions and mergers are highly restricted in China, the issue of foreign equity control over an alliance relates mainly to alliances in the form of joint ventures. The government has set restrictions on foreign control over joint ventures ever since 1979 when the Law of the People's Republic of China on Sino-Foreign Equity Joint Ventures was issued. In 1995 the Regulations on Guiding the Direction of Foreign Investment and the Guidance Catalog of Industries with Foreign Investment were issued, clearly specifying the industries in which foreign control over joint ventures through majority shareholding is not permitted.

As discussed in chapter 2, the Regulations and the Guidance Catalog divide all Chinese industries into four categories: encouraged, restricted, prohibited and permitted. In the category of restricted industries, one of the restrictions is that TNCs have to enter these industries in the form of a joint venture with 'the Chinese party as the controlling shareholder' or 'the Chinese party as the relatively controlling shareholder' (Lo and Tian, 2005, chap. 3). That is to say, the foreign party can neither have more than 50 per cent of the equity share of the joint venture nor have an equity share that is higher than that which its Chinese partner has in the joint venture.

Along with the progress in economic liberalization and opening up, the government gradually relaxed its policy on TNCs in the restricted industries. Up to 2002, however, the restrictions on foreign majority control of joint ventures still applied to nine industrial sectors: (1) the development and production of grains, cotton and edible oilseed; (2) the processing and mining of special and rare coals; (3) publication printing; (4) the production of addictive narcotic drugs and raw materials for medications for mental illnesses; (5) railway passenger transportation; (6) general aviation companies engaged in photography, mine exploration or industrial applications; (7) the construction and operation of cooking gas, heating and water supply and sewage pipeline networks in large and medium-sized cities; (8) the construction and operation of cinemas; and (9) measuring and mapping. According to the agreement on China's entry into the WTO, joint ventures with foreign majority share are not allowed in the following industries even after membership, or at least within a certain period of WTO entry: (1) telecommunications (no more than 49 to 50 per cent of the equity); (2) insurance (no more than 50 per cent of the equity for life insurance); (3) securities (no more than 33 per cent of the equity for joint ventures engaging in stock underwriting and trading, and no more than 49 per cent of the equity for joint ventures engaging in investment funds); and (4) transportation (no more than 49 per cent of the equity for joint ventures engaged in international freight and passenger transport, and for joint ventures engaged in international maritime agency services and for joint ventures engaged in domestic aircraft repairs and maintenance).

With these regulatory regulations, foreign control over joint ventures in these industries is not possible in China. TNCs should, nevertheless, keep a lookout for possible changes in governmental regulations to see whether China further relaxes its policy on foreign majority control over alliances that involve equity participation.

The relative strength of the partners in alliances

Even in industries in which the government allows a foreign partner to gain control of an alliance in terms of the equity, it is not always to the advantage of the foreign partner to take control. In other words, gaining control of an alliance is not always desirable. To understand this point, we need to review the resource dependence theory of business organization. According to this theory, the ability of one party to command the key resources in an organization gives that party control over it (Pfeffer and Salancik, 1978). In the context of international business alliances, therefore, whether or not a partner takes control of an alliance depends, to a large extent, on the relative strength of that partner in providing key resources for the alliance compared to others in the alliance. That is to say, the partner that commands the key resources that are crucial for the operation of the alliance should take control of the alliance, while the partner that does not have the resources should not take control.

Drawing on resource dependence theory, international business scholars break down not only control but also resources into different categories. On the basis of the classification, they attempt to identify particular kinds of control that depend on particular types of resources. It is argued that control can be classified in two categories: strategic control and operational control. Strategic control refers to control over the overall direction and operation of an alliance, including the appointment of senior management positions, the determination of strategic priorities and the command of key financial resources. In contrast, operational control refers to control over specific functional areas in the alliance, such as sourcing, product quality, promotion, distribution, R&D and the management of employees who work in these functional areas. It is important for a TNC to know just which kind of control it wants in the alliance in the first place.

Resources can be also classified in two categories: equity resources and non-equity resources. Equity resources refer to all kinds of tangible assets, including land, buildings and plants, cash, securities, etc. Non-equity resources refer to a wide range of intangible assets, including management know-how, technology, local knowledge, sourcing networks, promotion and distribution channels, service supports and social connections (*guanxi* in the Chinese context). Both the equity and the non-equity resources are essential for the operation of an alliance, and thus are the strength base on which partners can seek control over the alliance. TNCs should, therefore, ensure they are completely clear as to the relative strength they have in providing each type of resource compared to their local partner, and decide on whether and how to seek control of the alliance.

John Child and Yanni Yan (2001) argue that each type of resource provides a different source of power and different scope of influence, on the basis of which different kinds of control over an alliance can be established. Equity shares in an alliance primarily determine the degree to which partners in the alliance have the right to strategic control over the alliance. A majority equity share is often associated, for instance, with the right to appoint the majority members of the board of directors of the alliance, and the right to appoint the chairman of the board. The appointment of board members and board chairman is a crucial step towards strategic control, because the board and the chairman decide on business plans, strategic priorities and the allocation of key financial resources in the alliance, and also decide on the appointment of the chief executive positions. Of course, the appointment of senior executive officers influences, in turn, operational control. In a sense, therefore, having a majority equity share confers the right to strategic control directly and the right to operational control indirectly.

In contrast, non-equity resources in an alliance primarily determine the degree to which the partners have the right to operational control of the alliance. In most cases, non-equity resources are provided through contracts that specify clearly the right associated with the provision of these non-equity resources, including the right to control the management of these resources. The provider of management know-how, technology, the brand name, sourcing networks, promotion and distribution channels often, for instance, has control over the respective individual functional areas related to the specific non-equity resources it offers to the alliance. Even in cases in which non-equity resources are not provided through contracts, the provider can still achieve control over the related functional areas because it has the expertise that is essential for the operation of those areas.

According to the model developed by Child and Yan, TNCs that seek strategic control of an alliance should obtain a majority equity share, while TNCs that seek operational control over an alliance should, first and foremost, provide the key non-equity resources for the functional areas that they want to take control of. Child and Yan's model suffers from a vital drawback, however. It does not address the issue of key success resources (KSRs) – that is, the specific key resources needed for the success of an alliance. This issue is important, because these key resources are indispensable for the success of an alliance, and whoever has them should assume the strategic control of the alliance through a majority shareholding. As strategic control determines the general direction of an alliance directly and the operation of its specific functional areas indirectly, the relationship between key success resources and strategic control should, in light of resource dependence theory, be the focus of discussion on control over alliances.

Other things being equal, therefore, whether or not a partner should take strategic control over an alliance depends upon the relative strength of the partner in provision of the KSRs for the alliance. If the KSRs are the proprietary technologies or global marketing networks in which a TNC has obvious strength, the TNC should seek strategic control of the alliance through a majority shareholding. As shown in the case of Shanghai Foxboro Company, Limited (SFCL), a joint venture established by US-based Foxboro and a local Chinese company in Shanghai to produce and sell high-tech products in China, the American company had obvious strength in providing the advanced technology that was indispensable for the success of the joint venture and thus took strategic control of the joint venture (box 5.2).

Box 5.2 Control arrangements in Shanghai Foxboro Co. Ltd

In 1982, soon after China opened up to foreign direct investment, Foxboro, a US company in the high-tech industry, established a joint venture in Shanghai with a local partner – Shanghai Instrumentation and Electronics Holding Group. The joint venture, named Shanghai Foxboro Company Limited, produced such high-tech products as process control instruments and advanced distribution control systems for power plants and large manufacturing facilities. SFCL provided, for instance, reactor shut-down controls for at least 120 of the 180 active nuclear power stations in the world. When the joint venture was established, the demand for these high-tech products was so strong that customers literally had to line up outside the door to buy them.

To start with the Chinese side held 51 per cent of the equity share, while the American side held the rest. This was because the Chinese government then had very strict regulations on foreign majority control over joint ventures, and strategic control by a foreign company over a joint venture in the high-tech industry was not permitted. When the restrictions were relaxed in the 1990s, Foxboro decided to take strategic control of the joint venture by increasing its share to 51.5 per cent.

The decision to assume strategic control was based on the consideration that the key resources for the success of the joint venture were proprietary technologies owned by Foxboro. Foxboro had, in fact, already taken control of the majority of the joint venture's functional areas even before the change in equity structure. Of the 140 staff working on the manufacturing side, for instance, 125 were engineers trained by expatriate experts from Foxboro. For instance, Edmund J. Tarala, the expatriate chief engineer of SFCL appointed by Foxboro, spent 80 per cent of his time training local engineers. In addition, local engineers were so unqualified that Foxboro had to send them on overseas training programmes. The strength that Foxboro had in proprietary technologies therefore supported the transfer of strategic control of the joint venture from the Chinese side to Foxboro.

Lacking the key resources needed for the success of the joint venture, the Chinese partner was willing to hand control over to Foxboro. After the transfer of control the Chinese partner was happy to hang on to its minority share, because it could do little and still enjoy the fruits: sizeable returns on the equity shares it held. Following the transfer of control the joint venture has, reportedly, been running very well[3].

If the key success resources are the local service support systems or local connections in which a local partner has obvious strength, on the other hand, it may not be in the interests of the TNC to seek strategic control of the alliance through majority shareholding. If the TNC seeks strategic control despite its obvious weakness in providing the KSRs, the Chinese partner that commands the KSRs may be reluctant to collaborate with the TNC, which often results in disappointing performance, or even failure of the alliance. The experience of the Suzhou Industrial Park, a Sino-Singaporean joint venture, helps to illustrate this point. As mentioned in chapter 3, the industrial park was established in 1994 with support from top government officials in both countries. The park was designed to provide superior services and infrastructure for foreign companies operating in China, and the key resources for the success of the alliance were thus the service support systems and local connections, in which the Chinese side had obvious strength. However, the Singaporean side insisted on taking strategic control of the joint venture through a majority shareholding (65 per cent). The Chinese partner therefore had no incentive to collaborate with the Singaporean partner, and the joint venture ran very poorly. Although other factors, such as a failure to cultivate *guanxi* with the Suzhou local government, also contributed to the weak performance of the Suzhou Industrial Park, the inappropriate control structure arrangement was, arguably, the key source of the problem. In the end, the Singaporean side had to give up its strategic control of the joint venture by reducing its equity share to 35 per cent.

In sum, control over an alliance is a very important and complex issue. Although each partner tends to seek control of an alliance, this is not always achievable or even desirable. In making an alliance with a Chinese partner, therefore, TNCs need to think carefully about the conditions under which control over the alliance is not only achievable but also desirable. That is, they need to examine minutely the current restrictions on foreign majority control of alliances in China, and assess realistically whether they command the key resources that are indispensable for the success of the alliance.

Conflict management

Conflicts often occur between partners in alliances, particularly in international business alliances, where the partners are from different countries and cultural backgrounds. Anecdotal evidence suggests that conflicts may become very intense in international business alliances, and sometimes even lead to

soft-line approach, a partner takes into account what the other partner thinks and feels, and resolves conflicts through compromises, open and friendly negotiations, and reasoned argument and persuasion. This approach roughly corresponds to the problem-solving strategy and the compromising strategy. Under the hard-line approach, one partner imposes its will on the other party, sometimes by having recourse to the law, and resolves conflicts through non-compromising confrontation. This approach roughly corresponds to the forcing strategy and the legalistic strategy. As shown in box 5.3, the experiences of Volkswagen and BorgWarner help to illustrate these two approaches to conflict resolution.

Box 5.3 Two approaches to conflict resolution: BorgWarner and Volkswagen

Volkswagen, based in Germany, is one of the best-known and high-profile car makers in the world, while BorgWarner, based in the United States, is a leading maker of power train products for major automobile manufacturers worldwide. The two companies each established an alliance with local partners in the form of joint ventures in China, and experienced conflicts with their Chinese partners. The approaches to conflict resolution adopted by the two companies, however, were completely different.

Volkswagen established its joint venture in Shanghai in 1984 namely Shanghai Volkswagen. In the joint venture Volkswagen had more than one local Chinese partner, including Shanghai Automotive Industry Corporation (SAIC), the Bank of China, and China National Automotive Industry Corporation (CNAIC) – a quasi-ministry of the central government in charge of formulating and implementing automotive planning nationwide. Volkswagen held 50 per cent of the equity of the joint venture, while the Chinese partners shared the rest. The local partners were selected because of their presumed ability to help overcome the difficulties faced by the joint venture. The Bank of China, for instance, could provide or guarantee the necessary loans; SAIC would help to solve local problems in Shanghai; and CNAIC could serve as a link to the government in Beijing. Being the largest shareholder, moreover, Volkswagen took control of the joint venture. Nevertheless, Volkswagen experienced conflicts with its Chinese partners soon after the joint venture was established.

The most serious conflict occurred in 1988, when the head of CNAIC complained about the slow pace of component localization and asked Volkswagen to raise its local content utilization to 80 per cent as soon as possible. At that stage the local content level was only 12 per cent, and it was unrealistic to try and reach the CNAIC target in a short period of time as local suppliers could not provide high-quality components because of the low level of technology they were using. Disregarding these difficulties, CNAIC decided to curtail raw material supplies and limit the joint venture's output until the required local content target was achieved. This decision was not in conformity with the joint venture contract, in which it was clearly specified that the Chinese side was responsible for locally supplied high-quality components.

To resolve the conflict, Volkswagen did not choose a forcing or legalistic strategy to confront CNAIC openly through media-based or legal procedures. Instead, Volkswagen adopted a problem-solving strategy, explaining patiently to CNAIC the difficulties in content localization, and persuading the Chinese side through reasoned arguments to look for a solution to the problem. The soft-line approach worked. The Chinese partners stopped blaming Volkswagen, and worked together to form a suppliers association to resolve the technical problems in providing high-quality components (see chapter 7 for details). The joint venture survived the crisis, and is now understood to be doing well.

The experience of BorgWarner tells a different story. BorgWarner established its joint venture in Hubei province in 1995, together with a local partner, Shiyan Automotive Transmission Factory (SATF), to make five-speed manual transmissions for 1.5-ton light trucks produced by a Chinese truck maker for the domestic market. BorgWarner held 60 per cent of the equity and SATF held the rest. The joint venture had to be established from scratch, and each side of the alliance agreed to take certain responsibilities and follow a scheduled timetable to complete the project. If one side failed to fulfil its commitments, according to the contract, the other side would be entitled to apply directly to the Hubei Commission on Foreign Trade and Economic Cooperation (COFTEC) for liquidation and termination.

Soon after the contract was signed BorgWarner provided the joint venture with technology, a completed transmission design and a completed prototype transmission, thus fulfilling its commitments to the alliance within the specified time-frame. The Chinese partner, however, did not fulfil any of the commitments it had made, such as securing and providing a site for the manufacturing facilities, securing a facility lessor to finance, build and lease back the facilities to the and assisting the joint venture in obtaining a supply agreement with a potential customer.

BorgWarner called a couple of board of directors meetings to request that SATF fulfil its commitments. The SATF-appointed directors refused to admit that there were problems, however, and did not give any assurance that they would get the work done. Seeing this lack of progress, BorgWarner decided to adopt a hard-line approach. In line with the joint venture contract, BorgWarner unilaterally terminated the technology transfer agreement, the name licence agreement and the trademark licence agreement with SATF, and requested the return of its technology. SATF rejected the termination and refused to hand the technology back. In 1997, furthermore, SATF filed a lawsuit against BorgWarner for alleged breach of the joint venture contract at a local court, and won the case with the help of the SATF-appointed chair of the joint venture.

BorgWarner then had to engage in a lengthy battle to overturn the local court's decision. For seven years, from 1997 to 2004, BorgWarner petitioned numerous Chinese government agencies and officials, including the Supreme People's Court, the Supreme People's Procuratorate and the Governor of Hubei province. With assistance from the US Commercial Service in Beijing and the US ambassador a number of meetings were arranged between BorgWarner and Chinese ministries, including the Ministry of Foreign Affairs and the Ministry of Foreign Trade and Economic Cooperation (MOFTEC). Two US Secretaries of Commerce, William M. Daley and Donald L. Evans, raised the BorgWarner issue at meetings of the US–China Joint Commission on Commerce and Trade, as well as at meetings with China State Councillor Wu Yi. Finally, on 2 June 2004, an agreement was reached between BorgWarner and SATF, requesting SATF to return BorgWarner's technology, and terminating the joint venture[5].

The experiences of Volkswagen and BorgWarner help to illustrate the soft-line and hard-line approaches to conflict resolution. Choosing between the two approaches is dependent on the root problem of the conflicts in an alliance. In the case of BorgWarner, the root problem was the lack of willingness and ability on the part of the Chinese partner to fulfil its commitments to the alliance, so a hard-line approach was probably the best option. Whenever possible, however, TNCs should try a soft-line approach to conflict resolution, as in the case of Volkswagen, which is generally more likely to succeed than a hard-line approach because it fits in well with Chinese cultural traditions.

According to Xiaohua Lin and Richard Germain (1998), whether a transnational corporation should adopt a soft-line approach or a hard-line approach depends upon cultural similarities, the relative power of the partners and the age of the relationship. Their finding is that the more similar the partners are in cultural traditions the more likely they are to adopt a soft-line approach. TNCs from Singapore and other Asian countries are more likely to adopt a soft-line approach in China than TNCs from Western countries. They also find that the greater power and strength a partner has in the relationship the more likely that partner is to adopt a hard-line approach. If a TNC holds the key resources for the success of the alliance it is very likely to put pressure on the Chinese partner through legal channels. Furthermore, it is found that the longer the partners have known each other the more likely they are to adopt a soft-line approach. If a TNC has known its local Chinese partner for a long time and has established a good relationship with the partner that TNC is very likely to adopt a soft-line approach.

Moreover, Lin and Germain suggest that, in the Chinese context, the soft-line approach to conflict resolution appears to be more conducive to good performance by the alliance than the hard-line approach, which has significant implications for managing conflicts in international business alliances in the country. One key element of traditional Chinese culture, as discussed in the next chapter, is an emphasis on harmony and the avoidance of conflict. This cultural tradition fundamentally affects the way Chinese deal with conflicts in everyday life, and also, of course, the way Chinese deal with conflicts in international business alliances. Michael Morris et al. (1998) find, for instance, that Chinese managers tend to rely on an approach to conflict management that avoids confrontation, because of the relatively high value they attach to concord, while US managers tend to rely on a competitive approach to conflict management because of the relatively high importance they attach to individual achievement. Similar findings are reported in a recent empirical study conducted by Cheng Wang, Xiaohua Lin, Allan Chan and Yizheng Shi (2005), which was based on extensive surveys of managers of international joint ventures who were of Chinese origin, other Asian origin and Western origin. These findings indicate that, if TNCs adopt a soft-line approach to resolving conflicts with Chinese partners in international business alliances, they are likely to get along well with them because the approach accords nicely with Chinese cultural tradition, and thus there is a high probability that conflicts are resolved such that ventures achieve success. Indeed it is also true that a hard-line approach often leads to a deteriorating relationship between the partners, and the eventual failure of international business alliances adopting such a course. Whenever possible, therefore, the advice to TNC is to adopt a soft-line approach in dealing with conflicts.

While acknowledging the merits of the soft-line approach to conflict resolution, however, we should bear in mind that not all conflicts can be resolved this way. The choice of method depends primarily on the root cause of the conflict: if the fundamental problem is a lack of willingness or ability on the part of the Chinese partner to fulfil its commitments to the alliance, for instance, the adoption of a soft-line approach may not lead to a result in the best interests of the TNC, and adopting a hard-line approach may be the best option. Given the antipathy of Chinese cultural tradition to confrontation and legal action, however, TNCs going down this route should be prepared for a protracted and painful process of conflict resolution, as demonstrated by the case of BorgWarner.

Summary

The international business alliance has now become a normal way of doing business in China. It is popular because TNCs often need a local partner to gain easy access to local market, resources and personal networks (*guanxi*), while Chinese companies often need a foreign partner to secure ready access to foreign capital, technology, management know-how and global marketing networks. In addition, the Chinese government encourages TNCs to form alliances with Chinese companies so that China can benefit from the transfer of foreign technology without losing control of the economy.

There are four basic types of international business alliance in China: the short-term joint project agreement, the long-term joint functional agreement, the joint venture and equity participation by one partner in the capital of the other. The four types of alliance actually represent four strategic options for TNCs forming business alliances with Chinese partners. Each of the options has its own advantages and disadvantages, and TNCs need to select an alliance strategy that fits in with their needs and strategic objectives in the country.

To make an alliance a success, the partners in the alliance have to work together well, and therefore it is crucial that a TNC selects the right local partner for the alliance. In selecting a local partner, attention should be paid to the strategic fit, capacity fit and organization fit of the prospective partner, the aim being to select a partner with strategic objectives that are complementary to, and compatible with, the strategic objectives of the TNC, with the capacity to fulfil its obligations to the alliance and with an organizational structure that is conducive to the smooth functioning of the alliance. The selection of a good partner helps to avoid and minimize conflicts between the partners.

To make an alliance a success, moreover, its control structure has to be designed properly. TNCs need to take into account not just government restrictions and the changes in these restrictions over time but also, more importantly, whether they have the ability to provide the key resources that are indispensable for the success of the alliance. If their strength lies in this area they should take control without hesitation; if it does not, however, it might be to their advantage to leave control in the hands of the local partner. A properly designed control structure also helps to avoid and minimize conflicts in an alliance.

No matter how carefully TNCs select a Chinese partner and design a control structure for an alliance, conflicts may still arise, for a variety of reasons. TNCs have the choice of adopting either a soft-line approach or a hard-line approach to resolving such conflicts, depending upon the particular underlying problem, but anecdotal evidence indicates that a soft-line approach is more likely to achieve the desired outcome than a hard-line approach, because it fits in better with Chinese cultural traditions. Under certain circumstances, however, the hard-line approach is the right – if not the only – choice, even though it may lead to the break-up of the alliance.

FURTHER READING

Child, J., and Yan, Y. 2001. 'Investment and control in international joint ventures: the case of China'. In J. T. Li and P. N. Ghauri (eds.), *Managing International Business Ventures in China*. Amsterdam: Pergamon, 17–30.

Gelb, C. 2003. 'Investment pioneer: the first US–Chinese high-technology joint venture is alive and well'. *China Business Review* 30 (2): 70–4.

Jagersma, P. K. 2002. 'Upfront best practice: building successful China alliances'. *Business Strategy Review* 13 (4): 3–6.

Lasserre, P. 2003. *Global Strategic Management*. New York: Palgrave Macmillan, chap. 4.

Lin, X., and Germain, R. 1998. 'Sustaining satisfactory joint venture relationships: the role of conflict resolution strategy'. *Journal of International Business Studies* 29 (1): 179–96.

Luo, Y. D. 2001. 'Joint venture success in China: how should we select a good partner?' In J. T. Li and P. N. Ghauri (eds.), *Managing International Business Ventures in China*. Amsterdam: Pergamon, 108–30.

Questions for discussion

1. What are the basic strategic options for transnational corporations in forming an international business alliance in China? Discuss how to select an alliance strategy in China.

2. Apart from the criteria of partner selection discussed in this chapter, are there any other criteria that may be important for the selection of a local partner?

3. Other things being equal, according to the resource dependence theory, control over an international business alliance is determined by the relative strength of each partner in providing key success resources for the alliance. Do you agree? If not, present an argument as to how TNCs should design a control structure for an international business alliance in China, particularly one in the form of a joint venture.

4. For TNCs operating in China it is not always possible, or even desirable, to take control of an international business alliance. Do you agree?

5. List the factors that may lead to conflict in an international business alliance in China and discuss possible solutions to them.

6. It is argued that a soft-line approach to conflict resolution may, in general, achieve better outcomes than a hard-line approach in China. Do you agree? If not, discuss how TNCs should resolve conflicts in an international business alliance in the country.

NOTES

1. Lenova, for instance, acquired the personal computer (PC) business of IBM in 2005.
2. See Economist Intelligence Unit (2003), and Alon (2001).
3. See Gelb (2003).
4. For the four conflict resolution strategies, see Lin and Germain (1998).
5. For details of the two cases, refer to Peng (2000) and Bransfild and Schlueter (2004).

6 Negotiating with Chinese partners

The Chinese may be less developed in technology and industrial organization than we, but for centuries they have known few peers in the subtle art of negotiating. When measured against the effort and skill the Chinese bring to the bargaining table, American executives fall short (Lucian Pye (1992, p. 74)).

To do business in China, transnational corporations have to negotiate with local Chinese partners. Many TNCs have now come to the realization that the Chinese have their own negotiation style, and that they are, though less advanced in other areas, rather good at negotiation. Without adequate understanding of the characteristics and skills that the Chinese demonstrate at the negotiation table, TNCs are unlikely to succeed in striking a desirable deal with Chinese partners and in developing business in China. The aim of this chapter is to set out how to understand the Chinese negotiation style and how to negotiate with Chinese business partners.

First a theoretical debate on negotiation is briefly introduced, with a focus on cross-cultural theory, which can serve as an analytical framework for the Chinese negotiation style. Then, in section 2, we discuss the cultural roots of the negotiation style, which helps us understand why Chinese negotiators behave the way they do. In section 3 we illustrate the main characteristics of the Chinese negotiation style, and in section 4 we highlight some general rules that may serve as broad guidelines for TNCs in their negotiations with Chinese business partners.

Introduction

The word 'negotiation' refers to an interaction process in which two or more parties communicate with each other so as to reach a mutually acceptable agreement on certain matters (Clarke, 1993). It is well acknowledged that the negotiation process normally involves two key elements at the same time: common interests and conflicting interests. As Fred Iklé (1968) puts it, 'Without common interests there is nothing to negotiate for; without conflicting issues nothing to negotiate about.' There is controversy, however, as to how negotiators should proceed in a negotiation process in order to reach a mutually acceptable agreement. This issue has been debated by scholars from different disciplines, including organization science, social psychology, political science, cross-cultural management and communications.

To start with, social exchange theory and game theory dominated the debate. Social exchange theory tends to consider negotiation to be a process of social exchange in which the negotiating parties communicate with each other in a problem-solving manner to reach a 'win–win' agreement – that is, an agreement that benefits all the negotiating parties (McCall and Warrington, 1984; Graham, 1986). In other words, social exchange theory takes negotiation as a cooperative process in which the negotiating parties make efforts to maximize the benefits accruing to all parties involved. In this manner, the negotiating parties may maintain a positive relationship throughout the negotiation process, and all of them succeed in achieving what it is possible to achieve without hurting each other. Conflicts between negotiating parties are resolved in a way that benefits all.

Social exchange theory therefore proposes a cooperative strategy of negotiation. To pursue a cooperative strategy, all the parties need to collaborate with each other in the negotiation process and reconcile the interests of all in order to achieve mutual benefits. The basic rules of the cooperative strategy are best illustrated in so-called 'principled negotiation'. According to Roger Fisher and William Ury (1981), principled negotiation should (1) separate the people from the problem; (2) focus on interests rather than positions; (3) provide options for mutual benefits; (4) insist on objective criteria; and (5) employ no tricks and no posturing. By using a cooperative strategy, the negotiating parties can gain from the negotiation in a decent and fair manner.

Game theory, by contrast, tends to regard negotiation as a process in which the negotiating parties communicate with each other in a competitive manner to reach a 'win–lose' agreement – that is, an agreement that benefits one party but hurts the other (Raiffa, 1982; Siebe, 1991). In other words, game theory takes negotiation to be a 'zero-sum' game, in which each party tries to maximize its own benefits at the cost of the other. The extent to which one party can achieve maximum gains may be calculated accurately using mathematical methods. Conflicts between negotiating parties are resolved in a negative or hostile manner, and the common interests of all are not served in the end.

Game theory therefore proposes a competitive strategy of negotiation, which is also referred to as contending bargaining. In pursuing a competitive strategy, negotiating parties do all they can to fight with one another in order to maximize their own interests. The competitive strategy is characterized, therefore, by the large-scale employment of 'tricky tactics, tricky bargaining, and dirty tricks', through which the parties try to take advantage of each other in the negotiation process. According to Fisher and Ury (1981), these tricks basically consist of: (1) deliberate deception (phoney facts, ambiguous authority and dubious intentions); (2) psychological warfare (stressful situations, personal attacks, the 'good guy/bad guy' routine and threats); and (3) positional pressure tactics (refusal to negotiate, extreme demands, escalating demands, lock-in tactics, a calculated delay and 'take it or leave it').

Social exchange theory and game theory thus propose two diametrically opposed negotiating strategies. In recent years scholars have begun to consider the two to be complementary rather than contradictory. On the one hand, cooperation and competition can both be necessary, depending on the particular circumstances. On the other hand, a combination of both strategies may achieve the most desirable negotiation outcome. Within game theory, for instance, there emerged an argument that tends to take game as a co-opetition process in which both competition and cooperation between the participants are essential strategies for achieving the optimal outcome (Nalebuff and Brandenburger, 1996). In a co-opetition negotiation, therefore, negotiators can act both as collaborators and opponents.

In the meantime, there has emerged in recent years the cross-cultural theory of negotiation, which focuses on a specific type of negotiation – that between negotiating parties from different cultural backgrounds. According to cross-cultural theory, the broadly defined cultural environments in which negotiators are brought up have a significant impact on their behaviour and shape the different negotiation styles found in different nations (Hofstede, 1991; Weiss, 1994a, 1994b; Graham, 1996; Hendon, Hendon and Herbig, 1996; Usunier, 1996). In particular, Hofstede has proposed five dimensions of national culture that may differ from one nation to another: power distance, individualism versus collectivism, masculinity versus femininity, uncertainty avoidance, and long-term versus short-term orientation. He carried out surveys in fifty countries, and found some striking differences in the five cultural dimensions between nations and regions. Hofstede and others have tried to apply the concept of the five cultural dimensions to the study of cross-cultural negotiation (see, for instance, Hofstede and Usunier, 1996).

Given the striking differences in national culture, according to the cross-cultural theory of negotiation, the generalizations of such opposing negotiation theories as game theory and social exchange theory have very few implications for negotiation in a cross-cultural setting. What really matters is that negotiators from different cultural backgrounds should understand each other's cultural environments and negotiation styles; otherwise, misunderstandings can arise, and the negotiations might end up in failure. Cross-cultural theory has become increasingly influential with the rapid expansion of international business, and provides the framework that underlies, explicitly or implicitly, all current research on the Chinese business negotiation style. In this chapter we discuss negotiating with Chinese in the light of cross-cultural theory. We do not use Hofstede's five-dimension framework in the discussion, however, because the framework is too general to be applied to such complex cultures as the Chinese. Chinese culture, as shown below, is much more colourful than Hofstede's framework suggests. Consequently, the Chinese negotiation style should be examined in the context of the complexities of Chinese culture, and should be dealt with accordingly.

For simplicity, we treat the Chinese as a whole and do not address cultural differences across the huge country. As it happens, there are significant differences in cultural attitudes between Chinese living in different regions in China. Tony Fang (2005), for instance, has pointed out cultural differences in three regions: Beijing, Shanghai and Guangzhou. Apart from these three regions, Min Chen (2004) goes even further to discuss cultural differences in other regions: the North-east, Sichuan and Zhejiang. For those who are interested in cultural differences across the territory of China, please refer to the aforementioned publications for detailed discussions.

Cultural roots of the Chinese negotiation style

According to cross-cultural theory, the behaviour of negotiators is determined, to a large extent, by the cultural environment in which they live. There is controversy, however, over how this happens. Indeed, the concept of culture itself is a difficult-to-define construct. It may be defined, for instance, as a shared pattern of being, thinking and behaving, or something learnt from childhood through socialization, or something deeply rooted in traditions that permeate all aspects of any given society (Hofstede, 1991). In this chapter we define 'culture' as ways of thinking and feeling, consciously or unconsciously, that are shared by all members of a society and that determine their behaviour at a fundamental level. There are, obviously, different cultural elements in a society; certain cultural elements may play a particular role in shaping a particular kind of behaviour of the members of the society. It is argued here that the behaviour of Chinese negotiators is primarily shaped by, or rooted in, two sets of Chinese cultural elements. The first set refers to traditional Chinese culture, while the second set refers to contemporary Chinese political culture.

Traditional Chinese culture

The Chinese have a history going back more than 4,000 years, in which they have developed a colourful reservoir of traditional culture. Traditional Chinese culture includes such philosophical strands as Confucianism, Taoism and Buddhism, such military stratagems and conventional strategic wisdom as the Sun Tzu Stratagems and the Thirty-Six Stratagems, such embedded mentalities as agrarianism, and such daily communicating tools as the Chinese pictographic language. Here we focus our discussion on Confucianism, Sun Tzu's stratagems, agrarian mentalities and Chinese pictographic language, which are believed to have the most significant impact on the behaviour of Chinese negotiators.

Confucianism

Confucius was an ancient Chinese philosopher and educator (551–479 BC), and his teachings were developed later by his followers and students into a coherent system of theories, doctrines, beliefs, tenets and moralities – Confucianism. As the most influential Chinese cultural tradition, Confucianism permeates every level of Chinese society, including the daily life of ordinary people. Confucianism upholds five core values: moral cultivation, family and interpersonal relationships, respect for age and hierarchy, harmony, and face.

Moral cultivation

Confucianism requires people to act as gentlemen (*junzi*) with the so-called Five Constant Virtues (*wuchang*): human-heartedness and benevolence (*ren*); righteousness and justice (*yi*); propriety, rituals and rules of conduct (*li*); wisdom (*zhi*); and sincerity and trust (*xin*). According to Confucianism, people can become gentlemen only through the lifelong learning of the five virtues – that is, lifelong moral cultivation. Among the five virtues, that of sincerity and trust is the most important. It applies only to insiders, however, not to outsiders; that is, gentlemen must be sincere to family members and quasi-family members (see below), though they may be insincere to enemies. According to Confucianism, rulers should rule their subjects by these virtues or moral powers, rather than by laws. In daily life, the Chinese are taught to use moral cultivation rather than legal measures to regulate people's conduct.

Family and interpersonal relationships

Confucianism requires people to appreciate family and interpersonal relationships, as shown in the so-called Five Cardinal Relationships (*wulun*) in the Confucian doctrine: the relationship between ruler and subject; the relationship between father and son; the relationship between husband and wife; the relationship between elder and younger brothers; and the relationship between friends. Three of the relationships are purely family relationships, while the remaining two are considered to be as important as, if not more important than, family relationships: ruler and subject are like father and son or grandfather and grandson, while friends are like brothers or sisters.[1] These pure family relationships and quasi-family relationships are characterized by trustfulness and reciprocity, and are very important for the maintenance of any human society. According to Confucianism, members involved in the family or quasi-family relationships are insiders, who together constitute a 'walled castle' against outsiders. The emphasis on family and interpersonal relationships is, as explained in chapter 3, one of the main driving forces behind the prevalence of *guanxi* in Chinese society.

Respect for age and hierarchy

Confucianism requires people to show respect for age and social hierarchy. According to Confucianism, age represents progress in learning and an increase in wisdom. As people grow up year by year, they gain more virtues and knowledge through moral cultivation; therefore, elders should be respected by the young. By the same token, all junior or lower-level members of a social hierarchy should respect their senior or higher-level counterparts, who are supposed to be more morally cultivated than they are. Four of the Five Cardinal Relationships are strictly hierarchical – i.e. those between ruler and subject, between father and son, between husband and wife and between elder and young brothers. Even the relationship between friends is considered to be hierarchical, because close friends are normally called brothers and sisters, and are ranked according to age. The older friend is called elder brother (*xiongzhang*) while the younger friend is called younger brother (*didi*). People at the lower levels of the social hierarchy are expected to listen to those at the higher levels.

Harmony

Confucianism emphasizes the need for harmony in a society and, therefore, requires people to avoid conflicts in social life. According to Confucianism, social harmony is achieved if all the members of a society respect the Five Cardinal Relationships, exercise self-control and behave the way a true gentleman with the Five Constant Virtues should behave. To avoid conflict, people are not supposed to quarrel, lose their temper or make harsh and provocative criticisms against each other. The Confucian principle of harmony and avoidance of conflicts has a far-reaching impact on Chinese society, and finds expression in almost every aspect of social life in the country, including the Chinese attitude towards peace and warfare, the Chinese approach to poetry, painting and music, and the Chinese way of controlling emotions in daily life.

Face

According to Confucianism, if people act as a gentleman with the Five Constant Virtues, value the Five Cardinal Relationships, respect age and hierarchy and maintain harmony, they will have face. Otherwise, they will lose face. In this context, 'face' refers to one's credit, respect, good name, reputation and dignity. Confucianism believes that face is extremely important, and that people should feel ashamed of losing face. If people have lost face, they should try to save face by correcting their improper behaviour. Indeed, Confucianism uses loss of face and shame as means to educate people in how to behave themselves.

Sun Tzu's stratagems

Sun Tzu was a Chinese military strategist in the period of Warring States (*c.* 300 BC). His book *The Art of War* forms the earliest record of Chinese thinking about stratagems (*Ji*), and has now been translated into many languages. The English term 'stratagem' is probably the best match to the Chinese term '*Ji*', and is defined as a 'strategic or tactical act of trickery, deceit, or cunning in military affairs and especially war' (Wheeler, 1988). *The Art of War* contains thirteen chapters, with the first titled '*Ji*'. According to Sun Tzu, the art of warfare is more the manipulation of human wisdom to design various stratagems than resort to physical force. In fact, the primary theme of *The Art of War* is to show how to design and employ various stratagems to 'subdue the enemy without fighting' in different circumstances.[2]

This primary theme of *The Art of War* appears to be different from the primary theme of Western thinking about military strategy. The most directly comparable statement on military strategy in the West is Carl Von Clausewitz's *On War*, published in 1832. The difference between *On War*, and *The Art of*

Figure 6.1   Taoist yin-yang principle

War lies mainly in the thinking as to how a war should be won. According to Von Clausewitz (1984, pp. 76–7), people should win a war by absolute physical force rather than mental wisdom: 'Kind-hearted people might of course think there was some ingenious way to disarm or defeat an enemy without too much bloodshed [. . .] Pleasant as it sounds, it is a fallacy that must be exposed [. . .] War is an act of force, and there is no logical limit to the application of that force.' It would appear that this statement is fundamentally different from Sun Tzu's teaching of defeating the enemy without physical fighting.

Since Sun Tzu the Chinese people have developed many stratagems, including the famous 'Thirty-Six Stratagems', also known as the 'Secret Art of War: Thirty-Six Stratagems' in the West. The thirty-six stratagems were included in a booklet written by an anonymous Chinese writer in late imperial China (either the late Ming or the early Qing dynasty). In the booklet, each of the thirty-six stratagems is expressed in three or four Chinese characters. Consequently, the booklet is very short, consisting of a total of 138 Chinese characters only. The thirty-six stratagems represent a condensed summary of Chinese strategic thinking, which have permeated the minds of millions of ordinary Chinese for centuries. Expressed in different ways, the stratagems basically follow the primary theme of Sun Tzu's *Art of War*, and require people to defeat an enemy using mental wisdom rather than physical force. Examples of the thirty-six stratagems are provided in box 6.1 (see page 135).[3] Differing from Confucianism, which basically teaches how to deal with insiders, the Sun Tzu type of stratagems primarily shows how to deal with outsiders.

In a sense, stratagems of the Sun Tzu type are based on Taoism – a Chinese philosophical tradition that can be traced back thousands of years, to roughly the same time as the origin of Confucianism. Taoism follows a dualist philosophy, as shown in the famous yin-yang principle. As shown in figure 6.1, the yin-yang principle can be illustrated as a circle divided equally by a curved line. The dark area indicates yin, representing one side of the world, such as female, darkness, weakness, softness and passivity, while the white area indicates yang, representing the other side of the world, such as male, brightness, strength, hardness and activity. The two sides are not divided absolutely and exclusively, by a straight line, but instead they depend upon each other and exist within each other. Underlying the yin-yang principle is a belief that the weak, the soft and the passive can defeat the strong, the hard and the active in certain circumstances, which is taken as the theoretical foundation of the Sun Tzu stratagems.

Agrarian mentalities

As in the case of other ancient civilizations in Asia and Africa, China has had a large agrarian population for thousands of years. Even now about two-thirds of the 1.3 billion Chinese still live in rural areas, which is a sharp contrast with what happens in the industrialized countries, where rural residents account for less than 3 per cent of the population. As pointed out by John L. Graham and N. Mark Lam (2003, p. 84), even the Chinese who currently live in cities 'were born and raised in the country and have retained their agrarian values'. During the Cultural Revolution, moreover, millions of students in urban areas were sent to the countryside by Mao Zedong to be re-educated by the peasants. Most of these re-educated students returned to cities after the economic reform programme started in 1978, and many of them assumed important positions in the government or enterprises. They got married and had children, passing their re-educated value systems to their offsprings.

There is no denying, therefore, that agrarian mentalities continue to have a profound impact on the way of thinking of the Chinese, no matter whether they live in cities or in villages. Agrarian mentalities may find expression in a number of aspects, and may influence Chinese behaviour in many ways. So far as Chinese negotiation is concerned, however, thrift and endurance are probably the most outstanding characteristics of the agrarian mindset. To survive in an agrarian society with scarce resources the Chinese people have had to learn how to save, how to work hard during difficulties and how to endure suffering. The Chinese people are, therefore, well known for their thrift and endurance, characteristics referred to as 'long-term orientation' by Hofstede (1991). These characteristics find expression in Chinese negotiators, who, as shown below, tend to bargain tenaciously over the price.

(Farmland)   (Male)

Figure 6.2   Chinese pictographic language

Pictographic language and a holistic way of thinking

The Chinese language is pictographic: each Chinese word looks like a picture. This is quite different from Western languages, in which words are composed of sequences of letters. The difference between the two types of languages reflects a profound difference in the way of thinking in the two kinds of civilizations. It is argued that the Chinese way of thinking tends to start from the whole rather than from specific details, while the Western way of thinking tends to start the other way around. In other words, the Chinese are used to looking at the whole frame first and then moving on to the details, while Western people are accustomed to assembling the details first and then drawing the whole picture. As pointed out by Graham and Lam (2003, p. 85),

Just as Western children learn to read Roman letters and numbers at an early age, Chinese children learn to memorize thousands of pictorial characters. Because, in Chinese, words are pictures rather than sequences of letters, Chinese thinking tends toward a more holistic processing of information. Michael Harris Bond, a psychology professor at the Chinese University of Hong Kong, found that Chinese children are better at seeing the big picture, while American children have an easier time focusing on the details.

The different ways of thinking are presumed to have a fundamental impact on the way people behave in the two kinds of society.

Contemporary Chinese political culture

Differing from Chinese traditional culture, Chinese political culture is closely related to the contemporary rather than the ancient, although it may have some connections to the distant past. The term 'political culture' refers to widely shared beliefs, attitudes, values and feelings about political phenomena. In an authoritarian society such as China's, these beliefs, attitudes, values and feelings are shaped primarily by changes in political leadership, and the intellectual as well as institutional heritages of top political leaders. These beliefs, attitudes, values and feelings exert a significant impact on the way people behave, including the way people negotiate, in Chinese society. Although contemporary Chinese political culture includes many elements, the most important are undoubtedly Mao Zedong's bureaucratic heritage and Deng Xiaoping's pragmatism.

Mao Zedong's bureaucratic heritage

From 1949 onwards Mao Zedong, following orthodox Marxism-Leninism, established a bureaucratic Communist regime in China. Although Mao Zedong's bureaucratic system might have some connections to the bureaucratic regimes in feudal China, it was based primarily on orthodox Marxist-Leninist ideology. The bureaucratic system therefore had more connections with the Soviet Union as established and developed by Lenin and Stalin in the first half of the twentieth century than with the feudalism of Chinese history.

Mao Zedong's bureaucracy bore three outstanding features. First of all, it was characterized by personal rule at the top of the Party. This was related to the Chinese political system, in which the Communist Party was, and still is, supposed to assume political leadership, as stated clearly in the Chinese constitution. Party leaders were typically also the administrative leaders in the government and government-run enterprises, taking control of almost everything under their administration. Consequently, top Party leaders held the power to make all key decisions. In a sense, therefore, Mao Zedong's bureaucracy was extremely authoritarian, in that Party leaders had absolute control over political power, as was also the case with the Soviet Union under Lenin and Stalin.

Mao Zedong's bureaucracy was also characterized by fragmented and stratified bureaucratic agencies. This had to be understood in the broad context of the Chinese command economy, in which comprehensive economic planning generated the need for different agencies to take charge of many individual areas of economic activities, whether it be electronics, textiles, machinery or electricity. As a result, there emerged numerous ministries, departments and agencies in the government at the central and the local levels alike each of which had command over a distinctive set of resources and enjoyed a certain degree of autonomy. These ministries, departments and agencies bargained with each other over the allocation of the resources under their control, and developed great skill at bargaining within the system.

A third feature of Mao Zedong's bureaucracy was that the art of survival in the bureaucracy was to avoid responsibility. This had to be understood in the way in which the bureaucratic system worked. Power was everything in the political system, and government officials tried very hard to avoid making mistakes in order that they could remain in office; if they made a mistake they might lose their position. One way to avoid making mistakes was to do everything according to orthodox Marxist-Leninist doctrines, a policy that led to rigidly political decision-making. Another way was to avoid taking responsibility, shifting responsibilities onto others. This was the case in China even in the early years of economic reform, as pointed out by Pye (1992, pp. 18–19):

The Chinese system, while undeniably authoritarian, is in its essence a bureaucratic process in which the critical art is to avoid responsibilities, diffuse decisions, and blunt all commands that might later leave one vulnerable to criticisms. In short, there is usually no particular person in command who can cut through problems and procedures and produce effective command decisions in the way Americans fancy it to be possible [. . .] In Chinese political culture there is no assumption that power must be tied to responsibility; on the contrary, in the ranks of the powerful, proof of importance lies precisely in being shielded from accountability. All high officials like to convey the aura of omnipotence, but they also expect that those below them will protect them from criticism; and this means, above all, protecting them from their own mistakes . . . Hence, at all times, Chinese officials have to practice the bureaucratic art of 'covering their tails.'

Mao Zedong's bureaucratic system has undergone fundamental changes since the reform programme started in 1978, but it still exerts a significant influence on Chinese society even today.

Deng Xiaoping's pragmatism

From the late 1970s onwards Deng Xiaoping began to take power in China, and initiated market-oriented economic reforms. In the reform process, reformist leaders had to overcome the political barriers left over from the previous period when orthodox Marxism-Leninism and Mao Zedong's bureaucracy prevailed. To overcome these barriers Deng Xiaoping promoted pragmatist ways of thinking within the Party leadership, which has fundamentally changed the political beliefs, attitudes, values and feelings of Chinese society at large ever since. Deng Xiaoping's pragmatism is primarily characterized by an emphasis on practice rather than theory, and an emphasis on the ends rather than the means.

Immediately after Deng Xiaoping took power he and his colleagues initiated a nationwide debate on practice as the sole criterion of testing the truth. It was argued that orthodox Marxist-Leninist theories might not match exactly the reality of China and, therefore, might not be applicable to Chinese society. Given the possible mismatches between theory and reality, Party leaders should take reality as the basis on which to make decisions on issues emerging in the reform process, and use the outcomes of reform practices to test whether or not the theories were applicable to China. A theory or doctrine, no matter how good it might look, should be discarded if it turned out not to fit in with the Chinese reality in practice.

Deng Xiaoping and his colleagues also proposed that all methods can be used to achieve a goal. In other words, what matters is the end result rather than the means. This way of thinking is expressed clearly in Deng Xiaoping's famous motto: 'White or black, it is a good cat as long as it catches mice.' Given China's backward reality, in Deng Xiaoping's view, the Party should aim at achieving economic development and modernization in China; for that purpose, all possible means can be used, including market mechanisms, a capitalist style of management systems and foreign direct investment.

Deng's pragmatism provides the theoretical guideline for the current economic reform programme in China, and has had an immense impact on the way of thinking and behaving in contemporary China. In sum, the Chinese negotiation style is rooted in a complex mixture of Chinese culture, with both traditional and contemporary elements. As Pye (1992, p. viii) has pointed out, the cultural roots of Chinese negotiation style are 'a strange mix. It of course is founded on basic (traditional) Chinese culture, but it has been profoundly influenced by decades of Marxism-Leninism, and more recently by ambivalent reactions against that orthodox and uncertainty about the reforms. As we shall see, Chinese negotiators are driven by contradictory pressures.' Pye is right on that point.

Characteristics of the Chinese negotiation style

As determined by the mixture within Chinese culture, Chinese business negotiators bear some characteristics that differ in many ways from those that are found in business negotiators in other parts of the world, particularly in the West. These characteristics are considered to constitute a unique Chinese negotiation style. To provide vivid illustrations of the characteristics of this style, in what follows there are frequent references to observations made by

Western negotiators who have had extensive experience in negotiating with the Chinese. According to these observations, the characteristics of the Chinese negotiation style include, among others: (1) an emphasis on interpersonal trust, friendship and *guanxi* rather than legal contracts; (2) hospitality; (3) tackling general principles first; (4) effectively having the government behind the scenes; (5) having a large but indecisive negotiating team; (6) sudden changes from being stubborn to being flexible; (7) sensitivity to price; and (8) the use of tactics, tricks and ploys.[4]

The emphasis on interpersonal trust rather than legal contract

Chinese negotiators tend to pay much attention to interpersonal trust, friendship and *guanxi*, and prefer to do business with someone whom they know well and consider to be trustful. As observed by a Western negotiator, 'Business in China is not about doing business between organizations, but about doing business between people. If people are business partners, they get to know each other and become personal friends who visit each other frequently. So, you have business when you have established an interpersonal relationship ... As I perceive, Chinese do business with you, not with your company' (Fang, 1999, p. 235). With their emphasis on interpersonal trust, Chinese negotiators do not pay as much attention to legal contract as Western negotiators do. As Pye (1992, p. 88) has pointed out, 'The Chinese seem to have less feeling for the drama of agreement and little expectation that any formalized contract will end the process of negotiations. Several informants described their surprise that the Chinese brought up proposals for revising what had been agreed upon, right on the heels of signing a contract.' Clearly, this feature of the Chinese negotiation style is closely related to the Confucian cultural tradition that requires people to appreciate interpersonal relationships rather than laws and legal regulations.

To get to know foreign negotiators well and establish whether they are trustworthy, Chinese negotiators often try to engage foreign negotiators in informal personal contacts and social activities first before talking about business. As noted by a Western negotiator: 'While we would rather do business straight ahead, at once, the Chinese want to get acquainted with you first. And most probably, you may not achieve anything in the first meeting, which is more of a social gathering. But then, when you have met them at least twice, you become a friend. Afterwards, the atmosphere becomes better and you can begin negotiating with them in real terms' (Fang, 1999, pp. 232–3). Abundant social activities in the pre-negotiation period become, therefore, a striking feature of negotiations with the Chinese.

Hospitality

Chinese negotiators tend to show great hospitality to negotiators from abroad, and are willing to arrange lots of free-of-charge activities to entertain them. As observed by a Western negotiator, 'When you arrive at the hotel, full of anticipation, your Chinese contact says, "How about visiting the Great Wall tomorrow?" So you agree, but then the next day it is the Ming Tombs, then the Forbidden City, the Temple of Heaven, and so on. You came to do business and you expected them to be in a big hurry, and it turns out that they would rather spend time leisurely sightseeing and chatting' (Pye 1992, p. 16). It is not an exaggeration to say that almost all foreign negotiators have similar experiences when they visit China to negotiate a deal with Chinese partners.

Some Western negotiators are frustrated by this hospitality. Some American negotiators, for instance, are suspicious of the true intention behind the hospitality, feeling that 'the Chinese consciously use such slowdown techniques as bargaining ploys because they believe they can exploit a natural American tendency for impatience' (Pye, 1992, p. 16). By playing this kind of so-called 'home court advantage', they think, the Chinese can intentionally control the pace, agenda, timing and place of the negotiation process, making Western negotiators become impatient. Then the impatient Western negotiators may begin to say too much about their opinions about the deal, and reveal details of their plans to the Chinese side during sightseeing and dinners. Thus, when the negotiations finally start, the Chinese side is well prepared, while the impatient Western negotiators, knowing nothing about the Chinese side and in a state of exhaustion, are completely at a loss. It seems that the Chinese negotiators are employing one of the thirty-six stratagems – 'Await leisurely the exhausted enemy' (box 6.1).

Chinese hospitality can indeed be a stratagem in some circumstances, but it is not so most of the time. In a sense, the Chinese view of hospitality is deeply rooted in the Confucian tradition. As stated previously, one of the Five Constant Virtues of Confucianism is *li* (propriety, rituals and rules of conduct), which often translates into hospitality in dealing with visitors, particularly visitors from afar. One of the Confucian teachings requires people to treat visitors from afar nicely, as shown in the popular Chinese saying 'isn't it a delight that friends come from afar' (*you peng zi yuanfang lai, buyi lehu*). Furthermore, as stated previously, Confucianism emphasizes interpersonal

Box 6.1 Examples of Chinese stratagems

1. Await leisurely the exhausted enemy (以逸待劳)
This is the fourth of the thirty-six stratagems. By this stratagem it is meant that you should relax and preserve your own strength, and watch the enemy exhausting himself. To weaken the enemy, in other words, it is not necessary to attack him directly. It is better to tire the enemy by carrying out defensive action. In so doing, the strength of the enemy will be reduced, and you will gain the upper hand without fighting.

2. Shut the door to catch the thief (关门捉贼)
This is the twenty-second of the thirty-six stratagems. By this stratagem it is meant that you should encircle the enemy, close off all his escape routes and defeat him. When dealing with an enemy, in other words, it is necessary to surround him as tightly as possible, leaving him no way to retreat, and destroy him completely. If you leave an escape route open to the enemy, you will be in a disadvantageous position at a later stage.

3. Make a feint to the east while attacking in the west (声东击西)
This is the sixth of the thirty-sixth stratagems. By this stratagem it is meant that you should confuse the enemy by making a noise in one direction but attacking him from another direction. When the enemy is in confusion, he will be unprepared for any contingencies. That is, you should puzzle the enemy with a diversionary move, and then give him a decisive blow when he has dropped his guard.

4. Red-face and white-face stratagem (红白脸计)
The red-face and white-face stratagem is not on the list of the thirty-six stratagems, but it is very popular among the Chinese. The Chinese expression of the stratagem comes from Peking Opera, in which different actors play different roles. The role that an actor plays is clearly indicated by the colour of his/her face. A red face usually indicates the role of a good guy and bravery, uprightness and loyalty, while a white face indicates the role of a bad guy and sinisterness, treachery and guile. In daily life, Chinese people may assign someone to the role of a 'bad' guy (white face), and the other to the role of a 'good' guy (red face), in order to achieve certain objectives.

trust, friendship and *guanxi*. Chinese hospitality often represents an effort on the Chinese side to establish trustful friendship with foreign negotiators before the formal negotiation starts.

General principles first

Chinese negotiators tend to start negotiations on a few general principles first, leaving specific details to a later stage. As pointed out by Pye (1992, p. 49), 'This insistence on first achieving agreement on general principles is one of the most distinctive characteristics of the Chinese negotiating style . . . The Chinese approach is almost the exact opposite of the American belief that progress in negotiations is usually best facilitated by adhering to concrete and specific details, avoiding debates about generalities, which can easily become entangled in political or philosophical differences.' The general principles that Chinese negotiators propose often take the form of vaguely worded letters of intent, letters of interest or protocols setting out the intentions or long-term interests of both parties.

The insistence on tackling general principles first can be, as pointed out by some Western observers, a negotiating ploy. It is observed that Chinese negotiators often take advantage of the signed general principles at a later stage of the negotiations, particularly when the discussion moves on to specific details. Once the two sides at the negotiating table are in dispute over specific details, Chinese negotiators tend to attack the other side for not complying with the general principles that have been agreed upon earlier (Pye, 1992, pp. 49–54). It seems, therefore, that Chinese negotiators are employing one of the thirty-six stratagems – 'Shut the door to catch the thief' (see box 6.1).

This is not always the case, however. The insistence on addressing general principles first may be rooted in the holistic way of Chinese thinking, as indicated by the pictographic language. That is, the Chinese get used to looking at the whole frame first before moving on to the details. It may also be closely related to Mao Zedong's bureaucratic heritage. That is, the general principles are set by top Party leaders and they have to be agreed upon before any specific details can be discussed. Given the diversified cultural roots, it does not come as a surprise that the insistence on general principles first prevails in Chinese negotiations, political and business alike (Pye, 1992, pp.49–54).

Government behind the scenes

In the negotiating process, Chinese negotiators are often not in a position to take final decisions, the power to take these resting in the hands of government officials behind the scenes. As observed by one Western negotiator who participated in negotiations on a joint venture project in China, 'It is very difficult to negotiate joint ventures in China, because your Chinese partner does not represent himself. Instead, he represents the Chinese government . . . For example, the government authority may say: "This won't work, that condition is not OK." Your partner always has to come back to renegotiate with you. Therefore . . . you are not negotiating with your partner but with the Chinese government (Fang, 1999, pp. 199–200). As foreign businessmen are normally unable to negotiate directly with the Chinese government, they have to negotiate with their Chinese business partner, who actually serves as an agent of the Chinese government.

This feature of the Chinese negotiation style is obviously related to Mao Zedong's bureaucratic heritage. The party leaders are also the government leaders, with the final say in decisions on almost everything, particularly on matters of major significance, such as projects involving foreign investors. Bearing this in mind, it is not surprising to find that Chinese negotiators may suspend the negotiations from time to time because of the repeated need to seek approval from the government, and that negotiations with the Chinese can be a very lengthy process because they involve more than the two sides at the negotiating table.

Having a large but indecisive negotiation team

Chinese negotiation teams are often very large in size, consisting of many officials from various government departments. As observed by a Western negotiator: 'We do not involve anyone outside [our company]. But, in China, it is common that people from various government departments and commissions (e.g. planning, economic, and foreign trade commissions) are found sitting in the negotiation room. You have visits from ministerial or provincial officials. Your partners report not only to their corporate chiefs but also to the provincial government and the like. The Chinese must receive permits from the province. By contrast, it is up to [us] to decide everything we want to do' (Fang, 1999, p. 206). Apart from government officials, representatives from various departments of the Chinese company are often also invited to participate in the negotiating team, to avoid possible 'non-collaboration' in the future.

This feature of the Chinese negotiation style is related to Mao Zedong's bureaucratic heritage. Although China has been moving from a command economy to a market economy since 1978, economic planning still plays a key role. Consequently, fragmented bureaucratic institutions continue to maintain control over specific resources, which is true even at the enterprise level. Chinese negotiators have to involve these institutions in the negotiating process to ensure the smooth progress of the negotiations. As stated by a Chinese negotiator, 'When it comes to negotiation of a large project in which various departments are involved, if you do not ask each of these departments to come, they will probably make complaints and won't support your work very much in the future . . . Therefore, in order to coordinate our work, we asked every department to send one representative to form our negotiating team' (Fang,

1999, p. 208). These department representatives tend to avoid responsibility, needing to seek approval from senior leaders on all important issues, so ironically, the large negotiating team is unable to make final decisions of any significance.

Sudden changes from being stubborn to being flexible

Chinese negotiators are very stubborn at times, but may become very accommodating and flexible all of a sudden. As observed by Pye (1992, p. 78), 'At one moment they [the Chinese] are described as being stubborn, firm, and tenacious, willing to wait with Oriental patience for the other side to give in; but they are also said to be realists, ready to adjust quickly to imperatives of human relations, and always anxious to be conciliatory if given a chance. They are thus seen as being both unyielding and highly adaptable . . .' This feature of the Chinese negotiation style is closely related both to Mao Zedong's bureaucratic heritage and to Deng Xiaoping's pragmatist reactions against it.

Chinese negotiators are stubborn when they feel that the general principles set by the top Party leaders are being challenged, when they are faced with propositions on which they cannot make any compromises without asking for approval from the senior leaders. Chinese negotiators may suddenly become flexible, however, when they have received approval from top Party leaders, who either have realized that the demand on the Chinese side is, though theoretically correct, not realistic, or want to achieve a certain goal using every method possible. Consequently, Western negotiators often find that 'higher Chinese officials can more readily make concessions whereas lower officials have to be more careful and hence appear to be stubborn. The higher the official the greater the flexibility' (Pye, 1992, p. 80). This finding, as shown below, has important implications for negotiating with the Chinese.

Sensitivity to price

Chinese negotiators tend to be very sensitive to price. In the negotiating process they often keep bargaining for a lower price, and do so even at the expense of other aspects of the deal, such as the quality of the products and the time of delivery. As noted by a Western negotiator, 'It is so easy for the Chinese to say that everything is too expensive, and the price is too high. This has been applied by the Chinese to expatriates' salary, travel, allowances, product value, GSM prices, terminal prices, kits prices, and whatever. The Chinese assumed that everything they were going to buy was too expensive.

[. . .] They just bargain like that during the whole negotiation. Instead of saying "Good night!" the Chinese were saying "Lower your price tomorrow morning!" at the end of a meeting' (Fang, 1999, p. 227). This feature of the Chinese negotiating style is discussed in almost all influential studies on Chinese negotiation tactics, including Pye (1992), Fang (1999) and Graham and Lam (2003).

The sensitivity to price is closely related to the Chinese agrarian mentalities, which emphasize thrift. Arguably, it is also related to Deng Xiaoping's pragmatism, which stresses the backward reality of China. In a primarily underdeveloped Chinese society in which financial resources are scarce, the Chinese are overwhelmed by the need to buy more for less. As a matter of fact, many of the Chinese tactics, tricks and ploys, which are analysed below, are employed to lower the price. Chinese negotiators are so keen to cut the price that they tend to overlook the other party's interests, which has led some observers to conclude that the Chinese are more interested in a competitive win–lose solution than a cooperative win–win outcome (see, for instance, Fang, 1999, and Pye, 1992). The alleged win–lose tendency is probably not an intrinsic feature of the Chinese negotiation style but a result of the Chinese sensitivity to price. As China develops, the Chinese are expected to become less price-sensitive over time.

The use of tactics, tricks and ploys

Finally, but not exclusively, Chinese negotiators are found to use various tactics, tricks and ploys in the process of negotiation. Pye (1992, p. 60) points out: 'The Chinese often display a fascination for tactics that may be at the expense of any recognizable strategy. Some would classify this absorption with manipulation as the second most distinctive Chinese negotiating characteristics after their stress on agreement over general principles. Once the Chinese have achieved their general principles, it is often hard to discern precisely what they are after because of their use of ploys, tactics, and gamesmanship, often of a subtle nature, but frequently crude and transparent.' The use of tricks and ploys is obviously related to stratagems of the Sun Tzu type. As a Chinese negotiator admitted, 'In negotiation, ji (stratagem) thinking constitutes absolutely far more than 10% of Chinese mentality. I believe it accounts for more than 50%. I agree that ji (stratagem) is built into the Chinese mentality and the Chinese can adopt it *xia yi shi* (unconsciously)' (Fang, 1999, p. 245). There are numerous examples showing how the stratagems are used in the negotiating process, and we illustrate a few of them below.

For example, Chinese negotiators may raise demands that are, as even they themselves know very well, unacceptable to foreign negotiators. In the meantime, they carefully indicate that these demands may be revised if the foreign negotiators are willing to make concessions. Moreover, Chinese negotiators may begin a negotiation with demands that are not really what they want, hiding their true intention, which they indicate clearly only at a later stage of the negotiations. Tricks and ploys of this type constitute a typical employment of one of the thirty-six stratagems – 'Make a feint to the east while attacking in the west' (see box 6.1).

Before negotiation starts, furthermore, the Chinese may have made careful plans with regard to what role each member in the team will play, and use the role-play very skilfully in the negotiating process – as experienced by a Western negotiator in the course of a deal with a Chinese team in 1986. When the negotiation moved on to the question of price, one Chinese negotiator suddenly stood up and shouted angrily at the Western negotiator, who, completely shocked, had no idea what had gone wrong. Two years later, when the two met again, the Chinese negotiator admitted that, before the negotiations had started, the Chinese team had already allocated their roles internally. It was decided that, if the Western side raised a price above a certain level, this Chinese negotiator would show anger. If not, another member of the Chinese team would play the game differently (see Fang, 1999, p. 247). This is a typical example of the employment of the Chinese stratagem of red-face and white-face (see box 6.1). In sum, the use of tricks and ploys may indeed be part of the Chinese negotiating process, and the Chinese are very good at manipulating them to achieve what they want from negotiations.

Tips for negotiating with Chinese partners

Negotiating with the Chinese is a daunting challenge to foreign business people. Given the complex cultural roots of the Chinese negotiation style, it is difficult, if not impossible, to make a comprehensive strategic plan that covers every aspect. It is useful, however, to draw some general rules from our previous discussion, which may be of some help to foreign negotiators in China. These general rules should be taken as broad guidelines rather than fixed strategies, as negotiating with Chinese partners is a complicated process influenced by many variables, such as the specific issues involved, the nature of the initial problem, the composition of the Chinese negotiation team and changes in the general political and economic context in which the negotiating is taking place. In what follows, we discuss six broad guidelines for negotiating with the Chinese.

Identify the meaning of a particular negotiating behaviour

As determined by the complex cultural roots, a particular piece of behaviour on the part of Chinese negotiators may have different meanings in different contexts. It is crucial for foreign negotiators to identify the meaning of a particular behaviour by Chinese negotiators and adopt corresponding strategies to deal with it. If you misunderstand the meaning of a particular behaviour and adopt inappropriate strategies, you may experience frustration or even unnecessary conflict with Chinese negotiators, which may eventually lead to the negotiations failing.

As stated previously, Chinese negotiators may entertain you and engage you in various social and informal activities first before starting formal negotiations. This behaviour may be rooted in the Confucian cultural tradition, indicating Chinese hospitality in general or an effort to establish a trusting relationship, friendship and *guanxi* with you. In this case, you need to respond politely and reciprocally, seizing the chance to establish a trust-based relationship with the Chinese negotiators. Equally, though, this behaviour may be related to the Sun Tzu type of Chinese stratagems, indicating the employment of tricks and ploys. That is, the Chinese negotiators are taking the so-called home court advantage to 'await leisurely the exhausted enemy'. In that case, you need to take sufficient caution when taking part in these kinds of activities, and get yourself well prepared for the tough negotiating that is expected to follow. If you treat this behaviour as a trick or ploy when the Chinese are genuinely showing their hospitality and friendship the negotiations are unlikely to succeed. If you treat this behaviour as an indication of Chinese hospitality and friendship when the Chinese are indeed using deceits and tricks on you, you will be in a disadvantageous position at later stages of the negotiations.

As analysed previously, furthermore, Chinese negotiators may urge you to start the negotiating process with an agreement on some 'general principles' leaving specific details to the later stages. This behaviour may be rooted in the holistic way of Chinese thinking, indicating that the Chinese negotiators are unconsciously accustomed to starting with the whole picture rather than the details. It may also be rooted in Mao Zedong's bureaucratic heritage, indicating a kind of bureaucratic procedure in which top Party leaders set the general principles beforehand that have to be agreed upon first in the negotiation process. In both cases, you need to show understanding, and reach an agreement with the Chinese on some general principles that not only fit in with Chinese culture but also serve your own interests. This behaviour may, however, be related to the Sun Tzu type of Chinese stratagems, indicating employment of the stratagem of 'shutting the door to catch the thief'. In other words, the Chinese negotiators are trying to encircle you and close off all your escape routes at the very beginning so as to gain the upper hand in the negotiations at the end of the day. In that case, you should be careful when entering an agreement with the Chinese negotiators on general principles, and make sure that the wording of these general principles cannot 'encircle' you in the later stages of negotiations on specific details.

Given the complexity of the cultural roots of the Chinese negotiation style, it is very difficult for foreign negotiators to distinguish between the different possible meanings of a particular piece of behaviour on the part of Chinese negotiators and adopt appropriate strategies in response. However, it is essential to bear in mind that Chinese negotiators use stratagems, ploys and tricks primarily when they are treating you as an outsider rather than an insider. When they have got to know you well and established trustful friendship with you, they will treat you as an insider with genuineness, sincerity and trust rather than deceits. It is advisable, therefore, for foreign negotiators to try to become insiders in the eyes of Chinese negotiators, which can be achieved by following the second guideline.

Adopt a people-oriented approach

A people-oriented approach consists of focusing on the people whom you are negotiating and doing business with, and establishing a good personal relationship or even friendship with them. To adopt this approach, you need to devote time and effort to getting to know Chinese negotiators on a personal basis, through, for instance, such informal social activities as dining, parties, personal visits, family gatherings and exchanges of gifts. In the Chinese cultural environment, a people-oriented approach can benefit foreign negotiators in many ways.

A people-oriented approach can help you gain trust from Chinese negotiators, who will then treat you as an insider. As stated previously, the Confucian tradition requires the Chinese to behave like gentlemen with such virtues as sincerity, which applies only when the Chinese treat the other party as a trusted insider or friend. Stratagems of the Sun Tzu type, on the other hand, require the Chinese to behave like military strategists, using all sorts of tricks and deceits, which applies when the Chinese treat the other party as an outsider or enemy.

Once you have established a trusting friendship with Chinese negotiators, you will enjoy the 'treatment of insiders' in comfort, and avoid being subjected to the numerous ploys and deceptions that can be used in the negotiation process.

A people-oriented approach can also help you overcome the bureaucratic barriers you may encounter in China. As stated previously, Mao Zedong's bureaucratic heritage continues to have a profound impact on Chinese society today, and can still become a huge barrier to business development in the country. To strike a business deal, for example, you need to get approval from Party and government officials at a number of different levels. If you have established a trustful friendship with your Chinese negotiators, they will help you get through all the red tape with relative ease.

Set up an appropriate negotiating team

Given the complexity of the cultural roots of the Chinese negotiating style and the importance of the people-oriented approach to negotiating in China, it is advisable for a foreign negotiation team to include a member of Chinese origin. Knowing Chinese culture intimately, the ethnic Chinese member will be far better placed to understand what a gesture or a wink by the Chinese negotiators may mean in the Chinese cultural context – something that is essential for foreign negotiators if they are to distinguish between the different meanings of a particular behaviour by the Chinese negotiators and adopt corresponding strategies to respond. It would be even better if the Chinese member of the foreign negotiating team already had good personal relationships with the relevant government officials or had the ability to establish such relationships, which is especially helpful in negotiations over large projects that involve complicated approval procedures. Sometimes it is desirable to appoint an ethnic Chinese to head the negotiation process and the negotiated project, as shown in the experience of American car makers in China (box 6.2).

Given the importance of social hierarchy in Chinese culture, moreover, it is advisable for a foreign negotiating team to have a head whose rank and age are similar to those of his/her Chinese counterpart. The Chinese tend, as admitted by a Chinese negotiator, to think that 'negotiations should be held between people of similar age and rank' (Fang, 1999, p. 236). If you do not follow this rule, you will certainly suffer delays, or even failure, in negotiations with Chinese partners. Graham and Lam (2003, p. 87) report an interesting case to illustrate this point. In a high-level negotiation with a Chinese partner over an important project, an American company sent a young and low-level

Box 6.2 General Motors and Ford in China

With the rapid growth of a wealthy middle class, China is expected to become the largest automobile market in the world in the foreseeable future. Foreign car makers have been eager to enter this market. European car makers, such as Volkswagen and Peugeot Citroën, were among the early birds, investing in China as early as the mid-1980s. In the early 1990 American automobile giants such as General Motors and Ford began to look for opportunities to invest in China, while the cautious Japanese car makers were still mainly exporting cars to China.

From 1993 to 1995 GM and Ford competed with each other in negotiation with Shanghai Automotive Industry Corporation, a leading car maker in China, on a joint venture project, valued at more than $1 billion, to produce sedans in China. In October 1995 the Chinese side picked GM in preference to Ford for this project. Apart from the efforts made by GM to meet the requirements proposed by the Chinese side, the composition of GM's negotiating team was reported to have made a difference in the negotiation process.

GM had appointed Shirley Young, an ethnic Chinese and vice-president of its department of consumer market development, to head the negotiation team. Young, born in Shanghai and speaking fluent Mandarin, knows Chinese culture very well. Thanks to her family background – her father was a war hero and her stepfather served as China's ambassador to the United States, the United Kingdom and France – Young has very good *guanxi* with government officials in China. In the end, as pointed out by Graham and Lam (2003, p. 88), '[E]ven though Ford has been one step ahead in the initial bidding phase, Young was able to pass the final victory to GM.'

Ford's failure was partly attributed to the composition of its negotiating team. Ford had appointed an American engineer, Jim Paulson, president of Ford (China), to head the negotiations. Without knowledge of Chinese culture and *guanxi* networks in China, Paulson lost the battle to GM. As he later admitted in *Time Magazine*, 'We tried to find out more about how they were arriving at their decisions, but we didn't have enough Chinese-speaking people to establish close contact with the officials in Shanghai' (Graham and Lam, 2003, p. 88). In fact, Ford did have very competent ethnic Chinese candidates at that time for the position of chief negotiator, such as Lawrence T. Wong, then president of Ford's Taiwan operation. Unfortunately, Ford did not realize the importance of the composition of a negotiating team in the context of cross-cultural negotiations, and did not make use of its ethnic Chinese staff at hand.

Learning its lesson from the failure, Ford later tried to include ethnic Chinese in its team in negotiations with Chinese partners over other projects. In 1998 Ford appointed Meiwei Cheng, an ethnic Chinese, as senior executive in Beijing. In 2001 he played a key role in Ford's success in reaching agreement with Chang'an Automobile Industry Corporation, China's third largest automobile maker, over a joint venture project to produce 50,000 cars in China.[5]

gentleman to head the negotiation team. The head of the Chinese negotiation team said to his American counterpart: 'You are about the same age as my son.' The Chinese side felt insulted and doubted the sincerity of the American company. Consequently, the negotiations ended in failure. In negotiating with the Chinese, therefore, you need to select the members of your team carefully, particularly the chief negotiator.

Talk to top Party and government leaders whenever possible

In line with Mao Zedong's bureaucratic heritage, the power to make final decisions rests firmly in the hand of top Communist Party and government officials. It is advisable, therefore, for foreign negotiators to try as much as they can to talk directly to top Party and government officials, which often paves the way to success in negotiating with the Chinese. As a Western negotiator observed, 'I once did a project, selling to China a complete paper packaging production line. We had tried for many years but failed. It seemed that at that time, China did not foresee the potential demand. Nobody dared to make a decision. Finally, it was the then Chinese premier who made the buying decision during his visit to Sweden . . . We sat and discussed for about one and a half hours and settled the project' (Fang, 1999, pp. 201–2). The top-down approach has proved to be very effective in most cases of negotiating with Chinese partners, but it does not imply that foreign negotiators can neglect government officials at lower levels. Overlooking lower-level government officials may not have a negative effect on a project under negotiation to start with, but it may lead to disastrous consequences at later stages of the development of the project, as shown in the case of the Sino-Singaporean negotiations on the Suzhou Industrial Park joint venture (see chapter 3).

It is not always possible, however, for foreign negotiators to have access to such top Party and government leaders as the Chinese Premier. Whenever high-ranking Chinese government officials pay a visit to your country, as shown in the above case, you had better seize the opportunity to talk to them or establish contact with them. Furthermore, foreign negotiators may establish direct contacts with top Party and government leaders through various intermediaries in China. Given the prevalence of *guanxi* and the transferability of *guanxi*, as analysed in chapter 3, it is always possible for you to find someone who can establish direct contacts with top Party and government leaders if you really want to do so. Once again, this requires foreign negotiators to have a wide *guanxi* network in China.

Employ tactics when necessary and appropriate

When Chinese negotiators are indeed deploying stratagems of the Sun Tzu type, foreign negotiators need to employ certain tactics, tricks and ploys to respond. There are no fixed rules to follow as to how to deal with Chinese stratagems. In a sense, it all depends on the specific stratagem that Chinese negotiators are employing and the particular circumstances under which the stratagem is being employed. Michael Miles (2003) has produced a list of tactics that Chinese negotiators may employ, and provides a list of responding tactics for foreign negotiators to use.

According to Miles, for instance, Chinese negotiators tend not to show interest in what the foreign party proposes, and tend to let the foreign party make the initial statements of position and concessions. In response, foreign negotiators need to (1) gather information about what the Chinese are interested in beforehand, (2) present more than one area of potential collaboration and (3) show limited concern over short-term commitments. In addition, Chinese negotiators tend to use time strategically, delaying a reply to a proposal. In response, foreign negotiators should (1) not plan to sign the final contract on any specific occasion, (2) use trusted intermediaries to gather information and (3) hold back on committing themselves, using as an excuse the need to secure approval back home. Furthermore, Chinese negotiators tend to have recourse to real or fictional regulations or budget limitations to get concessions. In response, foreign negotiators need to (1) use a third party to find out what the situation really is and (2) refer to fictional or real policies and regulations back home as a counterbalance, and so on. As shown in the case of a Canadian negotiator (box 6.3), foreign negotiators may adopt some of these tactics in negotiating with Chinese business partners.

Pye illustrates some tactics used by Western negotiators in response to the Chinese tactics of blaming foreign negotiators for violating the general principles that had been agreed upon. Faced with this blame, some American negotiators tried to 'smooth ruffled Chinese feathers over "violations" of the spirit of agreements by symbolic gestures of continuing goodwill, even as they held firm on matters of details' (1992, p. 53). On another occasion, some Japanese negotiators dealt with the act of blaming by doing what the Chinese requested in one area while achieving what they requested in another area in the negotiated contract (p. 53). In both cases, the foreign negotiators did not suffer.

Although it is appropriate to adopt commensurate tactics, tricks and ploys in response to those exercised by the Chinese side, it is advisable for foreign

Box 6.3 The experience of a Canadian negotiator

Mike, who worked for a Canadian consultancy firm, went to Beijing to develop a consultancy business in China in 1997. Through his contacts in China, Mike learnt that the Chinese State Coordinating Agency (SCA) was planning a major human resource management training programme that fitted in well with his expertise. In fact, Mike had already established friendly relations with the heads of the SCA: he had hosted all the directors in his home in Canada in the past. He then managed to arrange a meeting with the current director of the SCA, Ms Wang, to discuss possibilities for him to work with the agency, particularly opportunities for long-term collaboration. Wang did not show any great interest in having Mike on the HRM training programme, however, even though she was well aware of his ability to run the programme. Nevertheless, the meeting ended up with an agreement to move the discussion forward.

Two days later Wang contacted Mike about the possibility of his running an HRM seminar in a city in western China, and asked for another meeting with him the next day. Prior to the meeting Mike contacted a Chinese friend to obtain information as to the specific details of the HRM seminar, including the target participants. At the meeting Wang asked Mike to provide an outline for the seminar and estimates for the costs involved before he left for Canada the following day. It appeared to be an urgent request, one that Mike could not meet. Mike then told her that he had to discuss it with his business partners and get approval back home before he could submit the plan. Wang then indicated that she respected the declared 'company policy'. As soon as he returned to Canada Mike sent the outline and cost estimates to Wang by fax. There then followed a long period of waiting.

Three months later Mike visited Beijing again. Before meeting Ms Wang, Mike met his Chinese friend, who knew her quite well, and who used to stay with Mike in Canada for extended visits of up to half a year. Mike discussed the business plan with him, and asked him for information about the delay and for advice. Then, the next day, Wang invited Mike, his Chinese friend and two government representatives from the city in western China for dinner. It was almost at the end of the meal that Wang started to talk about the seminar, saying that the SCA was keen to have Mike to deliver the seminar but had no budget to pay for the professional fees, and asking Mike to deliver the seminar, as an old friend, for free. In response, Mike described the costs involved and the difficulties in securing approval from his company for the free service, and suggested that both sides go away and think about a possible solution again.

Early the next morning Wang called Mike, saying that she had discussed the issue with her boss and would like to meet him again. At the meeting Wang proposed an inclusive professional fee of C$10,000. Mike replied that he had to discuss this proposal with his company back home. Immediately upon arrival in Canada, Mike sent Wang a letter by fax indicating that he and his company had agreed to the proposed professional fee, and that any reduction in the fee was unacceptable.

A few days later, however, Wang replied by fax, indicating a reduction in the proposed professional fee because of an increase in the expenses involved. Mike sent Wang a fax by return, stating firmly that it was impossible for his company to accept the revised payment for the service, and that he might have to withdraw from the negotiated training project. Soon Mike received a reply from Wang, to the effect that she had talked with the government official in the city in western China, who had agreed to stick to the original plan for the professional fee! The HRM seminar then proceeded as scheduled.[6]

negotiators to use these counter-tactics skilfully so as not to offend the Chinese negotiators. In so doing, friendship between the two sides may be established eventually, and then the foreign negotiators will no longer be subject to tricks and deceits.

Know the Chinese negotiation style but be yourself

In the debate on the cross-cultural theory of negotiation, some scholars have advocated that foreign negotiators should adopt a 'when in Rome, do as the Romans do' approach with local negotiators. Others, however, recommend that foreign negotiators should not completely accept what the local negotiators do and imitate them. Stephen Weiss (1994a, 1994b), for example, argues that simply accepting and imitating what local negotiators do is no guarantee of success. Indeed it is not always desirable for foreign negotiators to adapt to the Chinese ways of negotiating and imitate them. This is a very important point, which foreign negotiators would do well to bear in mind when negotiating with Chinese partners.

The Chinese emphasize interpersonal relations and *guanxi* in business negotiations for instance. Although it is important for foreign negotiators to learn about Chinese culture and adopt a people-oriented approach, it is equally vital for foreign negotiators to know the extent to which they can proceed in that direction. Given the prevalence of corruption in the Chinese government at present, the adoption of a people-oriented approach to establishing *guanxi* with government officials is very likely to lead to bribery, as analysed in chapter 3. While pursuing a people-oriented approach, therefore, foreign negotiators have to be aware of the ethical limits of the approach and refer to their own ethical standards for guidance when doing business in China.

The Chinese are, in addition, price-sensitive. They tend to ask for a lower price at the expense of quality, and tend to keep bargaining over the price throughout the negotiation process. It is, of course, unwise and inappropriate for foreign negotiators to adapt to the Chinese approach in this respect and imitate it: intensive haggling over the price would lead the negotiations nowhere. In the face of persistent bargaining over price on the part of Chinese negotiators, foreign negotiators should stress the importance of quality, and show their bottom line on price clearly and firmly, as the Canadian negotiator did regarding the professional fee in the case highlighted in box 6.3.

It is advisable, therefore, for foreign negotiators to know the Chinese negotiation style, but be themselves. As Pye (1992, p. 110) points out, 'Know the other culture, be sensitive to its distinctive characteristics so as not to unintentionally offend, but also be true to your own cultural standards.' This is also the case because Chinese negotiators need to adapt to other cultures and negotiation styles as well in the process of globalization. Since China began opening up to the outside world in 1978, the Chinese have found themselves immersed in the process of learning about different cultures and coming to terms with them. The convergence of cultures in the globalization process requires multilateral rather than unilateral accommodation.

Summary

According to the cross-cultural theory of negotiation, the cultural environments – broadly defined – in which negotiators are brought up have a significant impact on the behaviour of the negotiators, and shape the different negotiation styles found in different nations. This theory provides a framework that has underlain, explicitly or implicitly, all research on the Chinese negotiation style.

The behaviour of Chinese negotiators is rooted primarily in two sets of cultural elements. The first is traditional Chinese culture, including Confucianism, Sun Tzu's types of stratagems, agrarian mentalities and the pictographic language. The second is contemporary Chinese political culture, including Mao Zedong's bureaucratic heritage and Deng Xiaoping's pragmatism. These cultural factors contribute to the formation of a uniquely Chinese negotiation style.

Western negotiators have observed that the Chinese negotiating style is characterised by, among other things, an emphasis on interpersonal trust, friendship and *guanxi* rather than legal contracts, hospitality, addressing general principles first, government behind the scenes, having a large but indecisive negotiating team, sudden changes from being stubborn to being flexible, sensitivity to price, and the use of tactics, tricks and ploys. An understanding of these characteristics of the Chinese negotiating style must form the basis for any meaningful strategic thinking about negotiation with Chinese partners.

Given the complex cultural roots of the Chinese negotiation style, however, it is not at all easy to come up with a comprehensive strategic plan that covers every aspect of negotiating with Chinese partners. It is useful, however, to follow some general rules. Foreign negotiators are, for instance, advised to: (1) identify the meaning of a particular negotiating behaviour; (2) adopt a people-oriented approach; (3) set up an appropriate negotiating team; (4) talk to top Party and government leaders whenever possible; (5) employ tactics when necessary and appropriate; and (6) know the Chinese negotiation style but be yourself. These general rules should be taken as broad guidelines rather than rigid strategies.

FURTHER READING

Fang, T. 1999. *Chinese Negotiating Style*. London: Sage.

Graham, J. L., and Lam, N. M. 2003. 'The Chinese negotiation'. *Harvard Business Review* 81 (10): 82–91.

Miles, M. 2003. 'Negotiating with the Chinese: lessons from the field'. *Journal of Applied Behavioral Science* 39 (4): 452–72.

Pye, L. 1992. *Chinese Negotiating Style: Commercial Approaches and Cultural Principles*. New York: Quorum.

Questions for discussion

1. How should cultural differences be handled in negotiations between parties from different cultural backgrounds? Should foreign negotiators adopt a 'when in Rome, do as the Romans do' approach, and completely accept what the local negotiators do and imitate them? Illustrate your argument with examples of the experience of foreign negotiators in China.

2. To what extent is the Chinese negotiation style different from, or similar to, those in other parts of the world? Illustrate your argument with examples of the negotiation style of a particular country/region.

3. What is culture? How does culture influence the behaviour of people in general, and negotiators in particular? Are there negotiating behaviours that transcend cultural borders and thus can be found everywhere in the world?

4. Apart from the traditional cultural elements and the political cultural elements discussed in this chapter, are there any other Chinese cultural elements that may have an impact on the behaviour of Chinese negotiators?

5. How does Confucianism influence the behaviour of Chinese negotiators? What particular characteristics of the Chinese negotiation style are rooted in the Confucian tradition?

6. Are stratagems of the Sun Tzu type unique in China? Do negotiators in other parts of the world adopt tactics, tricks and ploys in negotiation? If so, what are they?

7. Explain why it is important for foreign negotiators to adopt a people-oriented approach to negotiating with the Chinese. Relate your argument to the cultural roots of Chinese negotiation style.

NOTES

1. In feudal times Chinese people often called the emperors by names that suggested the role of grandfather, such as Taisuiye, Qiansuiye and Laofuye, '*ye*' meaning 'grandfather' in the Chinese language.

2. Many scholars have now begun to discuss the application of the basic stratagems of *The Art of War* to strategic management. Mun (1990), for instance, summarizes fifteen principles from Sun Tzu's book, and believes that they can be applied to strategic management. The fifteen principles are comparison, leadership, shared vision, delegation of power, conquering by stratagems, creation of a situation, prudence, initiative, quick fighting, deception, extraordinary troops, flanking, flexibility, focus and espionage.

3. For details of the thirty-six stratagems, visit http://www.geocities.com/Area51/Shire/5882/36s.html.

4. Many books and articles have been published on the Chinese negotiation style, but two of them are most influential. The first is a book entitled *Chinese Negotiating Style: Commercial Approaches and Cultural Principles*. Written by Lucian Pye, an American political scientist at the Massachusetts Institute of Technology, it is considered to represent the Western view of the Chinese negotiation style. The other is a book entitled *Chinese Negotiating Style*, written by Tony Fang, a Chinese scholar working in northern Europe, it is considered to represent the Chinese view of the Chinese negotiation style. The two books are both based on extensive interviews with negotiators in the field, and they both contain abundant observations made by Western negotiators in China.

5. For the details, see Graham and Lam (2003).

6. For the details, see Miles (2003).

7 Production operations management

The need to successfully operate facilities in any location is clearly an important task for both subsidiary and headquarters management. As China continues to liberalize its economic and political regime, foreign firms have to work within the constraints and requirements of that environment while leveraging the advantages they possess in terms of size and resources, and their experience in the Chinese setting (Rajib N. Sanyal and Turgut Guvenli (2001, p. 45)).

Production operations are the 'processes that produce goods and services' or the 'processes that transform inputs into products and services' (Krajewski and Ritzman, 2002, p. 1). As such, they play a crucial role in the value creation of a firm, and need to be managed carefully. Production operations management in an international setting differs from production operations management at home in many ways. In managing production operations in China, transnational corporations need to take into account the Chinese business environment and the challenges that that environment poses for them. In this chapter we discuss some key issues that TNCs need to address in managing production operations in China, including the siting of their manufacturing facilities, the choice of location, localization of sourcing and localization of research and development.

The siting of manufacturing facilities

In establishing manufacturing facilities in China, transnational corporations need to think about the way in which the manufacturing facilities are arranged – that is, the siting of the facilities. China is a huge country with a vast territory. Investing in manufacturing facilities in China is different from investing in a small country such as Singapore, where all the facilities can be concentrated in a single place. In a large country such as China, TNCs have to make a decision on whether they should establish all their manufacturing facilities in one place or establish them in a number of sites across the country – that is, whether they should centralize or decentralize their manufacturing facilities in the country. Some TNCs have adopted the centralization approach to the siting of their manufacturing facilities in China, while others have adopted the decentralization approach.

Each approach has its advantages and disadvantages. If a TNC sets up all its production facilities in one place, for example, it is better placed to exploit economies of scale and reduce the unit cost and price of its output. The TNC may suffer, however, from poor responsiveness to possible differences in consumer preference in different localities, and from high transportation costs. If a TNC establishes its production facilities in many places, by contrast, it may benefit from better local responsiveness and low transportation costs, but it cannot make full use of economies of scale. What, then, should the choice between the two approaches to siting manufacturing facilities in China be determined by? Potentially there are many factors that could influence TNCs' decisions on centralizing or decentralizing their manufacturing facilities, but two stand out as the most important: the product's attributes and the technology attributes.

Product attributes

To a large extent, whether a TNC concentrates or decentralizes its manufacturing facilities is determined by the kind of products it manufactures. The most important product attribute that affects the siting decision is what is known as the value-to-weight ratio. If a product is expensive in price and light in weight then it has a high value-to-weight ratio. Examples of products with a high value-to-weight ratio include electronic components, pharmaceuticals, mobile phones, laptop computers, calculators, wristwatches, radios and jewellery. A high value-to-weight ratio ties in with the centralization of manufacturing facilities in China, because it is less costly to transport products with a high value-to-weight ratio across the country than products with a low ratio. Other things being the same, therefore, TNCs manufacturing products with a high value-to-weight ratio tend to set up all their manufacturing facilities in one location in China and serve the whole national market from there.

If a product is cheap in price and heavy in weight, by contrast, the product has a low value-to-weight ratio. Examples of products with a low value-to-weight ratio include refined sugar, cement, chemical fertilizers, paints, coal, petroleum goods, canned food and vegetables, mineral water and other inexpensive soft drinks. A low value-to-weight ratio does not fit in with centralizing manufacturing facilities in China because it is costly to transport products with a low value-to-weight ratio across the country. Other things being equal, therefore, TNCs producing output with a low value-to-weight ratio tend to set up manufacturing facilities in multiple places in China in order to minimize the transportation cost.

Another product attribute that affects the decision on siting manufacturing facilities is the needs that a product serves. Some products, such as industrial electronics, serve universal needs – that is, the needs are the same or similar all over China, or even all over the world. Manufacturers of these products do not, therefore, have to respond to differences in consumer preference between different localities in China. Other things being equal, therefore, TNCs manufacturing products that serve universal needs tend to centralize their manufacturing facilities in China. By contrast, some products, such as canned foods and vegetables with specific local flavours, serve the particular needs of consumers in certain locations, and manufacturers of these products have to respond to differences in consumer preference across the regions in China. Other things being the same, therefore, TNCs producing goods of this type tend to decentralize their manufacturing facilities in order to achieve better local responsiveness. More often than not, however, other things are not the same, and TNCs are obliged to take into consideration other factors, such as the technology attributes.

Technology attributes

In some circumstances, the decision whether to centralize or decentralize manufacturing facilities is dependent on the technology attributes of a transnational corporation, including the fixed cost, minimum efficient scale and flexible manufacturing or lean production.

The fixed cost is the cost that does not vary significantly with the volume of output, including the cost of capital goods (building, machinery, etc.), the cost of land, the cost of property taxes and the cost of various types of insurance. The amount of fixed cost involved in setting up a manufacturing base in China varies from one type of manufacturer to another. The manufacturing of semiconductor chips, for example, requires very expensive precision machinery and a well-maintained production environment, so the fixed cost to set up a manufacturing base for semiconductors is relatively high. In contrast, the manufacturing of furniture is not very demanding in precision machinery and production environment, so the fixed cost of setting up a furniture manufacturing base is relatively low. In principle, if the fixed cost of establishing a manufacturing base is high, a TNC should consider setting up all its manufacturing facilities in one place so as to minimize the cost. If the fixed cost of establishing a manufacturing base is low, by contrast, a TNC should consider setting up the facilities in multiple places in order to avoid the disadvantages of centralizing manufacturing facilities, such as high transportation costs if the value-to-weight ratio of the product is low and poor local responsiveness if the product does not serve universal needs.

The minimum efficient scale refers to the level of output at which the economies of scale of a plant are exhausted, and the plant thus cannot benefit from the low cost and low price brought about by economies of scale any more. As mentioned in chapter 1, economies of scale occur when the cost of producing one unit of output decreases with the increase in the volume of output. That is, the average cost of producing a unit of output diminishes as each additional unit of output is produced, primarily because the fixed costs are shared over an increasing number of units of output. There is, however, a limit to the utilization of fixed capital investments, and thus a limit to economies of scale. A machine cannot, for instance, be used twenty-four hours a day; otherwise, it breaks down. In addition, it needs maintenance periodically. On average, a machine can be utilized for rather less than twenty-four hours a day – say, twenty hours – to ensure that it keeps functioning well. Beyond that point, therefore, any additional output cannot lead to reductions in unit cost and price any more because it will be achieved at the expense of the machine. The breakdown of the machine will add to the overall cost structure of the plant and thus push up the unit cost. The same analysis applies to other fixed capital investments, such as workshops, that help to realize economies of scale. Therefore, a plant is able to benefit from economies of scale only under a certain level of output, beyond which any additional output cannot lead to further reductions in unit cost and price. That level of output is called the minimum efficient scale – that is, the scale of output at which a plant has to operate in order to realize economies of scale at the minimum average cost.

It would appear that the larger the minimum efficient scale is the stronger the argument becomes for the centralization of manufacturing facilities. If the minimum efficient scale is large, for example, a TNC is able to set up all its manufacturing facilities in one place and produce all its output there without exhausting economies of scale. If the minimum efficient scale is small, by contrast, a TNC may choose to establish its facilities in multiple places so as to avoid the disadvantages of centralization: high transportation costs and poor local responsiveness.

The third technology attribute is flexible manufacturing, also called lean production. As already mentioned, one disadvantage resulting from the

Table 7.1 Factors influencing the decision on the siting of manufacturing facilities

Factors	Centralization	Decentralization
Product attribute		
Value-to-weigh ratio	High	Low
Universal needs	Yes	No
Technology attribute		
Fixed cost	High	Low
Minimum efficient scale	Large	Small
Flexible manufacturing technologies	Available	Not available

centralization of manufacturing plant is that it achieves economies of scale at the expense of local responsiveness. Flexible manufacturing helps to resolve this problem; it refers to the manufacturing technologies that can reduce the set-up time for complex machinery, increase the utilization of machinery through better scheduling and improve quality control at all stages of production. Flexible manufacturing therefore allows a TNC to cluster all its facilities in one place so as to make use of economies of scale and yet achieve good local responsiveness. With flexible manufacturing technologies, a TNC thus has the ability to engage in so-called 'mass customization' – that is, the ability to produce a variety of products to meet the needs of different local markets at low unit cost. As shown in the next chapter, this ability is sometimes referred to as economies of scope. To some extent, therefore, a TNC's decision as to whether it should centralize its manufacturing facilities depends on whether the company is able to deploy flexible manufacturing technologies.

In theory, all these product attributes and technology attributes may influence a company's decision on whether or not to centralize its manufacturing plant in China. Table 7.1 summarizes the influence of these attributes. The degree to which these attributes have an influence on the siting decision varies from one transnational corporation to another. In practice, a TNC may be subject to the influence of some factors more than others, so it needs to pay special attention to the most relevant factors. A comparative study of the cases of Motorola and Coca-Cola may help to illustrate this point.

Coca-Cola and Motorola: a comparison

Motorola and Coca-Cola are both large TNCs based in the United States, and they both began to move to China in the 1980s. The two American giants chose to adopt completely different approaches, however, to the siting of their manufacturing facilities in the country. Motorola established almost all its manufacturing facilities not just in one city, Tianjin, but in one district of the city, the Tianjin Economic Development Area. By contrast, Coca-Cola established its facilities in no fewer than twenty-one cities across China, with its headquarters in Shanghai. In other words, Motorola adopted a centralized siting strategy while Coca-Cola adopted a decentralized strategy.

Many factors undoubtedly influenced the siting decisions of the two companies, but two of them featured most prominently. The first was the value-to-weight ratio. Motorola's main product, mobile cellphones, had a value-to-weight ratio much higher than Coca-Cola's main product, bottled soft drinks. The second factor was the fixed cost. In the case of Motorola, the production of semiconductor chips and mobile cellphones was very exacting in terms of precision machinery and the production environment, and therefore had a high fixed cost structure. It is estimated that more than a half of Motorola's total investments in China were used to set up its semiconductor manufacturing plant in Tianjin. In the case of Coca-Cola, by contrast, the production of bottled soft drinks not being very demanding with regard to precision machinery and the production environment, there was a low fixed cost structure. As can be seen, therefore, both the value-to-weight ratio and the fixed cost question led Motorola to adopt centralization as its siting strategy, and Coca-Cola to adopt decentralization as its.

The choice of location

No matter whether a transnational corporation sets up its production facilities in one place or in multiple places, it has to decide on the location where the facilities are to be established. As is well acknowledged in the business literature, the location has a significant impact on the performance of a company, particularly a TNC operating in a country with a complex business environment, such as China. In 1998 a group of scholars at the City University of Hong Kong collected data on 257 TNCs operating in China, and found that location-specific factors accounted for 17 per cent of the variation in their performance.[1] To succeed in China, therefore, a TNC needs to choose the location for its manufacturing facilities with care.

To arrive at this decision a number of factors need to be taken into account, but four carry particular weight in the context of China. To begin with, a TNC needs to pay attention to the geography of China, as there are striking differences in geographical features across the country's vast territory. The climate differs significantly, for instance, from one region to another, tending to be dry and cold in the north but humid and warm in the south. This variation in climate may have important implications for the location choice of some TNCs, especially those producing climate-sensitive products. One case in point is Mary Kay, a US company that produces and sells cosmetics and skincare products. Entering the China market in 1996, Mary Kay has now established at least seventeen branches, which are mainly located in north-east China. According to Paul Mak, president of Mary Kay China, the climate has been a key factor here: he believes that people in eastern and northern China use Mary Kay's products more often than people in the south, because of the differences in climate and skin types between the two regions (Hulme, 2001). This case highlights the fact that a TNC needs to locate its production facilities in those geographical regions where its products are most needed.

The second factor that needs to be taken into account in making location decisions is the variation in the quality of the infrastructure across China. The infrastructure is the whole suite of basic supporting systems that enable a society to function, including transportation, telecommunications, power supply and education. Production facilities have to be established in a location where the infrastructure is good enough for them to function properly. As is the case with other developing countries, however, the infrastructure is generally poor in China, though there are very great differences in the level of infrastructure development across the regions. In general, the infrastructure is relatively good in the eastern, or coastal region and relatively poor in the western region. The central region lies somewhere in between. The literacy rate, for instances, is roughly 88 per cent in the eastern region but only 74 per cent in the western region. In Tibet and Qinghai, the poorest provinces in the western region, the literacy rate is only 48 per cent and 58 per cent, respectively. The railway coverage is about 153 km per 10,000 sq. km in the eastern region but only 26 km per 10,000 sq. km in the western region. There are more than ten internet subscribers in every 10,000 people in the eastern region but only one in every 10,000 in the western region. Even within the eastern region, moreover, the infrastructure may vary from one city to another.

These wide regional differences in the infrastructure explain why TNCs have established their affiliates mainly in the coastal region. As mentioned in chapter 1, nearly 90 per cent of foreign direct investment has been directed towards this region, and the good infrastructure here is clearly one of the key factors. As shown in the aforementioned study by Liu, Li and Gao (1999), the better the infrastructure a region has the more likely it is to be chosen as a location for FDI. In making its location decision, however, a TNC needs to think about the specific infrastructural requirements of its production operations. If the production operations require good transportation, the manufacturing facilities should be established in a location where the transport infrastructure is sufficiently developed. If the production operations require good human resources, a TNC should set up its plant in a location where local Chinese talents are abundant. The experiences of Butler and Microsoft help to illustrate this point. As a transnational corporation engaging in the marketing, design, fabrication and supply of building systems, Butler deals with heavy products and needs, therefore, to establish its production facilities in locations where the transportation infrastructure is well developed. In the end, Butler chose to set up all its manufacturing facilities in three coastal cities in the eastern region, where the shipping and railway transportation systems are among the best in China: Shanghai, Guangzhou and Tianjin. As a software developer, in contrast, Microsoft needs a good pool of human resources for its production operations. Microsoft thus chose to establish its manufacturing facilities in Beijing, the capital, where the most prestigious Chinese universities and research institutes are located.

The third factor that a TNC has to take into consideration in making location decisions is the variation in market structure across the country. China's move from a plan-based to a market-based economy has proceeded unevenly across the regions. In regions where the transition has been rapid a market system is already in place to provide a supportive institutional environment for TNCs' operations. In regions where the transition has proceeded slowly, by contrast, a market system has not yet fully taken shape and the institutional environment is not very conducive. China's variation in market structure is mainly a reflection of differences in the degree of transition to a market-based economic system. The differences may be found in many aspects of the transition process, including the protection of property rights, the development of the private sector, the degree of opening up to foreign direct investment, and the legal environment for market competition. In making location decisions, therefore, a TNC should take all these aspects into account, and locate its production facilities in places where property rights are well protected, private enterprises are flourishing, FDI is most welcomed and the legal environment is conducive to competition. In general, it is the eastern region that has been moving well ahead of other regions in terms of market-oriented reforms and opening up, and thus provides the most favourable market structure for the operation of TNCs in China, which is why most have chosen to establish their production facilities here.

The fourth factor that needs to be taken into account in making location decisions is the degree of government support. China is still an authoritarian state, and the government is a major player in society and the economy. The influence of government on economic activities is much stronger in China than in Western democracies, and this has been noticed by many transnational corporations. To a large extent the success or failure of a TNC in China depends heavily on whether it can gain support from the government. As a result, it is vital for a TNC to locate its production facilities in places where it can gain the maximum support from the Chinese government. In consideration of the importance of this factor, we discuss it in greater detail.

To encourage foreign direct investors to move into certain regions, as discussed in chapter 2, the government has established various special zones in these regions. TNCs that establish production facilities in these special zones can thus receive full governmental support and enjoy various preferential policy treatments, and many TNCs have located their manufacturing facilities in them. These special zones are established for different purposes, however, and are designed to attract different types of FDI (see chapter 2 for details). When establishing production facilities in these special zones, TNCs need to compare them and choose the kind that are designed to encourage the type of investment they want to make in China. As a high-tech corporation, for instance, Motorola chose to set up almost all its production facilities in the Tianjin Economic Development Area, which was created to encourage FDI in high-tech industries, and thus gained the full support of the Chinese government.

Moreover, although China remains an authoritarian state, local governments now have much greater autonomy than before and can exert considerable influence on local affairs. They can, for instance, decide on many issues related to the operation of TNCs in China, including the taxes levied by local governments, the approval procedure for projects, and the provision of electricity, water, gas and basic social services. In making location decisions therefore, it is crucial for TNCs to gain the support of local governments if they want to make sure of avoiding difficulties and frustrations. The case of Suzhou Industrial Park, mentioned in chapter 3, clearly illustrates this point. In deciding where to locate the industrial park, a Sino-Singaporean joint venture, the Singapore side did not consult with the Suzhou local government, even declining an offer it made. The local government then established its own industrial park, the Suzhou New District Park, to compete with the Suzhou Industrial Park, which suffered huge losses and, in the end, had to come back to negotiate with, and seek support from, the Suzhou local government.

Furthermore, the national government can change regional development policy from time to time. In the first two decades of the economic reform programme, for example, the authorities adopted the policy of accelerating the development of the eastern region, conferring on it many preferential policy initiaties. From 2000 onwards, however, the government began to shift the focus of economic development to the western region, offering it preferential policy treatment instead. It is important that TNCs take into account this change in China's regional policy in making their location decisions, but not to the extent of following it blindly, as they still have to consider whether the newly targeted region has the necessary resources for their companies' functioning. When the eastern region was being promoted most TNCs moved there, and certainly benefited greatly from the preferential policy initiatives and from the region's good infrastructure and resources. By contrast, when the government switched to promoting the western region TNCs were cautious, and very few of them made direct investment there because of the poor infrastructure. It is not, for instance, in the interests of Butler and Microsoft to move their production facilities to the region because their production operations require good transportation and good human resources, respectively, neither of which is available in the west. It may, however, be in the interests of TNCs operating in the agriculture, food and beverage industries to establish production facilities in the western region, as the infrastructural and human resource deficiencies will matter less to them, and they will benefit from the full support of the government.

In making their location decisions, of course, TNCs cannot give equal weight to all the factors discussed here, and have to prioritize the factors that carry most weight with them. Other things being equal (infrastructure, resources, etc.), however, it is advantageous for TNCs to set up their production facilities in locations targeted and supported by the Chinese government at both the central and local levels. This is, indeed, the approach adopted by many TNCs in China, as illustrated by the case of Seagram, a Canadian company in the beverage industry (box 7.1).

Box 7.1 The location choice of Seagram

Seagram, a Canadian company specializing in beverages and entertainment, moved into China in 1988. In the early 1990s the chairman, Edgar M. Bronfman, proposed a project to process orange juice in China. In 1997 Seagram signed a memorandum of understanding (MOU) with two Chinese partners, Chongqing city government and the Three Gorges Construction Group, to build a modern orange juice plant from scratch, with multiple functions including research, production, processing and marketing. Seagram promised to invest $11 million to build up the nursery centre and demonstration groves.

In selecting the location for the plant, Seagram was initially in favour of Guangxi province. This was because Seagram owned a firm, Tropicana Products, that already had a packaging factory in Guangxi, which would make it easier for Seagram to streamline the production operations if it set up the new plant nearby. As reported by Virginia Hulme, assistant editor of *China Business Review*, however, 'The central government did not consider development of the citrus industry in Guangxi a priority, so Seagram decided to look for a site that was more consistent with Chinese development priorities.'[2]

Seagram's choice was a location in the Three Gorges region. The decision was made on two grounds. First, the climate in this area is suitable for oranges. The relatively cold winter helps to control pests and infectious agents, so the region is free of citrus diseases. Also, as winter comes on slowly in this region, the trees have time to adjust to the change in the weather and the fruit has a deeper and more attractive colour than oranges grown in warmer regions. Secondly, and more importantly, the central government had already targeted this area for the construction of the Three Gorges Hydropower Station, and was very keen to create employment opportunities there for people displaced by the massive project.

After careful deliberation, Seagram finally chose Zhongxian county in the Three Gorges region as the site for its plant. Zhongxian was chosen, according to Hulme, not only because it was suitable for growing citrus but also because it lay within the Three Gorges resettlement region.[3] Some 3 per cent of the total land area of the county would be inundated once the reservoir was full and about 6 per cent of the 1 million residents of the county would have to be resettled. By locating the plant in the county, Seagram could help to create employment opportunities for the resettled local residents and therefore would gain the full support of the authorities, at both the central and local levels. The scheme indeed won backing from the Chinese government, and Seagram qualified for access to the official resources earmarked for counties involved in resettlement. The orange juice plant, which was set up in Zhongxian one year later, has reportedly been operating smoothly since then.

The localization of sourcing

Sourcing is the securing of parts, supplies and other items necessary to produce goods or services for sale. In sourcing, almost every firm has to make the so-called 'make-or-buy' decision. That is, a firm needs to decide whether it should manufacture the components and materials itself or buy them from independent suppliers. If a firm manufactures them itself, it is engaging in vertical integration – that is, it integrates vertically into the manufacture of the components and materials that go into the final product. If a firm buys them from independent suppliers, it is conducting outsourcing. Given the growing complexity of the required components and materials and the prevailing trend towards specialization, it is increasingly difficult, if not impossible, for a firm to manufacture all these components and materials on its own. In practice, therefore, almost every firm has to outsource at least some of the required components.

For a transnational corporation entering a new market, it faces not only the make-or-buy decision but also the decision on whether or not to localize its sourcing – that is, whether or not it should make or buy the components and materials inside the new market. In making decisions on the localization of sourcing, TNCs need to think about the benefits they can gain from doing so, and the difficulties they may encounter in sourcing in China.

Sourcing in China can help TNCs keep down costs. In theory, a TNC should localize its sourcing if the cost of producing the components and materials at home, and then importing them into China, is higher than purchasing or producing them in China. Due to its massive population and the widespread underemployment in rural areas, China enjoys an obvious advantage in terms of low labour costs compared to most other countries in the world. Firms in China can therefore make full use of the abundant, cheap labour force to produce the components and materials required by TNCs at a very low cost. For TNCs, therefore, the cost of either purchasing components and materials from independent local Chinese suppliers or producing them themselves in China is normally much lower than producing them at home and importing them into China.

Sourcing in China can also help TNCs win support from the Chinese government. If they outsource components and materials to local firms or produce them (often together with a local partner, as discussed below) in China, they create employment opportunities in the country and transfer advanced technology and management know-how to it. The Chinese authorities, both at the central and the local level, are thus very keen to encourage TNCs to localize sourcing in China. In some industries, in fact, the government even requires TNCs to reach a certain level of localization within a certain period of time, and the requirement is written into the agreement that they sign when they apply for entry into those industries. For example, when Peugeot, a French car maker, established a joint venture with a Chinese car maker in Guangzhou in 1985, it signed an agreement that the vehicles produced by the joint venture should reach a 90 per cent Chinese content level within five years. Localizing sourcing in China, therefore, can help TNCs maintain a good relationship with the government.

The localization of sourcing is by no means an easy task in a developing country such as China, however, where technology is relatively backward and government intervention still occurs frequently. In localizing sourcing in China, TNCs have encountered many difficulties. The low level of technology, for instance, is sometimes reflected in the poor quality of locally supplied components and materials. Owing to local protectionism, moreover, TNCs located in one part of China are often not allowed to look for local suppliers from other parts of the country. For example, soon after establishing the joint venture in 1985, Peugeot realized the great difficulty it would have in trying to meet the 90 per cent local content target, because it 'found few suppliers of quality parts in Guangdong and was prohibited by local officials from sourcing from other regions in China' (Harmit, 1997, p. 10). TNCs need to come up with the appropriate approaches to overcoming these difficulties.

As a first step, they may help to organize associations of local suppliers and local research institutions. This can strengthen the coordination of local suppliers and promote cooperation between them and local research institutions in improving the quality of supplies. As it is difficult for TNCs to organize associations of this kind on their own, this approach relies heavily on support from the Chinese government. As the localization of sourcing serves the interests of both the government and the TNCs, as shown in the case of Volkswagen (see box 7.2), these kinds of associations are very likely to gain official backing.

Moreover, TNCs may establish affiliates in China to produce high-quality components and materials themselves. This approach is very costly, so it is adopted most often for components and materials that are so demanding in technology that they cannot be produced by local suppliers and research institutions. Foreign affiliates of this type normally take the form of joint ventures in China, because the government does not want TNCs to enter high-tech industries in the form of wholly foreign-owned enterprises. Therefore, as the Volkswagen case demonstrates, some TNCs establish joint ventures in China to produce the components and materials that go into the final product. As joint ventures of this kind produce components and materials involving the proprietary technology that TNC's own, the TNCs need to adopt measures, such as majority shareholding, to prevent possible technology leakage.

Box 7.2 Volkswagen's localization of sourcing

Volkswagen began its move into China in the early 1980s, and has now set up two large automobile joint ventures in the country. The first, called Shanghai Volkswagen, was established in Shanghai in 1984, the main Chinese partner being the Shanghai Automotive Industrial Corporation. The joint venture is well known in China for producing Santana sedans. The second joint venture, called FAW-Volkswagen, was established in Changchun in 1996, with the Chinese partner being the First Automotive Works (FAW). This joint venture is well known in China for producing Audi sedans. In both joint ventures Volkswagen holds 50 per cent of the shares, and the Chinese partners hold the remainder.

In establishing these two joint ventures, Volkswagen promised to move towards the localization of sourcing and to increase the local content step by step. However, the company was unable to make the move as rapidly as expected, because of the poor quality of the local supplies, and the Chinese government began to complain about the slow pace of localization. The government 'called for a goal of quickly reaching 80 per cent local content', and even began to 'limit the production of Shanghai Volkswagen by curtailing raw material supplies until the venture reached higher local content requirement'.[4] Under this pressure, Volkswagen had to work out ways to overcome the difficulties it was encountering, and to accelerate the pace of sourcing in China.

To begin with, Volkswagen tried to secure collaboration with, and support from, the government, explaining the practical difficulties in the localization of sourcing, and negotiating for a possible solution. The effort paid off. With the support of the government, Volkswagen established the Shanghai Santana Local Content Cooperative in 1988. The cooperative served as a suppliers' association, bringing together the parts makers, banks, universities and research institutes to resolve the problems in producing the required high-quality components and materials. The cooperative has now reached a total of 176 members, and has played a key role in Volkswagen's localization drive.

Furthermore, Volkswagen established joint ventures in China to produce quality components and materials. In 1993, for instance, Volkswagen established a joint venture in Shanghai, together with its long-time Chinese partner, SAIC, to produce gearboxes, primarily for the automobiles that Volkswagen produces in Shanghai. In 2004 Volkswagen signed a contract with another of its long-time Chinese partners, FAW, to establish a joint venture to produce running gear components, primarily for the automobiles that Volkswagen produces in Changchun. As the two joint ventures were designed to produce components with a high-tech content, Volkswagen insisted on holding the majority share holding in each case (60 per cent).

The two approaches have achieved good results. Volkswagen has made great progress in its localization of sourcing in recent years, and reached the highest local content rate among TNCs in the Chinese car industry. The local content rate for the Santana B2, for example, reached, 94 per cent in 2005. Thanks to this localization of sourcing, Volkswagen has managed to cut the cost, and therefore the price, of the cars it produces, and it has now become one of the most competitive foreign car makers in China.

TNCs may also provide technical and financial assistance to help local suppliers improve the quality of supplies. The experience of Coca-Cola illustrates this approach. The supplies that Coca-Cola needs to produce its drinks include packaging materials, drink ingredients, bottling-line equipment, construction services, etc. When Coca-Cola first moved to China, in the 1980s, it had to import such basic materials as glass and aluminium from abroad because of the lack of high-quality supplies in China. As a result, Coca-Cola suffered from a high cost structure. To promote the localization of sourcing, the company offered financial assistance and technical advice to help its Chinese suppliers improve their production processes, and in return required all supplies to comply with 'stringent quality standards set by the Coca-Cola Company' (Weisert, 2001, p. 54). In addition, Coca-Cola set up, together with the Chinese government, the Tianjin Soft Drink Training Centre in 1988, to provide training in technical skills for local suppliers. The endeavour has achieved great success. Although Coca-Cola does not own a single share in any of its suppliers, the level of localized sourcing reached as high as 98 per cent in 2001. This approach is particularly useful when the locally supplied components and materials do not involve the proprietary technology owned by a TNC.

The localization of research and development

R&D covers a combination of complex activities, including (1) scientific and technological research; (2) the development of new products and production processes; (3) manufacturing and marketing support; and (4) the provision of technical services. In standard textbooks, R&D is often discussed in relation to marketing management, particularly in relation to new product development. In fact, as shown in the activities it covers, R&D is closely related to production operations management, and accordingly it is discussed in this chapter. The focus is on a major challenge faced by transnational corporations in connection with their research and development in China: the localization of R&D. We first discuss the trend towards R&D localization in general, and the extent to which TNCs are localizing R&D in China. We then turn to address some managerial issues connected with the localization of R&D.

The trend towards R&D localization

We are currently in an era in which there is an explosion of knowledge. Science and technology are both developing at an unprecedented pace, and are fundamentally changing the way people live and work. As a result, product life cycles are being shortened dramatically. New products are created every day, and established products become obsolete overnight. The business world has become more dynamic today than it has ever been. To survive the competition in this dynamic business world, firms have to stay at the technological cutting edge, and keep developing new products and production processes in order to meet the changing needs of customers and the changing requirements of production environments.

Despite the increasing importance of R&D as a consequence, international evidence suggests that the failure rates of R&D projects have been very high in recent years. Based on data derived from firm-level surveys, for instance, some studies found that only 20 per cent of R&D projects resulted in commercially successful new products and processes, while other studies found that about 30 per cent of R&D projects were actually commercialized and only 12 per cent of the projects earned a profit (Mansfield, 1981). It is argued that R&D projects failed primarily because they did not meet customers' needs and the requirements of actual production environments. The problem is most outstanding in the context of TNCs, where R&D is often conducted in the headquarters far away from the production sites in host countries. The problem therefore raises an important question that TNCs have to think about: where they should carry out their R&D activities.

The success of R&D projects depends heavily on the interaction of scientific research, a competitive environment and market demand. Scientific research enables a TNC to keep abreast of new technologies, while competition among TNCs helps to stimulate ideas about new products and production processes. Only in places where market demand is strong, on the other hand, can new products and production processes be tested in a timely manner to see whether they really meet the needs of consumers and the requirements of production environments, and whether they can then be commercialized successfully. In theory, therefore, R&D activities should be conducted in locations where the resources for scientific research are flourishing, competition is intense and market demand is strong.

At the end of the Second World War the United States appeared to be the only place where the three conditions for R&D were met, and thus it became the world centre for R&D activities. The situation began to change subsequently, as some countries and regions recovered from the damage caused by the war during the second half of the twentieth century, and began to rise in the world economy: first Europe and Japan, and then the four 'small dragons' in East Asia (Singapore, South Korea, Taiwan and Hong Kong) and most recently mainland China and India. These countries and regions began to invest heavily in science and education, to generate strong market demand and to become a competitive battlefield between TNCs from all over the world. These countries and regions have increasingly become the places where R&D activities are most likely to succeed. For various reasons, however, TNCs have been slow in moving their R&D activities to the emerging markets, particularly the emerging markets in the developing world, which led to a 'gap' or 'unfit' between R&D projects on the one hand and the practical needs of marketing and production operations on the other. This may help to explain the high failure rates of R&D projects in recent years.

For TNCs operating in the Chinese market, therefore, a key decision that they have to make is whether or not they should localize their R&D activities in the country – that is, establish R&D centres or the like in China so that the R&D activities can better serve the needs of local customers and the requirements of production environments there. Localizing R&D has the advantage of close integration between three core functional areas involved in the development of new products and production processes – R&D, production operations and marketing – and therefore can increase the probability of success for these R&D projects in China. The integration between R&D and production operations helps to ensure that R&D projects fit in well with the Chinese production environments, and that new production processes are applied successfully in the country. The integration between R&D and marketing helps to ensure that R&D projects are driven by the needs of local customers, and that new products sell well in the local market.

After testing the water in the 1980s TNCs came to realize the benefits of R&D localization, and began to establish R&D centres in China one after another. The move towards localizing R&D was encouraged by the fact that China has abundant and yet cheap human resources for R&D activities. It is estimated that China ranks second only to the United States in the number of scientific researchers, and at the same time the Chinese researchers are paid much less than their counterparts in developed countries. The level of Chinese education, particularly basic science education, is among the highest in the world, and Chinese students are diligent and well equipped with the basic knowledge and skills needed for R&D activities.

The move towards the localization of R&D was also aided by the fact that the rapidly growing Chinese economy generates strong market demand in the country. For the past three decades the economy has grown at an annual rate of about 10 per cent, the highest in the world, and the Chinese people have become steadily richer. The sustained income increase in a country with a population of 1.3 billion generates the strong market demand that is essential for the development of new products and production processes. Furthermore, the trend towards R&D localization was underpinned by the fact that China has now become one of the largest recipients of FDI in the world, and that most of the world's largest TNCs have moved to the country. The intensified competition among TNCs helps to stimulate new ideas, thus facilitating R&D activities. The final factor in the increased localization of R&D was the support of the Chinese government; as it increasingly realized the benefits that China can gain from the R&D centres set up by TNCs in the country, it

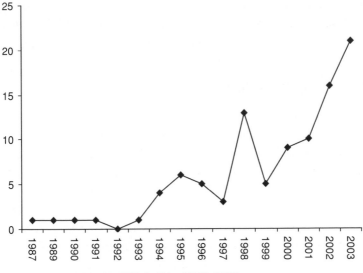

Figure 7.1   R&D centres established by TNCs in China (1987–2003)
Source: Zedtwitz (2004).

issued regulations to encourage the trend still further. According to the regulations, foreign R&D centres enjoy such preferential treatment as import tariff exemptions for equipment and instruments.

The combined effect has been an upsurge in R&D localization in China in recent years. As shown in figure 7.1, the number of R&D centres established by TNCs has increased rapidly, gaining momentum particularly in the late 1990s and early 2000s, such that by 2003 there were at least ninety-seven. Because of problems with the definition of what constitutes an R&D centre on the one hand and the difficulties of gathering reliable figures on the other, this is an area where there are serious data problems, and this number may not reflect the true scale of foreign R&D centres in China. According to Zedtwitz (2004), by 2004 there were 199 R&D centres that had either been established or were in the process of being established by TNCs in China. According to the *People's Daily* for 28 October 2002, however, there were already 400 R&D centres in China by 2002! A recent article published in *Technology Review* put the total number of R&D centres set up by TNCs in China at some 600 in 2005 (anonymous, 2005). Although, as this demonstrates, it is very hard to come up with precise figures for the number of foreign R&D centres in the country, anecdotal evidence also suggests strongly that R&D localization has accelerated in China in recent years. Newly established foreign R&D centres include such major examples as the Roche R&D centre in Shanghai (2004) the Sony R&D centre in Shanghai (2004) and the Nokia R&D centre in Chengdu (2005).

Key issues of managing R&D in China

There are many approaches to R&D localization, but the establishment of wholly owned independent R&D centres is the most popular among transnational corporations operating in China. This is because R&D activities often involve proprietary technologies that the companies do not want to transfer to local competitors, and sole ownership can control technology leakage better than joint ownership, as discussed in chapter 4. For TNCs that do not have sufficient resources to establish wholly owned R&D centres, localization can be promoted through other routes; for example, such activities can be conducted by the R&D departments of their affiliates in China, or by their China affiliates in cooperation with Chinese research institutes and universities. Given the importance of wholly owned independent R&D centres in China, we focus our discussion on the major issues related to managing these centres, although some of the discussion may also apply to other R&D localization activities.

The first issue relates to the objectives of the R&D centres. In establishing such centres in China, TNCs may have in mind a range of different objectives and purposes. In general, however, the R&D centres have been set up in the country primarily to achieve two objectives. The first is to ensure that R&D projects do indeed work well locally – that the new products meet the needs of local Chinese consumers, and the new production processes fit in well with the specific production conditions and requirements in China. To develop localized new products, for instance, the Microsoft R&D centre in Beijing, Microsoft Research Asia, aims to 'develop a better understanding of the Chinese language for next-generation voice and handwriting recognition systems' (Huang, 2004, p. 34). Similarly, according to Dr Al Pretty, the director of the R&D centre of Proctor and Gamble (P&G) in China, the centre's aim is 'to make absolutely sure that our global products are meeting the needs of Chinese consumers' (Walfish, 2001, p. 4). Given the particular Chinese cultural traditions and environments, as shown in the experience of P&G (box 7.3), foreign R&D centres have to make great efforts to learn about Chinese customers and market conditions in order to achieve this objective.

Box 7.3 The R&D centre of Proctor and Gamble in China

In 1998 P&G, a consumer products company based in the United States, set up an R&D centre in Beijing, the Chinese capital. Dr Pretty, who had been working for P&G since 1973, was appointed the director of the Beijing R&D centre. The centre now employs more than 200 researchers and engineers, and nearly 90 per cent of them are local Chinese. The centre conducts R&D activities in connection with two product lines. The first is the laundry programme, which focuses on the Tide and Ariel brands of detergents, and the second is the oral care programme, focusing on Crest toothpaste and toothbrushes. Two-thirds of the researchers at the centre work on the first programme while the remaining work on the second.

According to Dr Pretty, the R&D centre was established to accomplish two missions. The first is to develop localized products for Chinese consumers. To develop customized products, the centre requires researchers to study Chinese people's tooth-brushing and laundry-washing habits and preferences. The researchers watched Chinese people doing their laundry at home and brushing their teeth aboard a bus equipped with bathrooms, and certainly found some interesting characteristics. Differing from American consumers, for instance, the Chinese like different toothpaste flavours, and they would also like to have a lot of foam in their mouths. In addition, many Chinese actually do their washing at home by hand, and thus would like 'suds to be generated and removed at rates different from the rates produced by detergents sold in America'.[5] As a result of this research, the R&D centre tries to develop new tooth-brushing and laundry-washing products that meet Chinese customers' needs.

The second mission of the Beijing R&D centre is to conduct 'technology mining' in order to gain access to untapped research and innovation opportunities in China. The centre requires all researchers to be 'on the look-out for potentially valuable ideas – among former colleagues, for example'.[6] The researchers searched for new ideas at universities, research institutes and conferences. In one case, for example, they learnt that some local people working at an institute of traditional Chinese medicine had found a vegetable extract with a particular health effect. The researchers reported the finding back to the director to see whether P&G could work with the local institute to 'find a way of synthesizing the product so it can be incorporated into an over-the-counter medicine'.[7] Beijing is home to the most prestigious universities and research institutes in China, and thus is an ideal place for P&G to carry out its technology mining.

In working on the two missions, the centre tried to integrate its R&D activities with what was being conducted in other centres that P&G had set up elsewhere; before the establishment of the Beijing centre, P&G had already established sixteen R&D centres around the world. The R&D projects conducted in the Beijing centre in the oral care product line and the laundry product line are also aimed at improving the products that P&G sell globally. The centre therefore looks for innovative ideas in China that are applicable not only to the product lines in China but also to those that P&G has set up in other parts of the world. That is to say, the Beijing R&D centre actually has a global role to play, and serves P&G's global ambitions.

The Beijing centre has encountered many difficulties. It is very hard for instance, to get the local Chinese community to see that cooperation with P&G is beneficial to both sides. In addition, it is very difficulty to find qualified Chinese research staff who can really take initiatives and risks. Much effort has to be made to overcome these complications. Despite all these problems, however, the Beijing centre has been doing quite well, and has already yielded a good number of patent applications.

Another objective of the R&D centres is to make use of the location advantage of China to strengthen their parent companies' technological competencies. As mentioned earlier, innovative ideas are most likely to develop in China because of the strong market demand, the intense competition between the world's most powerful technology giants, and the hard-working and talented local workforce. TNCs therefore, attempt to use their R&D centres in China as a bridgehead to strengthen their technological competencies in order to remain as technology leaders. Consequently, almost all the R&D centres aim to tap the potential of Chinese technology – or, in the words of Dr Pretty, 'technology mining' in China.

The second managerial issue is concerned with the choice of location for the R&D centres in China. With few exceptions, almost all of them have been established in large cities on the east coast. It is estimated that more than 97 per cent of all the R&D centres established by TNCs are located in cities in the eastern region, particularly Beijing and Shanghai. In 2004, according to statistics provided by Maximilian von Zedtwitz, there were seventy-eight foreign R&D centres in Beijing and sixty-one in Shanghai, accounting for 39 per cent and 31 per cent of the total R&D centres established by TNCs in China, respectively. The location choice is closely related to the location advantages of the eastern region. To start with, it enjoys the highest rate of GDP growth, the highest level of personal income, and thus the strongest market demand in the country. Moreover, nearly 90 per cent of foreign direct investment is located there, so competition among TNCs is especially intense. Finally, and most importantly, most of China's prestigious universities and research institutes are located in the region, particularly in such large cities as Beijing and Shanghai, so local Chinese talents are plentiful there.

In making decisions on setting up a R&D centre in a particular city, however, TNCs need to take into account some specific factors. It is found, for instance, that TNCs tend to locate research-intensive R&D centres in Beijing. This is because Beijing, as the country's academic centre, is most conducive to scientific research. There are about 100 universities in Beijing, including China's top two universities – Tsinghua University and Beijing University. The

Chinese Academy of Science is located in Beijing, as is the Zhongguanzun – China's largest high-tech zone. In contrast, TNCs tend to set up development-intensive R&D centres in Shanghai, primarily because Shanghai, as the most open city in the country, is already home to many large TNCs' headquarters. As product development depends greatly on the interaction of related business activities, development-intensive R&D centres can benefit enormously from proximity to the centre of international business activities in China. Resources permitting, of course, TNCs may consider establishing R&D centres in multiple locations in China. Motorola, for instance, has set up R&D centres in six cities in mainland China: Beijing, Shanghai, Tianjin, Suzhou, Nanjing and Chengdu.

The third managerial issue is related to staffing in the R&D centres. TNCs need to decide on who will lead and manage the centres in China. Despite the general trend towards staffing localization in China in recent years (as shown in chapter 9), TNCs tend to appoint home-country nationals to head and manage their R&D centres in the country, particularly development-intensive R&D centres, where familiarity with internal networks is more important than external contacts. For example, Zedtwitz found, in a survey, that 'more than two-thirds of the initial R&D directors in this study were non-Chinese, and many had no or little China experience before being assigned to the job'. He continues that the staffing approach is related to the concern over intellectual property protection 'in a country that has a notorious reputation of uncontrolled knowledge diffusion' (2004, p. 446). Expatriate directorship is taken to be a firewall to protect IPR in the R&D centres. Chinese are sometimes hired for management positions in research-intensive R&D centres where external contacts are crucial, but they are mostly overseas Chinese trained in the West. Since the establishment of Microsoft Research Asia, for example, all three directors have been overseas Chinese trained in the United States.

Transnational corporations primarily recruit local Chinese for professional research and engineering positions in the R&D centres, however, because Chinese researchers and engineers are talented, hard-working and yet paid much less than their counterparts in the West. In Microsoft Research Asia, for instance, all the researchers and engineers are local Chinese, and in P&G's R&D centre nearly 90 per cent are. A key function of directors of foreign R&D centres in China is to recruit local researchers and engineers. In recruiting from universities and research institutes, TNCs have encountered some resistance from the academic authorities, worried that the best local graduates and researchers are taken away and ensconced in foreign R&D laboratories without any contact with Chinese academic communities. TNCs therefore often need to make efforts to strengthen the academic links between their R&D centres and local academic communities in order to assure the Chinese side that China can benefit from the recruitment of local talent by foreign R&D centres. In so doing, they gain understanding and support from the Chinese academic communities and the government.[8]

The fourth issue is related to the coordination of the R&D centres with their parent companies. In the initial stages an R&D centre normally starts up quite autonomously. The director has to establish the centre all on her/his own, and often has to make decisions independently in China. Soon after the centre has been set up, however, coordinating it with the parent company becomes a daunting challenge. Although a primary objective of R&D centres in China, as discussed previously, is conducting projects that fit in specifically with the needs of Chinese consumers and the local production requirements, it is crucially important to incorporate the Chinese R&D activities into the global research and development ambitions of the parent company. As shown in box 7.3, P&G's R&D centre in China plays an important role in integrating R&D projects conducted in the country with activities that the parent company conducts elsewhere, making new ideas and innovations generated in China available to its R&D centres in other parts of the world.

It is essential, therefore, for the R&D centres in China to interact well with centres established by the parent company elsewhere, particularly the R&D centre at the TNC's headquarters. Good internal coordination is key to achieving this. According to a survey conducted by Zedtwitz, the internal coordination is often carried out through formal procedures, and some R&D centres in China have 'formalized program and project management to ensure integration of their lab with other R&D labs and headquarters' (2004, p. 447). R&D programme managers in a TNC are often called for coordination meetings, and these meetings are held with the help of advanced information and communication technologies, such as computer-supported discussion. In some cases internal coordination is carried out informally, through personal contacts and communications between R&D personnel across the corporation. However it is carried out, the internal coordination helps to ensure that the Chinese R&D centre becomes integral to the transnational R&D network.

Summary

In this chapter we have discussed the major issues that TNCs need to address in managing their production operations in China, including the siting of their manufacturing facilities, the choice of location, the localization of sourcing and the localization of R&D. When tackling these issues TNCs must take into account the different aspects of the business environment in China, and the challenges that these may pose to the company.

With regard to the siting of production facilities, TNCs need to take into consideration the sheer size of the Chinese territory, and decide on whether they should centralize or decentralize their plant in the country. In making the siting decision, TNCs should think about such product attributes as the value-to-weight ratio and the needs that the product serves, and such technology attributes as fixed costs, the minimum efficiency scale, and flexible manufacturing or lean production.

In making decisions as to the specific location for their manufacturing facilities, TNCs have to take into consideration the variation in geographical features, infrastructure and market structure across China's regions. In addition, they need to pay particular attention to the Chinese authorities, at both the central and local levels, and think about whether the location choice can gain governmental support.

In connection with the localization of sourcing, TNCs face two major difficulties in China: the low quality of locally supplied components and materials and local protectionism. To overcome these difficulties, TNCs may try to establish, with the backing of the Chinese government, a suppliers' association, or provide technical and financial assistance in order to help local suppliers improve the quality of their products, or establish their own affiliates in conjunction with Chinese partners to produce high-quality components and materials locally themselves. The choice of solution is dependent on the type of difficulties a TNC faces, and the type of technology involved.

As to the localization of R&D, TNCs need to understand and address the major issues concerned with managing R&D centres in China, including identifying the objectives of the centres, deciding where to locate them, staffing in the R&D centres and the coordination of the centres with the parent company. These managerial issues should be considered in the light of the specific environment in China.

FURTHER READING

Huang, G. T. 2004. 'The world's hottest computer lab'. *Technology Review* 107 (5): 32–42.

Hulme, V. A. 2000. 'Seagram juices up the Three Gorges'. *China Business Review* 27 (5): 16–22.

Liu, A., Li, S., and Gao, Y. 1999. 'Location, location, location'. *China Business Review* 26 (2): 20–5.

Mansfield, E. 1981. 'How economists see R&D'. *Harvard Business Review* 59 (6): 98–106.

Peng, M. W. 2000. 'Controlling the foreign agent: how governments deal with multinationals in a transition economy'. *Management International Review* 40 (2): 141–65.

Von Zedtwitz, M. 2004. 'Managing foreign R&D laboratories in China'. *R&D Management* 34 (4): 439–52.

Walfish, D. 2001. 'P&G China lab has global role'. *Research Technology Management* 44 (5): 4–5.

Questions for discussion

1. Why do some transnational corporations centralize their manufacturing facilities in China while others decentralize them? Relate your argument to the advantages and disadvantages of each of the two siting strategies, and TNCs' product attributes and technology attributes.

2. What are the key factors that influence TNCs' decisions as to the location of their production facilities in China? Why is it important for TNCs to gain support from the Chinese government in making location decisions?

3. What is meant by the localization of sourcing? What are the benefits that TNCs may gain from localizing their sourcing? What are the main difficulties that TNCs face in the localization of sourcing in China and, how can they overcome these difficulties?

4. What is meant by the localization of R&D? Why have more and more TNCs begun to localize their R&D in China? What are the key issues that TNCs face in managing R&D centres in China?

NOTES

1. See Liu, Li and Gao (1999). Apart from location-specific factors, firm-specific factors accounted for 72 per cent of the variation in performance, while industry-specific factors accounted for 11 per cent.

2. See Hulme (2000).

3. See Hulme (2000).

4. See Peng (2000, p. 154).

5. Walfish (2001, p. 4).

6. Walfish (2001, p. 5).

7. Walfish (2001, p. 5).

8. The experience of Microsoft Research Asia helps to illustrate this point. See Walfish (2001).

8 Marketing management

Multinationals must squarely face the fact that the competitive edge that is potentially available to them from superior technologies, products and systems will be severely blunted unless they build much stronger local competencies. In many cases, that will require a new willingness and determination to master the complexities of distribution, sales and service in China's secondary cities and rural heartland and to learn how to more sensitively adapt everything from products and processes to marketing messages to the peculiarities of the Chinese market – competencies in which their local competitors are currently far ahead (Peter Williamson and Ming Zeng (2004, p. 91)).

In general, marketing involves making decisions on the so-called 'four Ps': product, price, promotion and place (distribution). In this chapter we discuss the challenges that transnational corporations face in marketing in China, and the strategies and approaches that they may adopt to deal with them. In section 1 we review a debate triggered by Levitt on marketing in the context of the globalization of markets, and discuss the implications of the debate for TNCs operating in the Chinese market. In sections 2, 3, 4 and 5 we discuss the major issues that TNCs need to take into consideration in making decisions on product, price, promotion and distribution in China, respectively. The final section summarizes.

The Levitt debate

In 1983 Theodore Levitt, professor in marketing at Harvard University Business School, published a paper entitled 'The globalization of markets' in the *Harvard Business Review*. In this article, Levitt argues that people in different parts of the world are increasingly connected to each other, and the world is moving towards a 'converging commonality'. People tend to become similar to each other in terms of what they want and what they like, so 'everywhere everything gets more and more like everything else as the world's preference structure is relentlessly homogenized' (Levitt, 1983, p. 93). Accustomed differences in national or regional preferences have disappeared, giving way to the needs for standardized consumer products and marketing practices. The markets are, therefore, globalizing.

Underlying the globalization of markets is the advance of technology, which has made it increasingly easy and cheap for people in previously isolated parts of the world to move around and communicate with each other. Consequently, as Levitt (p. 92) puts it, 'Almost everyone everywhere wants all the things they have heard about, seen, or experienced via the new technologies.' Another underlying force behind the globalization of markets is competition, which forces companies to explore economies of scale over the whole planet to cut down costs and prices. Consequently, as Levitt (p. 94) argues, 'If a company forces costs and prices down and pushes quality and reliability up – while maintaining reasonable concern for suitability – customers will prefer its world-standardized products.' These attractive, low-priced and standardized products play a key role in reshaping and homogenizing consumer preferences and marketing practices in different parts of the world.

Faced with the irresistible globalization of markets, according to Levitt, companies need to abandon the outdated marketing practices of the so-called multinational corporations, which operate in different countries and adjust their products and marketing practices in each of these countries, at relatively high cost. Instead, companies should adopt the marketing practice of the so-called global corporations, which operate in different countries with resolute constancy and sell the same products in the same way everywhere at relatively low cost. The global corporations will not just passively accept the vestigial national or regional differences in consumer preferences and marketing practices, but will actively make efforts to narrow these differences by standardizing what they sell and how they sell in every corner of the world. This is because these global corporations are fully aware of 'the absolute need to be competitive on a worldwide basis' and the advantage of standardization over customization in maintaining competitiveness. They believe with confidence that standardized products and marketing practices, combined with aggressively low prices, will eventually circumvent, shatter and transform the widely differing consumer preferences, pricing practices, promotion media and distribution systems.

The ideas that Levitt expressed in the article were very powerful, and sparked a fierce debate in the field of marketing. It was argued, for instance, that, along with the advance of new technologies, economies of scope might offset

---

Box 8.1 Economies of scale and economies of scope

The notion of economies of scale is one of the cornerstones underlying Levitt's argument for a standardization strategy in the process of globalization. Economies of scale refer to the reduction in unit cost with an increase in the volume of output. That is, the average cost of producing a unit of product diminishes as each additional unit of product is produced, primarily because the fixed cost is shared over an increasing number of products with the increase in output. Companies that produce standardized products in large quantities can, according to Levitt, make full use of economies of scale, offer cheap products to customers and thus beat companies that produce customized and expensive products.

By contrast, the notion of economies of scope is said to undermine the Levitt argument. Economies of scope refer to the ability to produce a variety of fairly customized products at low cost. It is argued that the advance of technology, such as computer-aided design and manufacturing, enables a company to change products and product features quickly without halting the manufacturing process. The company can therefore produce broad lines of customized products without sacrificing the benefits of economies of scale. That is to say, companies that produce customized products can still offer cheap products to customers through economies of scope, and thus compete fairly and squarely in the process of globalization.

---

economies of scale, and customization might not give way to standardization in the globalization process (see box 8.1). The debate was so fierce that in May 2003, twenty years after the publication of the article, Harvard Business School (HBS) organized a colloquium at which some seventy faculty members and top executives convened to debate Levitt's argument. Participants tended to think that Levitt's argument was one-sided, and that 'much of what Levitt predicted did not come true – if anything, there has been a consumer uprising against homogeneity and the "Americanization" of the world'.[1] As Pankaj Ghemawat puts it, 'The global standardization hypothesis has less momentum behind it than what is often supposed to be the case.'[2] Nevertheless, almost all agreed that the issues Levitt raised in the article 'were profound, and still carry important implications for companies selling products internationally'.[3] These issues were so profound that, as Richard S. Tedlow and Rawi Abdelal have observed, 'everyone says the article is wrong, and everyone reads it twenty years later.'[4] It is useful, therefore, for us to analyse the strong points as well as the weak points in Levitt's argument, so as to reach a more balanced view on marketing in an international setting.

The strength of Levitt's argument lies in the fact that he correctly pointed out the emergence of a 'global market', and the role of technology (such as TV and the internet) and economies of scale in the globalization process. Admittedly, the sense of 'globalness' has grown stronger and stronger all over the world in the past two decades or so. Levitt also correctly discerned the trend towards the standardization of certain products, including basic industrial products such as steel, chemicals and semiconductors, as well as certain consumer products with an established brand name, such as Coca-Cola, KFC and McDonald's. Coca-Cola certainly produces globally standardized products, which are 'sold everywhere and welcomed by everyone', and which 'successfully cross multitudes of national, regional, and ethnic taste buds trained to a variety of deeply ingrained local preferences of taste, flavor, consistency, effervescence, and aftertaste' (Levitt, 1983, p. 93). Today you can see people drinking standardized Coca-Cola products in almost every corner of the world.

The weakness of Levitt's argument lies in the fact that he overstated the tendency towards globalization and underestimated the persistence of national or regional differences in consumer preferences and marketing practices. Consequently, he exaggerated the need for standardization and overlooked the need for customization/localization in the globalization process – that is, the need to customize products and marketing practices to satisfy specific local conditions in individual national markets. Even such global giants as Coca-Cola, McDonald's and KFC, cited by Levitt to support his argument, have to respect differences in consumer preferences and marketing practices in different national or regional markets and pursue a customization/localization strategy in these markets to a certain degree. When Coca-Cola moved into Japan, for example, it had to adapt to the local marketing practice of providing vending machines that sell everything from beer to egg salad sandwiches and hot drinks on almost every street. Coca-Cola soon produced a canned coffee called Georgia and put it in these vending machines. It turned out that Georgia sold so well that it even outsold Coca-Cola's standardized drinks, becoming the most popular canned coffee in Japan. Coca-Cola then produced dozens of new localized drinks, hot and cold, to meet the demand of local customers, including Nagomi (green tea), Fanta Asari Berry (a cola blending raspberry, blueberry and gooseberry) and Hachimittsu (a honey and grapefruit drink). Today localized drinks account for two-thirds of the total product range that Coca-Cola sells in Japan, while they account for only 10 per cent of what Coca-Cola sells in other parts of the world. As A. R. C Allan, president of Coca-Cola's Asian unit, said, 'That is unique, and we thought it would stay unique. But now we are taking the Japanese model and applying that learning to the rest of Asia to come up with new products' (Flagg, 2001). As shown below, Coca-Cola also produced localized drinks to suit the tastes of Chinese consumers when it moved into China.

Bearing in mind the strengths and weaknesses of the Levitt argument, we can see that the marketing practice of the so-called global corporations and the marketing practice of the so-called multinational corporations are both one-sided. A transnational corporation can neither ignore national or regional differences in consumer preferences and marketing practices nor blindly accommodate those differences. It should try to standardize its products and marketing practices as much as it can on the one hand, and adapt to long-standing national or regional differences in customer preferences and marketing practices on the other. The decision-making on the marketing four Ps is, therefore, contextual, depending on the kind of products a TNC produces, the kind of country markets it enters, the number of country markets it deals with, and so on. When a TNC deals with many country markets simultaneously, for instance, it may think more about the need for standardization. When a TNC deals with a single foreign country market, on the other hand, it may think more about the need for customization/localization. In the case of marketing in the Chinese market, it would appear that TNCs should pay most attention to the specific local consumer preferences and particular marketing practices in the country.[5] We illustrate this point in greater detail in the following sections.

Product

On entering the Chinese market a TNC has to decide, first of all, what kind of product(s) to produce and sell in this market. It may, for example, adopt a strategy of product standardization to produce and sell the same goods or services as it does on its home market or other overseas markets. Alternatively, it may adopt a strategy of product customization/localization to produce and sell goods or services that fit in with the specific needs of the local customers. Indeed almost all TNCs have to think about the standardization versus customization issue. Before reaching their decision, they need to ask themselves the question: do the two product strategies necessarily contradict each other?

As discussed in the previous section on the Levitt debate, regional or national differences in consumer preference may persist despite the trend towards a homogenization of preference structure in the globalization process, and there are needs for both standardization and localization. Product standardization and product customization are not, therefore, necessarily contradictory. On the contrary, they are complementary to each other. As pointed out by Luc Wathieu, Gerald Zaltman and Yu Lien, global and local marketing efforts are at the opposite sides of the spectrum, and both actually 'ignore crucial aspects of consumer behaviour'.[6] There is a way to combine the best of both: a TNC may, for instance, adopt a combination product strategy, in the sense that it standardizes its core products while customizing its other products.

For a TNC entering a new market such as China, product customization rather than product standardization is the most challenging task. This is because, normally, they have already standardized their products before entering a new overseas market. However, these corporations know little, if any, about the consumer preferences in the new market, and have to learn about these preferences and make an effort to customize their products to meet local consumers' needs. All TNCs entering the Chinese market therefore need to familiarize themselves with Chinese consumers' preferences and localize their products accordingly; many have genuinely made the effort, and invested much of their R&D in customizing their products to meet these needs. There are many factors to take into account in the process of product localization in China, but two stand out as being of particular importance. We now illustrate these two factors using real-world examples of transnational corporations currently operating in China.

The first factor is cultural differences. As discussed in chapter 5, culture is a difficult-to-define concept, but it refers primarily to a shared pattern of being, thinking and behaving. Cultural differences may be small between two Western countries – say, the United States and United Kingdom – but they can be huge between a Western and a non-Western country – say, the United States and China. In some cases, cultural differences can also be large even between two countries in the non-Western world. In marketing products in China, therefore, TNCs, particularly those from Western countries and those from non-Western countries with cultural traditions fundamentally different from those in China, need to adjust their product attributes to accord with Chinese cultural traditions.

Take TNCs in the food and beverage industry as an example. Western-style foods and drinks such as sandwiches, cheese, coffee and Coca-Cola were not known to the majority of Chinese until TNCs began to move into China in the 1980s. Straightaway they vigorously promoted standardized Western-style products in China, because they knew, from their past experience in other non-Western countries, that customer preferences could – as Levitt correctly pointed out – be changed and transformed in the process of globalization. Indeed, these standardized Western-style foods and drinks are now increasingly being accepted by Chinese customers; as a symbol of being modern and Western, they are particularly popular among the younger generations of Chinese in the cities, and are expected eventually to win favour with Chinese youth in the rural areas. While promoting these standardized Western-style items, however, almost all the TNCs in the food and beverage industry have also had to learn about the preferences of Chinese customers that have been embedded in their cultural traditions for thousands of years, and customize their products to local needs. Otherwise, they will lose Chinese customers to local companies operating in the food and beverage industry.

A combination product strategy would appear to be an appropriate option, and TNCs in this industry have, indeed, adopted such a strategy in China in practice. That is, they have standardized their core product offers on the one hand, while localizing their other products so as to accommodate Chinese cultural traditions on the other. A case in point is KFC. KFC began to enter the Chinese market in 1987, when it set up the first Western-style fast food restaurant in Beijing; now it has hundreds of outlets in more than eighty cities. While providing the standardized fried chicken and associated foods and drinks as its core products, KFC also tried to provide products that fitted in well with the preferences of local Chinese customers. In the 1990s, for instance, KFC developed a new product called 'Dragon Twist' – a Western-style food item incorporating the flavour of a famous local Beijing dish. The combination product strategy has also been adopted by other foreign food and beverage companies, including the global soft drink giant Coca-Cola (box 8.2).

Another example can be found in the computer software industry. As discussed in chapter 5, the Chinese language is pictographic, and is different from Western languages, which have words that consist of sequences of letters. This difference causes difficulties for TNCs that produce language-sensitive products, such as computer software. When foreign computer software was first introduced into China most of it was in English. Although more and more Chinese have started to learn the language, the majority still know little about English, and even those who have learnt it have serious problems in really mastering the language. To reach the most Chinese customers, therefore, TNCs have to customize their products to specifically Chinese language traditions and produce computer software in Chinese.

For example, when Microsoft began to move into China in 1992, setting up its headquarters in Beijing, from the very beginning it faced the challenge of translating its software from English into Chinese. It invested a large portion of its R&D in the project and employed many talented local Chinese to work on it. Although the project proved very difficult, Microsoft made impressive progress. Starting from 1995, for instance, Microsoft began to produce a new version of Microsoft Windows in simplified Chinese language. It was reported

---

Box 8.2 Coca-Cola's product strategy

Coca-Cola began its move into China in the early 1980s, and has now set up one wholly foreign-owned enterprise and more than twenty-five joint ventures in the country. Coca-Cola has invested more than $1.1 billion in total over the past two decades, and it has now annual sales of more than $1.2 billion. It has reportedly earned a gross profit in China each year since 1990. Fundamental to the success of Coca-Cola in the country has been the adoption of a combination product strategy.

Coca-Cola sells all four of its globally standardized core products in China: Coca-Cola, Diet Coke, Sprite and Fanta. These global brands have attracted many Chinese people, particularly the younger generations in the urban areas, who admire Western culture. In 2001, for example, the four brands captured almost 50 per cent of China's carbonated soft drink market, while the three globally standardized core products of its competitor, Pepsi, accounted for only 20 per cent of the market.

In the meantime, Coca-Cola devotes major efforts to developing localized soft drinks specifically for Chinese consumers. Coca-Cola has learnt from its successful experience in Japan, and takes a 'think local, act local' approach in China as well. In the second half of the 1990s, for instance, Coca-Cola introduced two new localized brands in Asia outside Japan, and both of them were in China. The first was introduced in 1996, and was called Tian Yu Di, or Heaven and Earth. This brand is a line of non-carbonated drinks that include mango and lychee flavours, oolong and jasmine teas, and bottled water. The second was introduced in 1997, and was called Xing Mu, or Smart. This brand is a line of carbonated fruit drinks that includes green apple, grape, watermelon, coconut and other flavours. The two localized brands have been well received by Chinese consumers, and it is reported that, in terms of sales value, Smart is now among the top five brands in China's carbonated soft drink market.

Nevertheless, the success of Coca-Cola's brands, whether standardized or localized, is mainly limited to urban China. It is estimated that, on average, each urban resident in China drinks sixty Coca-Cola products a year, while each rural resident drinks only three. As rural residents account for roughly 70 per cent of the total Chinese population, this represents a huge potential market. As Ms Lee, director of external affairs of Coca-Cola (China), said: 'Imagine if we have 500 million people in the countryside. If we can get each of them to buy just two more drinks, maybe at festivals, that will be a billion beverages.'[7] To attract rural consumers, Coca-Cola may have to develop new brands that appeal to the tastes of rural residents in China. This is a major challenge for Coca-Cola (China) in the coming years.

---

that it then took eight months to translate Microsoft Windows 95 from English into Chinese. From then on the translation time gradually began to shorten: the gap between the release of the English version and the release of the Chinese version was narrowed to one month for Microsoft Windows Me, and to fifteen days for Microsoft XP! While still selling its computer software in the English version, Microsoft vigorously promoted the Chinese version as well. Microsoft is growing very rapidly in China, such that it has now become the largest foreign software developer in the country, and product localization has been key to its success in the Chinese market.

The second factor that TNCs need to take into account in product localization is the difference in the level of economic development between developed and developing countries. As determined by the level of economic development, and thus the level of personal income, consumer behaviour in developing countries may differ significantly from consumer behaviour in developed countries. Consumers in developed countries are, for instance, willing to pay more for products that have additional features and attributes, such as cars with air-conditioning, DVD players and TV-style displays. Consumers in developing countries prefer to pay less for products that have few new attributes because they do not have much money to spend. Although China has developed rapidly since it started its reform programme, it is still a developing country, and the majority of Chinese customers have limited income. Companies from developed countries need to pay attention to the price-sensitive behaviour of Chinese customers in the process of product localization, and customize their products to Chinese consumers's needs. The experience of a US air-conditioner maker helps to illustrate this point. It was reported that the company established a joint venture in China to produce two models of central-comfort air-conditioner. One model was more advanced, with many new features that had been developed in the 1990s, while the other model was less advanced, with features developed in the 1980s. To the great surprise of the company, the less advanced model sold much better than the more advanced one in China, because it was much cheaper (Chen, 2003, p. 45).

To offer low-end products and services to meet the price-sensitive Chinese consumers is not necessarily the best product strategy for all TNCs at all times, however. For TNCs with globally acknowledged brand names and a well-established reputation for good quality, for instance, they may still succeed in China by providing the same standardized high-end products that they provide in other countries. For example, the famous products of Eastman Kodak and Fuji are priced much higher than those of their local counterparts, but yet they account for 90 per cent of the sales of rolls of film in the Chinese market. This kind of approach can succeed only when indigenous Chinese companies are still not strong enough to compete with the TNCs in providing high-quality products; once local companies have reached a sufficient level of maturity, the TNCs will have no choice but to customize their products for the price-sensitive Chinese consumers. As shown below, the price-sensitive behaviour of Chinese consumers influences the decisions that TNCs make not only on what kinds of products to offer in China but also on how to price their products there. This influence became most noticeable in the recent price wars in China (see below).

It should be noted that the Chinese market is not homogeneous. There are considerable differences in cultural traditions, level of economic development, and geographical features between the regions in China – say, between the eastern and the western regions, or, as shown in chapter 7, between the north and the south. In addition, there are also marked differences between urban and rural residents, between the rich and the poor and between the older and the younger generations. As determined by these differences, the preferences of Chinese consumers may vary from one location to another and from one group to another. TNCs should pay attention to the within-country differences when localizing products in China.

Price

After a product has been produced it needs to be priced in a way that maximizes the interests of the TNC that produced it. If the product is priced too high, it is not competitive and cannot be sold in the market. If the product is priced too low, it can be sold in the market but the TNC may make a loss. In theory, ideal price-setting occurs when the price maximizes both the competitiveness of the product and the profitability of the company. In reality, however, the price-setting decision is heavily influenced by many factors, particularly by the marketing environment of the country that the TNC has entered, and changes in that marketing environment.

Price wars in China

As mentioned in the previous section, Chinese consumers, like those in other developing countries, are quite sensitive to price. In the face of these price-sensitive customers, indigenous Chinese companies vie with each other in cutting prices, triggering constant price competition. From the mid-1990s onwards this intensified into outright price wars.

The price wars started in the TV industry. In March 1996 Changhong, Konka and TCL announced, one after another, price cuts of 30 per cent on each television set sold in China. From 1997 to 1998 the contest was carried on by Konka, TCL and Conrowa. Then, in 1999, Changhong initiated a new round in the price wars by cutting the price of its 21-inch and 25-inch TV sets, and other TV manufacturers followed suit. Although nine top Chinese TV

manufacturers convened in Shenzhen in June 2000 for a 'Chinese TV manufacturers' summit' to form a price alliance to end the fighting, the agreement
reached at the summit was shattered three months later when Konka declared
a nationwide price cut, slashing the price of its flagship products, the 29-inch
and 34-inch TV sets, by 20 per cent. Only twenty-four hours later Changhong
announced a price cut of up to RMB 3000 for its products. A few days later
other Chinese TV manufacturers also cut the price of their products.

The price wars quickly spread to other industry sectors. In 2000 the price
of various game, education and translation software packages produced in
Zhongguancun, China's Silicon Valley, was cut by a large margin, roughly
from RMB 150 per package to RMB 35. Some anti-virus software and stock
market analysis software packages were sold at only RMB 28. In the same year
large Chinese DVD manufacturers, such as Shinco, Idall, Panda, Doingding
and SAV, together announced a price cut of 20 per cent for their products.
Galanz, a leading Chinese microwave manufacturer, cut the price of its product by 40 per cent, and offered a popular free gift promotion. Price cuts then
took place in the washing machine sector, the gold jewellery sector and even
the healthcare sector. In mid-2000 the Concord Hospital in Wuhan, the capital
city of Hubei province, announced a price cut of 50 per cent for four major
cardiological operations, and a price cut of 40 per cent for a videoscopic coro-
nary artery examination. Other hospitals soon followed suit, reducing the
charge of medical services by a large margin, such as a 50 per cent price
cut for haemorrhoidectomy operation and waivers for some consultation
fees.

By the end of the 1990s, in the meantime, some indigenous Chinese companies had managed to improve the quality of their products through the
introduction of advanced foreign technology, which enabled them to compete
not only with their local counterparts but also with TNCs operating in China.
These indigenous companies know much better than their foreign counterparts where to find low-cost materials, components and other resources, so
they have an advantage in cutting prices. Based on their improved quality and
low price, indigenous brands have developed and compete with established
foreign brands in the country. This competition has exerted huge pressures
on TNCs and forced them to adjust their pricing strategies.

Adjustment of pricing strategies

In theory, a TNC can choose from a variety of pricing strategies in a national
market it enters, but particular attention needs to be paid to three strategies.

The first is indiscriminate pricing; this is the practice of setting the same price for a product in all countries, regardless of the differences in the level of economic development, cultural traditions, and so on between these countries. Under this strategy, for instance, a microwave oven produced by a US company is sold at the same price in the United States as in China. The US company will enjoy an extremely high profit rate in China thanks to the low labour cost structure there. This strategy works well when competition is weak, and it was adopted by most TNCs when they first moved to China in the 1980s. Until the early 1990s this strategy worked fine, and the high-priced products of TNCs sold well in China due to the lack of competition from indigenous companies. A microwave oven, for example, sold then for about $300, more than 80 per cent of the annual income of an ordinary Chinese worker. A 29-inch TV set sold at more than $1500, about three times the annual income of an ordinary Chinese worker. TNCs earned high profits in China by pursuing the indiscriminate pricing strategy.

The second strategy is discriminate pricing, which refers to charging different prices for the same product in different countries. A microwave oven produced by a US company may, for example, sell at $300 in the United States but $200 in China. The US company will still make a profit in China, albeit a smaller one than with indiscriminate pricing, thanks to the low labour cost structure. This strategy is adopted when competition in the local market intensifies to the extent that indiscriminate pricing fails to work. The competition drives the price down, and TNCs have to sell their products at a price lower than that on the home market or other overseas markets. From the mid-1990s onwards China's domestic companies grew strong enough to compete with the TNCs, forcing them to shift from indiscriminate to discriminate pricing and cut the prices of their products sold in the country.

Discriminate pricing works only when the two markets where products are priced differently are separated. Otherwise, individuals or companies may take advantage of the price discrimination through arbitrage. Arbitrage occurs when individuals or companies capitalize on price discrimination by purchasing the products in the market where the price is low and reselling them in the market where the price is high. Individuals or companies may, for instance, purchase cheap goods from China and sell them in the United States to make a profit. Due to strict antidumping regulations and the tariff and non-tariff trade barriers in the United States and other developed countries, however, it is very difficult for individuals and companies to take advantage of the pricing differentials between China and developed countries through arbitrage. To an extent, therefore, TNCs are able to charge a lower price in China than they do in developed countries for the same product; and, having the ability, they have indeed adopted a discriminate pricing strategy in China.

The third strategy is predatory pricing, (also called pre-emptive pricing or strategic pricing), which refers to the use of price as a competitive weapon to drive weaker competitors out of a national market. A TNC may suffer a temporary loss of profitability by pursuing a predatory pricing strategy, but once the competitors have been driven out of the market it can raise its prices and enjoy high profitability. Predatory pricing enables a TNC to take over a national market and exploit experience curve economies (as explained in chapter 1) in the long run. Predatory pricing is often adopted when competition is, or is expected to be, very intense. In recent years, since indigenous Chinese companies have become increasingly competitive, some TNCs have begun to pursue this pricing strategy in order to drive domestically based competitors out of the Chinese market. Roger Chen (2003, p. 45) has reported a case of a US TNC in the electronics industry in China. The firm first sold its electronics components in China for RMB 6 a piece in 1995. Faced with intensive competition, the company then aggressively cut the price by 67 per cent in the following three years. In the end, as Chen points out, 'This preemptive strategy effectively curtailed the development of local competitors and deterred new entrants. Today, the US firm controls almost 100 per cent of that market.'

For a predatory pricing strategy to work, furthermore, a TNC must normally have a profitable position in another market, so that it can use the profits it earns in that market to offset the loss it makes in the market where it is pursuing a predatory pricing strategy. The experience of some Japanese companies helps to illustrate this point. As the Japanese market is largely protected from foreign competition by high informal trade barriers, Japanese companies can charge very high prices and make massive profits in their home market. They then pursue a predatory pricing strategy overseas to drive foreign competitors out of overseas markets, using the profits earned at home to subsidize the overseas strategy. Once the Japanese firms have occupied the overseas markets, they raise the price and reap the large profits that result. Matsushita, a Japanese TV maker, is reportedly an example of a company that adopted the predatory pricing strategy to penetrate overseas markets.

The pursuit of predatory pricing may, however, fall foul of antidumping regulations in the country where the strategy has been adopted. Dumping occurs when a company sells a product for a price that is less than the cost of producing it. Under this definition, predatory pricing is hardly possible in countries where antidumping regulations are in place and are well enforced. In practice, however, most regulations define dumping vaguely, and they are not implemented effectively. The Chinese government has issued regulations against unfair competition, including dumping, and began to follow the WTO antidumping regulations after it joined that organization in 2001.[8] These regulations are not effectively enforced in China, however. Consequently, TNCs can, and some of them actually did, adopt a predatory pricing strategy in China.

To summarize, faced with price-sensitive Chinese consumers and intensified price wars in China, many TNCs have shifted from an indiscriminate pricing strategy to either discriminate pricing strategy or a predatory pricing strategy so as to compete with indigenous Chinese companies. The shift in pricing strategy reflects the efforts made by these TNCs to adapt their marketing practices to the realities of the Chinese market.

Promotion

In order to sell a product, companies need to make it known to customers in the overseas market they have entered – that is, they need to promote the product. TNCs can use many standard promotion tools to sell their goods and services in overseas markets. They may, for instance, promote their products through mass media advertisements, through direct marketing without the use of an intermediary, through exhibitions, and through such sale campaigns as free give-aways, vouchers for gifts, coupons and combination offers. They may also promote their products through public relations campaigns, including donations to social welfare projects and the provision of after-sale customer services. Except for direct selling, particularly in the form of pyramid schemes, TNCs are allowed to use all the promotion tools in China (see box 8.3). They can use these promotion tools individually or simultaneously, depending on the kind of product they are promoting and where it is being promoted. Nonetheless, there are some strategic issues that TNCs need to take into account in connection with the promotion of their products in China.

The first issue is how to deal with the conservative behaviour of Chinese consumers. Many TNCs have found that they are much more conservative than those in other parts of the world, generally tending to be reluctant to spend even an extra yuan on an unfamiliar product. This conservative behaviour is presumably related to the low level of economic development in China, but it has been remarked, however, that consumers in some other countries with a comparable level of development are not as conservative as Chinese consumers. Consumers in the Philippines, for instance, are more adventurous,

Box 8.3 Direct selling in China

Generally, direct selling refers to the direct, person-to-person sale of goods or services to consumers without the involvement of a wholesaler or/and a retailer who has a fixed place of business. Direct selling can be used for both the promotion and the distribution of products. Direct selling may take various forms. For instance, a direct salesperson may obtain income primarily through commissions from product sales, which is an accepted and lawful practice in many countries. Alternatively, a direct salesperson may recruit a series of new salespeople and obtain income mainly through the initiation fees of, and sales made by, the new recruits, which is usually referred to as pyramid selling. In a pyramid scheme, new recruits must make an initial investment to sign up as members. Members who joined earlier earn sizeable commissions because of the multi-layered recruitment, while the latecomers may receive little return. A pyramid selling business generates income primarily through the recruitment of salespeople rather than the sale of goods or services, and it is outlawed in many countries.

Direct selling, including pyramid selling, was introduced to China in the early 1990s. The terms 'direct selling' (直销) and 'pyramid selling' (传销) have been used interchangeably in China. Prior to 1998 there were many direct sellers in China, including such American giants as Amway and Avon. There were also some lawless individuals, however, who used pyramid selling schemes to engage in smuggling, the selling of counterfeit and low-quality products, and other illegal activities. Consequently, the Chinese government decided to ban direct selling in the form of pyramid schemes. On 18 April 1998 the State Council promulgated the Circular on the Prohibition of Business Activities by Pyramid Selling, forbidding all businesses from engaging in pyramid selling activities or pyramid selling in disguise. Two months later, on 18 June, the Ministry of Foreign Trade and Economic Cooperation, the State Administration for Industry and Commerce, and the State Domestic Trading Bureau jointly issued the Notice on the Relevant Issues concerning the Conversion of Sales Methods by Foreign-Funded Pyramid-Selling Enterprises, which urged foreign enterprises and foreign investment enterprises engaging in pyramid selling to change their sales methods. Then, on 4 February 2002, the State Administration for Industry and Commerce, MOFTEC and the State Economic and Trade Commission issued the Rules on Relevant Questions regarding the Execution of the 'Notice on the Relevant Issues concerning the Conversion of Sales Methods by Foreign-Funded Pyramid-Selling Enterprises', explaining China's policy on foreign direct sellers in details. The main provisions in these documents in relation to foreign direct sellers can be summarized as follows.

Foreign-funded direct selling businesses are urged to adopt measures to convert their businesses into legal operations. They may choose to convert their businesses into one of the two types: (1) those with hired salespeople who are not regular employees and who receive wages through product sales, and (2) those without any hired salespeople. To become the latter, the business has to satisfy three requirements: (1) the business must be established with approval from the government in accordance with the law; (2) the business must be a production enterprise and can sell only the products it produces; and (3) the business must not have violated the law and must have passed the 1998 annual review. To convert into the former, the business must satisfy the preceding three requirements plus two further requirements: (1) its total amount of capital must be more than $10 million, not including investment in sales branches; and (2) the principal business must be direct selling.

Furthermore, a transformed business must first establish a retail shop in the place where its branch is located before hiring salespeople, provided that the branch has been granted approval to hire salespeople. Each salesperson is allowed to conduct selling activities only in the area where his or her shop is located. Besides, a transformed business must ensure that consumers can purchase all its products at the shop. Moreover, a transformed business must submit a biannual report, on the number of its salespeople in each province and relevant matters, to the State Administration for Industry and Commerce, MOFTEC (now the Ministry of Commerce) and the State Economic and Trade Commission.

After entering the WTO China began to work on its commitments to the organization and draft new legislation on direct selling. This came to fruition in late 2005, when the new regulations on direct selling were issued, confirming the ban on pyramid selling since such schemes have been used to commit crimes while removing the ban on other types of direct selling. According to the regulations, however, direct sellers have to meet very strict requirements in order to get a licence from the government. Avon has been successful in its application for a licence, which it received on 22 February 2006, but it remains the only licensed foreign direct seller in China at the time of writing (November 2006).

and they tend to be willing to try new products at least once. Therefore, the Chinese consumers' conservative behaviour may be related to Chinese culture as well – a subject that needs to be studied further by cultural anthropologists and cultural historians. No matter what the roots of this behaviour are, TNCs need to do all they can to overcome the conservative hurdle and promote their products in such a way that Chinese consumers are willing to give them a try.

McCormick, a spice company based in the United States, provides a case in point. The company moved into China in 1988, establishing a joint venture in Shanghai, Shanghai McCormick Foods, to produce and sell spices. Originally it was charged with exporting Chinese spices to other parts of the world, but it soon shifted its focus to the domestic market and tried to sell most of its output inside China. The shift put the joint venture in the front line of producing localized products and promoting them to Chinese customers. In time, the company managed to develop many new types of spices specifically for Chinese consumers, such as Four Seasoning Mix, 'Sichuan Pepper Salt' and Jelly Mix. After putting the new products on the market, however, the joint venture came up against the conservative behaviour problem and found that Chinese consumers were reluctant to try them. To overcome the hurdle the firm adopted a number of promotion methods, such as launching in-store demonstrations with free samples of mapo tofu (a popular Chinese dish) and hot and sour soups prepared from the spices that it produced. It also inserted flyers in local newspapers inviting customers to mail in tickets for free prizes, and provided bonus packs associated with the sale of their products. These methods worked well, and Shanghai McCormick Foods has now become the only company in China that sells spices and seasonings nationwide.

The second issue is the question of how to make use of the right 'heroes' in promotion campaigns. As is well acknowledged, a powerful promotion method is to associate a product with a hero – a famous athlete, movie star, etc. This is because consumers, no matter in which country they live, tend to admire heroes' behaviour or what the heroes symbolize, and they are drawn to certain celebrity images either consciously or subconsciously. Many famous transnational corporations, including Philip Morris, Walt Disney and Nike, have succeeded in marketing their products through promotion campaigns that feature such powerful figures as Marlboro man, Mickey Mouse and Michael Jordan. The use of heroes is sensitive to culture and nationality, however, and TNCs entering the Chinese market need to think carefully about the kind of heroes they should have in their promotion campaigns.

The *International Advertising Magazine* (*Guoji Guanggao*) carried out a survey a few years ago in five large Chinese cities, Beijing, Dalian, Guangzhou, Qingdao and Shanghai, asking Chinese consumers to rank their favourite celebrities. The results showed that all the top twenty celebrities nominated were of Chinese origin. The top five were Liu Dehua, Gong Li, Guo You, Liu Shaoqing and Wang Chen. Some celebrities who are very popular in the West – such as Nike sponsors Michael Jordan and Pete Sampras, Pepsi spokesman Michael Jackson, and Lishi cosmetics endorser Nastassja Kinski – failed to make their way into the top twenty list. Other Western celebrities, including Hollywood movie stars Arnold Schwarzenegger and Sharon Stone, were even not nominated at all. The survey suggests clearly that the Chinese admire local heroes more than foreign ones; TNCs will have to take this into account in their promotion campaigns (Scarry, 1997, p. 42).

To start with TNCs used Western celebrities almost exclusively in advertising their products in China, paying little attention to local heroes. From the early 1990s onwards, however, as they began to appreciate the importance of featuring celebrities of Chinese origin in their promotions, they made use of them in a number of advertisements. For instance, Proctor and Gamble ran an advertisement in China featuring Chinese–American tennis star Michael Chang. Recently, a Chinese basketball player, Yao Ming, who is now playing for the Houston Rockets on the National Basketball Association (NBA) circuit in the United States, has become a popular hero, particularly with young people, and many TNCs have tried to use his image in their promotion campaigns. In 2003, for instance, Coca-Cola used Yao Ming's portrait and name on the packaging of its products in an attempt to attract Chinese consumers. However, it is imperative that attention is paid to the legal issues involved in using images of local celebrities; in the case of Coca-Cola, as it had not asked Yao Ming for permission to use his image, the TNC ended up being sued by him.[9]

The third issue is to do with respect for Chinese customs and feelings. Chinese consumers, as is the case with consumers in other parts of the world, have customs inherited from the past. For example, the Chinese take kneeling down as the highest and most revered form of etiquette; normally the practice is reserved for when children show their gratitude to the parents who gave them birth and brought them up. In addition, due to the humiliations that China has suffered in modern times, the Chinese are very sensitive to anything that may hurt their national pride. These customs and feelings have now become part of Chinese cultural tradition, and have tremendous influence on the behaviour and thinking of Chinese people, young and old alike. TNCs need to understand Chinese customs and feelings, and show respect for them in their promotion campaigns, the danger being that, if they they do not, may run into trouble or even end up facing a lawsuit.

Some recent cases illustrate this point. In December 2003 the Japanese car maker Toyota published an advertisement in the *Friends of Automobile Magazine* (*Qiche Zhiyou*), in which a Japanese car stops in front of two stone lions. One lion raises its right front leg to give a salute while the other bows its head in submission. The background of the advertisement looks very much like the Lugou Bridge, where the Japanese invasion of China started in 1937. This advertisement provoked tremendous resentment in the Chinese people. In November 2004 Nike ran an advertisement on the CCTV Sports Channel in China, showing an American NBA basketball star knocking down, with a basketball, an old Chinese man who looks like a master of traditional Chinese martial arts. The advertisement aroused such strong resentment among the Chinese that the Central Broadcasting and TV Administration of China had to order CCTV to remove it from its programming. Then, in June 2005, McDonald's launched a promotion campaign in Xi'an, the capital city of Shanxi province. In a TV advertisement that was shown both on city buses and in McDonald's outlets, a Chinese customer falls to his knees to beg for a special offer. Many Chinese people thought that the advertisement was an insult to Chinese customers, and the city authorities ordered McDonald's to stop showing it. It is reported that the authorities considered taking legal action against McDonald's for this insulting advertisement. All these cases indicate that TNCs should understand Chinese customs and feelings, and try not to violate or hurt them in their campaigns.

The fourth issue concerns the importance of public relations to promotion. In marketing, the term 'public relations' refers to deliberate efforts to establish and maintain mutual understanding between a company and its public, or conscious and positive attempts to maintain a company's image. Public relations activities are aimed at different groups of people closely related to the operation of the company, particularly its customers and potential customers. As a company has to sell its products to customers to make a profit, it is essential that the company engages in active public relations so as to maintain a good corporate image with its customers or potential customers. In the marketplace, more often than not, a product may sell well simply because the company that produces it enjoys a good public image, or sell poorly simply because it has a negative public image. Because of the need to show sensitivity to the humiliation that China experienced in the past, it is very important for TNCs to maintain a good corporate image in China through active and effective public relations campaigns.

The Toshiba Event vividly illustrates this point. In March 1999 two American consumers sued Toshiba for quality problems in some Toshiba laptop computers they had bought, and a year later Toshiba paid $443 to each of the 500,000 American Toshiba laptop users as compensation. However, there were 200,000 Chinese users of the same Toshiba laptop, to whom Toshiba did not offer any compensation at all. The Chinese users felt that they were being treated unequally, and complained to Toshiba. Toshiba did not handle the complaints well. It did not, for instance, produce a Chinese version of an explanation for the problems on the Toshiba website until six months after the English version had been published online. It did not even have a public relations department to deal with consumer complaints in China. At a Beijing press conference the company's failure to provide explanations that satisfied the Chinese Toshiba laptop users led to their taking out a lawsuit against Toshiba. Most importantly, the event reminded the Chinese people of the historical grievances against Japan: they felt that their national pride had been insulted once again, and so launched a nationwide campaign against all goods with the Toshiba brand name, which led to a sharp decline in the company's sales in China.

Learning from the Toshiba Event, more and more TNCs have begun to pay attention to public relations in order to maintain a good corporate image. In early August 1999, five months after the Toshiba Event, a local newspaper in Zhengzhou, the capital city of Henan province, published a report on complaints about defective Motorola mobile phones. Motorola took the report very seriously, and sent a crisis management team to Zhengzhou the following day. The team opened a service centre in the city immediately after their arrival, and offered a week of free repairs for any Motorola cellphone. The team also opened a hotline to answer questions raised by Motorola phone users, and reported to the local press on the progress it made each day. As Motorola handled the event very well, complaints about the firm's products declined sharply, and the sales of Motorola products continue to grow in the country. It is reported that Motorola has now occupied nearly 30 per cent of the Chinese mobile phone market.

Distribution

A company needs not only to make its products known to customers but also to distribute those products to the customers in adequate quantities, in convenient locations and at the right times. In making decisions on distribution, transnational corporations need to take into account the existing distribution system of the country they are entering, and deal with the challenges posed by that system. In a large developing country such as China, where the retail sector is fragmented, the most challenging task that TNCs face is making the right choice from among the various potential distribution channels so as to create an appropriate distribution strategy.

Essentially, as shown in figure 8.1, a TNC can choose from four distribution channels to sell its products to a new overseas market if it has not yet established a manufacturing base in that market. The first, which is the longest, is to sell its products to import agents, who then sell the products to wholesalers, or retailers or direct to consumers. The second is to sell its products to wholesalers, who then sell the products to retailers or consumers directly. The third is to sell its products to retailers, who then sell the products direct to consumers. The fourth, also the shortest channel, is to sell its products to consumers directly, without going through any of the intermediate stages. If a TNC has already established a manufacturing base in the new market, of course, it can choose only from the last three channels. No matter whether a TNC has established a manufacturing base in the new market or not, in principle, the shorter the distribution channel is the more the corporation can benefit, because each intermediary in the distribution system adds his/her own mark-up to the product and thus increases the price of the product, which weakens its competitiveness in the market. To the extent that it is possible, therefore, a TNC

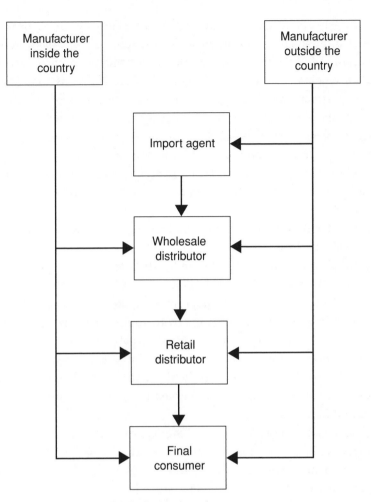

Figure 8.1   Transnational corporations' distribution channels

should choose a shorter distribution channel to strengthen the competitiveness of its products in the new market it is entering.

The selection of shorter distribution channels is restricted by many factors, however, in the new market that the TNC is entering. In China, two factors are especially significant. The first is regulatory restriction. For example, as mentioned earlier, direct selling in pyramid schemes is not allowed in the country. TNCs can do little about such government regulation, which they have no option but to observe. The second factor is the degree of concentration of the retail sector in China. If the retail sector is fragmented, in theory it becomes very costly for TNCs to distribute their products through a large number of retail distributors.

Largely due to state protection, China's retail sector remains weak and is, indeed, fragmented. Although such large foreign retailers as Wal-Mart and Carrefour have entered the Chinese market, they are limited in scale because of the regulatory restrictions. Large domestic retailers exist mainly in the form of department stores, and they do not give satisfactory service to customers. Thousands of urban and rural residents have moved into the retail sector to set up their own small businesses, and most Chinese customers rely mainly on these small retailers and vendors for their daily consumer goods, particularly foodstuffs, in both urban and rural areas. It is not in the interests of the TNCs, therefore, to distribute their products through these millions of small retailers individually.

Faced with this highly fragmented retail sector, TNCs can choose different strategies to distribute their products in China. They can, for instance, establish their own retail networks, and distribute their products to consumers through these networks directly. Kodak, for example, established its own retail networks to distribute its products in the country. Kodak currently has more than 5000 retail outlets in China, with about thirty liaison offices to coordinate the operation of these shops. Alternatively, TNCs can diversify their distribution channels, using a combination of shorter and longer channels simultaneously. As it is very costly to establish a retail network of their own, most TNCs have, in practice, adopted the strategy of distribution channel diversification.

Coca-Cola is a case in point. To overcome the difficulties posed by the fragmentation of the retail sector in China, Coca-Cola sells its products primarily through Chinese wholesale distributors. These include large sugar, tobacco and wine enterprises that are still under state ownership, former state-owned distribution enterprises that have now been privatized and independent wholesalers that have just emerged. These wholesale distributors then sell on the Coca-Cola products to small retailers. In the meantime, Coco-Cola also sells a small portion of its products directly to larger retailers. To handle this distribution and the sales to these larger retailers, Coca-Cola established at least one wholly owned sales centre in most Chinese cities with a population above 1 million. These sales centres run their own fleets of delivery trucks, coordinate deliveries and sales of Coca-Cola products locally, send personnel to retailers on a regular basis to take orders, and report to Coca-Cola's regional office periodically. The diversification distribution strategy works quite well, and Coca-Cola has now reached more than 200,000 active retail outlets in China.

It should be noted that, since the WTO accession, China has been trying to remove its protection in the retail sector, and the regulatory restrictions are now being relaxed. With the rapid development of foreign retailers, China's retail sector is expected to move from fragmentation to concentration in the future. TNCs need to adjust their distribution strategy to take into account the changing marketing environment in China.

Summary

Marketing in an international context is different from marketing at home. To sell goods and services in overseas markets, a TNC needs to address the following questions: whether consumer preferences and marketing practices are becoming homogenized worldwide in the process of globalization or remain different from country to country, and whether it should standardize its products and marketing practices to conform to the homogenizing trends or customize its products and marketing practices to suit the specific conditions of individual local markets. The answers to these questions will have a major impact on whether a company succeeds or fails in overseas markets.

The Levitt debate, although very enlightening and powerful, is somehow one-sided as an answer to these questions. The argument overstates the tendency towards globalization and underestimates the persistence of national or regional differences in consumer preferences and marketing practices. Consequently, it exaggerates the need for standardization and overlooks the need for customization/localization. In the process of globalization, in fact, although consumer preferences and marketing practices do indeed tend to become similar across the globe, some regional and national differences are proving persistent, and remain to varying degrees. Therefore, standardization and localization are not contradictory but complementary.

As shown in the experience of TNCs operating in China, it is localization rather than standardization that is the most challenging task for them. This chapter has shown how they try to be accommodating to Chinese consumer preferences and marketing practices when they make decisions as to what products to produce, how to price them, how to promote them and how to distribute them. There are many issues that these TNCs have to address. In deciding what products to produce, they need to pay attention to Chinese culture and the low level of economic development in the country. In pricing their products, they need to learn about the strong tendency towards price wars in China, and adjust their pricing strategies accordingly. In promoting their products, they have to deal with the conservative behaviour of Chinese consumers, look for local heroes for their advertisement campaigns, respect Chinese customs and feelings and maintain a positive corporate image. In distributing their products, they need to understand the regulatory restrictions and the retail fragmentation in China, and adopt an appropriate distribution strategy. Many lessons can be drawn from the successes and failures that the various TNCs have experienced in China.

FURTHER READING

Chen, R. 2003. 'Price wars'. *China Business Review* 30 (5): 42–6.
Gelb, C. 1997. 'Spicing up the Chinese market'. *China Business Review* 24 (4): 25–9.
Levitt, T. 1983. 'The globalization of markets'. *Harvard Business Review* 61(3): 92–102.
Scarry, J. 1997. 'Making the consumer connection'. *China Business Review* 24 (4): 40–4.
Weisert, D. 2001. 'Coca-Cola in China: quenching the thirst of a billion'. *China Business Review* 28 (4): 52–5.

Questions for discussion

1. Comment on Theodore Levitt's argument about the 'globalization of markets', and discuss the strengths and weaknesses of the argument.
2. Are product standardization and product localization complementary to each other? Why?
3. How have the intensified competition and price wars impacted on the pricing strategies of TNCs in China?
4. What are the main issues that TNCs should pay attention to in promoting their products in China? Relate your argument to Chinese culture and history.
5. Are Chinese consumers more conservative than consumers in other parts of the world? If so, what do you think the best promotion approaches are in dealing with the conservative behaviour of Chinese consumers?
6. How should TNCs deal with a fragmented retail sector in China? What are the rationales for TNCs to use diversified distribution channels in the country?

NOTES

1. See 'Theodore Levitt's Globalization of Markets is still powerful (if wrong) twenty years later', HBS Working Knowledge, HBS conference coverage, at http://hbswk.hbs.edu/specialReport.jhtml?id=3540&t=special_reports.
2. See 'Researchers contribute Globalization of Markets papers', HBS Working Knowledge, HBS conference coverage, at http://hbswk.hbs. edu/specialReport.jhtml?id=3540&t=special_reports.

3. See 'Theodore Levitt's Globalization of Markets is still powerful (if wrong) twenty years later', HBS Working Knowledge, HBS conference coverage, at http://hbswk.hbs.edu/specialReport. jhtml?id= 3540&t=special_reports.

4. See 'Historical perspective: Levitt shaped the debate', HBS Working Knowledge, HBS conference coverage, at Http://hbswk.hbs. edu/ specialReport.jhtml?id=3540&t=special_reports.

5. The local consumer preferences and marketing practices may vary from one region to another and from one group to another within China.

6. See 'Researchers contribute Globalization of Markets papers', HBS Working Knowledge, HBS conference coverage, at http://hbswk.hbs.edu/specialReport.jhtml?id=3540&t= special_reports.

7. See Simons (2003).

8. For instance, the Chinese government issued the Law of the People's Republic of China against Unfair Competition in 1993.

9. Yao Ming later withdrew his lawsuit after an agreement had been reached: Coca-Cola openly apologized to Yao Ming and paid a symbolic fine of one yuan.

9 Human resource management

The strategic role of human resource management is complex in a domestic firm, but it is more complex in an international business, where staffing, management development, performance evaluation, and compensation activities are complicated by profound differences in labour, markets, culture, legal systems, economic systems, and the like (Charles W. L. Hill (2003, p. 458)).

All business activities, no matter whether negotiation, production or marketing, have to be carried out by people in a business organization. People are, therefore, valuable assets or human resources, and should be properly managed. Human resource management is about how to use human resources effectively and efficiently in an organization. As people are different from machines or products, in the sense that they can think and feel, managing people is probably the most difficult task that a company undertakes. HRM has to deal with many complex issues, such as how to recruit employees, how to retain them and how to motivate them. The complexity of these issues is exacerbated in an international setting, where a company has to manage human resources in an environment different from that at home. A transnational corporation needs to learn how to manage its human resources efficiently and effectively in the different countries in which it operates. The aim of this chapter is to analyse the main challenges faced by TNCs in human resource management in China, and the various approaches to dealing with these challenges. In so doing, we focus on three of the most outstanding challenges: staffing, retaining Chinese employees and managing expatriates.

Staffing

Staffing is concerned with selecting and recruiting employees. Entering a new market, a TNC has to think about what kinds of people it should select and employ for the management positions of its affiliates in the host country. Should it select parent-country nationals and bring them to the host country? Should it recruit locals in the host country? Should it select and recruit the best people regardless of their nationality? Clearly, the answers to these questions will have a major influence on staffing strategies. In this section we first look at the staffing strategies that TNCs may adopt from a theoretical perspective, and then discuss the shift towards localization in the staffing strategy of TNCs operating in China and the key issues involved.

Staffing strategies from a theoretical perspective

In theory TNCs may adopt a number of staffing strategies, but three of them have most relevance here: ethnocentric staffing, polycentric staffing and geocentric staffing.

Ethnocentric staffing is a strategy in which all key management positions are filled by parent-country nationals. This strategy was widespread in TNCs all over the world at one time, and was adopted by such TNCs as Proctor and Gamble and Philips. Even today, some Japanese and South Korean TNCs still fill all their key management positions with parent-country nationals. The ethnocentric staffing route is often taken when there are few host-country managers who are qualified for senior management positions, or when TNCs want to maintain a unified corporate culture through the use of home-country nationals, or when TNCs intend to use the home-country nationals to transfer core competencies to a foreign affiliate.

The ethnocentric staffing strategy suffers from a number of drawbacks. It tends to lead, for instance, to so-called 'cultural myopia' – that is, management failure due to a lack of understanding of the host country's culture and environment. As mentioned in chapter 8, differences in consumer preference and marketing practice persist despite the globalization process. It takes time for expatriate managers to understand these differences and learn how to deal with them. During the long learning process there is the possibility of making mistakes that could have a disastrous impact on the company. Furthermore, this strategy leaves host-country nationals no opportunities for career advancement within the company, and thus leads to resentment on their part. In the case of Philips, for instance, Dutch nationals used to hold all the key management positions in almost all foreign affiliates, and were referred to, cynically, as the 'Dutch Mafia' by non-Dutch employees. Moreover, it is very costly, as expatriate managers are normally paid much more than their local counterparts and they need removal subsidies. In a sense, polycentric staffing and geocentric staffing emerged as a response to these shortcomings in ethnocentric staffing.

In polycentric staffing, parent-country nationals fill the senior management positions at the corporate headquarters at home, but host-country nationals are hired for the senior management positions in the affiliates located in the host country. It would appear that polycentric staffing can help to resolve the cultural myopia problem associated with ethnocentric staffing, in that host-country nationals know much better than parent-country nationals how an affiliate should be run in the particular business environment of the host country. Polycentric staffing can also help to resolve the problem of the high cost structure in ethnocentric staffing, because host-country nationals are normally paid less than expatriates and do not need removal subsidies. Furthermore, polycentric staffing provides opportunities for host-country nationals to move into senior management positions in the affiliates, and can therefore alleviate resentments from local employees.

The polycentric staffing strategy also has some weaknesses, however. Its most pressing problem is the potential for a divide to develop between the host-country management team and the parent-country management team. Owing to differences in cultural traditions and national loyalties, a schism may emerge between the two groups of managers, and thus a lack of integration between corporate headquarters and foreign affiliates. As a result, a TNC may become a de facto federation, in the sense that its foreign affiliates become 'little kingdoms' with only nominal links to the corporate headquarters. The formation of the little kingdoms makes it very difficult for the TNC to function effectively and efficiently. Another weakness with polycentric staffing lies in the fact that local managers have no chance to move beyond management positions within the affiliates located in the host country, which can lead to resentment.

In geocentric staffing, by contrast, a TNC selects and recruits the best talents, regardless of their nationality, for key management positions throughout the corporation, headquarters and affiliates alike. It would appear that the geocentric staffing strategy is best able to resolve the resentment problem found with both ethnocentric staffing and polycentric staffing. As the most talented locals are very likely be employed for the key positions in foreign affiliates, it can also overcome the cultural myopia problem with ethnocentric staffing. In addition, because the management teams in both parent headquarters and foreign affiliates are not divided by nationality any more, the problem of a lack of integration between headquarters and affiliates with polycentric staffing is mitigated. By utilizing a geocentric staffing strategy, a TNC can make best use of all the human resources available, at home and in the host country, and thus build up a pool of senior managers who can work internationally. From a theoretical perspective, therefore, geocentric staffing seems to be the most appropriate strategy that a TNC can adopt.

In practice, however, the adoption of this strategy is restricted by the protectionism that prevails in the labour market in most countries in the world. Many countries, including such liberal countries as the United States, the United Kingdom, Canada and Australia, issue immigration regulations requiring foreign affiliates to hire their citizens in the first instance. If foreign affiliates want to hire citizens of other nationalities to fill certain positions, they have to prove that there are no qualified locals for these positions. The process of providing the relevant documents is often so long and so troublesome that TNCs are forced to give up. In addition, the strategy often requires a standardized compensation scheme throughout a TNC and a standardized removal subsidy scheme across all countries where it has affiliates, adding to the company's cost structure.

In theory, as analysed above, there are both advantages and disadvantages, albeit to different degrees, with each of the three staffing strategies that a TNC can adopt when it operates in overseas markets. Because the ethnocentric staffing strategy is most problematic, it has become less and less popular among TNCs in recent years. As there are drawbacks and limitations with both polycentric staffing and geocentric staffing, very few TNCs adopt either of these two strategies in its pure form, tending in practice to adopt a mixed approach so as to avoid the drawbacks of individual staffing strategies while combining their strengths. No matter what kind of mixed staffing approach a TNC may adopt, staffing localization – the selection and recruitment of talented host-country nationals for management positions – appears to be inevitable. The question is not whether or not to localize managerial staff, but how and to what extent to do so. As shown below in the case of China, the most practical challenges faced by TNCs in staffing are localization, localization, and localization!

The trend towards staffing localization

In the 1980s, when transnational corporations first moved into China, most of them adopted an ethnocentric staffing strategy, filling all their key management positions with parent-country nationals. The adoption of this staffing strategy was justified then by the fact that there were few, if any, local Chinese who were qualified for senior management jobs. Formal management education, such as Master of Business Administration (MBA) programmes, did not start in China until the early 1990s, and the lack of qualified local managers was a nationwide phenomenon. Due to the relatively low level of intensity of competition in China at that time, furthermore, the high cost structure of ethnocentric staffing had not yet posed a severe challenge to TNCs operating in the country.

However, the drawbacks of ethnocentric staffing soon loomed large, and TNCs had to take action. To overcome the cultural myopia in a country where qualified local talents were not available, some TNCs worked out an ingenious approach to staffing, namely the hiring of talented overseas Chinese for senior management positions with their affiliates in China. These overseas Chinese were born and brought up either in mainland China or in an environment strongly influenced by traditional Chinese culture, such as Singapore, Taiwan, Hong Kong, Macao or local Chinese communities within Western countries. These overseas Chinese were later educated in the West, so they were familiar with Chinese culture as well as Western culture. They played an important role in bridging the two cultures, as shown in the case of Wilson Wang, IBM chief representative in China, and helped TNCs avoid cultural myopia in China (box 9.1).

The overseas Chinese staffing approach failed to overcome the other two shortcomings in ethnocentric staffing, however. The overseas Chinese managers were given the same compensation package (salary and reallocation subsidy) as was given to Western managers, so the cost structure remained high. In addition, the overseas Chinese managers were still considered by local Chinese as belonging to a high-class expatriate group that they could not join, which still caused resentment. The high cost structure and the widespread resentment from local employees increasingly became a barrier to the success of TNCs in the 1990s, when competition intensified in China. By the mid-1990s, for instance, some indigenous Chinese companies had begun to make full use of their low cost structure, staff solidarity and introduced foreign technology to compete successfully with TNCs, or even kick them out of the Chinese market. Under the pressure, TNCs were compelled to move further and further away from ethnocentric staffing, and began to localize managerial staff. In the meantime, the body of local Chinese talent widened in the 1990s when more and more graduates from MBA programmes, both local and foreign, became available on the Chinese labour market, which provided the much-needed sources for staffing localization.

From the mid-1990s onwards, therefore, staffing localization became increasingly popular among TNCs operating in the country, and more and more local Chinese began to fill senior management positions in foreign

---

Box 9.1 The story of Wilson Wang

Wilson Wang, born in China in 1930, went to Taiwan with his family in 1948. He left Taiwan for the United States in 1962 to study computer science and management, and later graduated from Washington University with an MBA degree. Wang worked as a software programmer in a transportation company in the United States before he joined IBM, a computer giant, in 1969. From 1983 onwards IBM began to develop its business in China, and Wang was in charge of selling IBM software to China. In 1991 IBM (China) was established in Beijing, and Wang was appointed the chief representative and one of the directors of the IBM affiliate in China.

Knowing both IBM corporate culture and Chinese culture, Wang played a key role in the development of IBM (China). Whenever there emerged difficulties and problems, it was Wang who acted as a bridge between the company and its Chinese business partners. As an employee of IBM, on the one hand, he defended the interests of IBM in negotiating with Chinese business partners. As an overseas Chinese, on the other hand, he understood Chinese culture and the Chinese way of thinking, and often thought the matter over from the perspective of the Chinese partners. He was then able to propose suggestions and business solutions acceptable to both sides. As he said in an interview, 'The reason IBM gave me the important duty is that I often noticed what they might miss'.[1] The bridging role was welcomed by both IBM and its Chinese business partners.

In addition, Wang understood how important *guanxi* is in China. He invested time in making friends with Chinese, including both high-level government officials and ordinary young people. Whenever he was free, he would invite Chinese friends round for dinner and entertain them. He believed that foreign executives should make friends not only with high-level officials and businessmen but also with ordinary people. In China, if someone wants to disrupt your plans, it is relatively easy. It is, therefore, in your interests to make as many friends as you can.

Indeed, Wang was very successful in his China mission, contributing significantly to IBM's rapid expansion in the country. In 1994, when he retired after working for IBM for twenty-five years, a number of important Chinese officials attended his farewell party, including Hu Qili, then Minister of Electronics Industry, and Zeng Peiyan, then director of the State Planning Commission and now a Vice-Premier of the People's Republic. Following his retirement, Wang still works for some large companies in China even now, serving as the honorary chairman of the board of directors for the Oriental Credit Company and the chief representative of the Flagtelecom Beijing office.

---

affiliates in China. In an article published in the *China Business Review*, Sheila Melvin, director of the Shanghai office of the US–China Business Council, gives a concise account for the driving forces behind the trend toward staffing localization in China. She writes: 'Localization is an ongoing struggle for HR managers in all FIEs [foreign-invested enterprises] . . . since local Chinese are generally perceived as better able to function in the China market and local managers usually cost less than expatriates. It also plays a role in retention – if expatriates fill all top-level jobs, talented local managers unable to break through a glass ceiling will simply go elsewhere' (Melvin, 2000, p. 49). Take the cost consideration as an example. In the late 1990s, according to Melvin's estimate, a typical annual compensation package for an expatriate manager ranged from \$250,000 to \$350,000. In contrast, a typical annual compensation package for a local Chinese manager was no more than \$20,000. Therefore, as pointed out by Melvin and Kissten Sylvester (1997, p. 32), 'The cost of sending an employee to China has many firms wishing [that] localization could happen tomorrow.' The driving forces behind staffing localization are real, and irresistible! By now, local Chinese have filled the majority of the senior management positions in most foreign affiliates in China.

In pursuing staffing localization, TNCs in China tried to avoid the drawbacks in polycentric staffing and geocentric staffing. While hiring local Chinese for most senior management positions, for instance, TNCs often kept some key senior executive positions for parent-country nationals or overseas Chinese in order to avoid the 'federation' problem in polycentric staffing. While seeking the best people for key senior management positions regardless of their nationality, furthermore, TNCs often provided a differential compensation scheme, in which local Chinese were paid less than parent-country nationals, so as to avoid the high cost structure problem in geocentric staffing. As a result, the approach to staffing currently adopted by TNCs in China is in fact a mixture of the staffing strategies discussed previously.

The experience of Butler, a building company based in the United States, helps to illustrate this point. Butler pursued a typical ethnocentric staffing strategy when it first moved into China in the early 1990s, with all twelve of its staff being parent-country nationals. Then, in the face of intensified competition, Butler began to hire local Chinese for management positions, such that by 1999 local Chinese accounted for the majority of management positions in Butler. Nevertheless, Butler still kept five expatriates in key senior management positions in its China affiliates. A similar story can be found in the case of Motorola. When Motorola first moved into China, in 1987, all the management positions were filled by parent-country nationals. By 2003, however, local Chinese accounted for 84 per cent of all the management positions in Motorola's affiliates in China. The remaining 16 per cent of key management positions were filled either by parent-country nationals or by overseas Chinese. Two of the vice-presidents of Motorola (China) were, for instance, overseas Chinese: Bingron Lai (a Malaysian Chinese) and Timothy Chen (a Taiwan Chinese). In both cases there were compensation differentials between expatriate and local managers, and very few, if any, Chinese were recruited for senior management positions in the parent company. In practice, therefore, the staffing localization of TNCs in China moves neither in the direction of polycentric staffing nor in the direction of geocentric staffing, despite what it says in standard textbooks.

The search for local talents

The move towards staffing localization has led to increasing demand for talented local Chinese individuals, while the supply of these talents remains limited. As pointed out by Rebecca McComb, chief representative of Norman Broadbent International (China), 'But as MNCs [multinational corporations] turned to the local market, the gap between their staffing requirements and the supply of qualified locals became clear . . . In the 1990s . . . the demand for qualified local managerial candidates has continued to soar exponentially, while the supply remains small' (Mc Comb, 1999, p. 31). Although the number of MBA programmes is increasing, MBA graduates still cannot meet the soaring demand; it is estimated that current MBA graduates can meet less than a half of the demand for management positions in China. Consequently, TNCs compete with each other, and also with indigenous Chinese companies, for valued local Chinese managers.

Under the pressure of this competition, TNCs have to go all-out to search for qualified local candidates for senior management positions. There are many ways by which TNCs can look for local talents in China. They can, for instance, do so through government agencies. The most renowned government agency is Foreign Enterprise Service Company (FESCO), which was established in the early 1980s to deal specifically with issues related to staffing in TNCs operating in China. At first FESCO helped only with the hiring of basic staff, but more recently it has begun to help TNCs recruit senior local Chinese managers. FESCO also provides assistance in managing new local recruits in TNCs. As a rule, TNCs pay a monthly fee to FESCO for each new local employee, while FESCO takes care of the local employee's state-supported benefits in relation to retirement, healthcare, childcare, etc. Moreover, TNCs can also look for talented local individuals through private recruiting firms in China, foreign and domestic alike, which began to emerge in China in the early 1990s. Today almost all the world's top executive recruitment firms have set up offices in China, and the number of local Chinese private recruiting firms is on the rise. The majority of clients of these private recruiting firms are TNCs operating in China.

Apart from formal government and private recruiting agencies and firms, TNCs can also look for local talent through other channels, including local newspaper advertisement, on-campus recruiting events, manpower fairs and online recruiting. As discussed in chapter 3, *guanxi* plays a very important role in Chinese society, so TNCs may also take a *guanxi*-based approach to recruiting in the country. That is, they can seek skilled local Chinese people through the *guanxi* network that its current personnel, particularly the personnel in the HRM department, have already established. To make better use of *guanxi*, as pointed out by Rebecca McComb (1999, p. 33), from the mid-1990s onwards TNCs began to hire 'experienced, English-speaking, local human resources managers . . . [. . .] The Chinese human resources manager was charged with finding all staff for the MNC by tapping into his or her local connections and network.' Due to intensifying competition, it will become more and more difficult for TNCs to find the most sought-after local Chinese talents. Recruiting valued local Chinese is only the first step, however, in fighting the war for local talent, and the next – also the most important – step is to adopt appropriate methods to retain the new local recruits. Otherwise, they will go elsewhere.

Retaining Chinese employees

Along with the move towards staffing localization and the resulting war for local talent, the Chinese labour market has become increasingly volatile in recent years, being characterized by double-digit turnover rates. Talented local individuals now have numerous career opportunities, and they move from one job to another frequently. The volatile labour market poses a severe challenge to the human resource management of TNCs in China. As pointed out by Melvin (2000, p. 39), the retention of valued local Chinese employees is 'a pressing concern for all foreign invested enterprises. HR managers spend considerable time and energy working with management to create incentives and an environment that will keep key staff happy and loyal.' There are many approaches to retaining talented local employees, but the three that have been adopted by TNCs operating in China stand out as the most important.

Retention through compensation and benefits

According to a recent survey conducted by Watson Wyatt in China, the number one reason for local Chinese employees to leave their company is to find a better-paid job (Leininger, 2004, p. 17). Offering an attractive compensation and benefits (C&B) package is, therefore, one of the most effective tools for retaining talented local employees in the country. All TNCs now try to offer generous compensation and benefits to talented Chinese employees, but the C&B package tends to differ from one type of foreign affiliates to another. Generally speaking, representative offices offer the highest compensation and benefits, followed by wholly foreign-owned enterprises and then joint ventures. The components of a C&B package vary from one case to another, but the following are normally included in the packages that TNCs offer to local employees, and therefore they are discussed here in detail.

The first element is the salary. Generally speaking, the salary is the largest component in a C&B package. In deciding on the salary level for Chinese employees, TNCs need to take into consideration a number of factors. For instance, China is a huge country with substantial regional differentials in the level of economic development and the cost of living, so the salary for equivalent positions may vary significantly from one place to another. The salary level is normally higher in the eastern (coastal) region than in the inland regions, because the level of economic development and the cost of living are higher in the former. Even within the eastern region, salaries may vary from one city to another. According to a recent survey conducted by Watson Wyatt in four coastal cities in China, Beijing enjoys the highest salary level, followed by Shanghai, Guangzhou and then Shenzhen. In acknowledgement of the differences, some TNCs have established a general salary structure that carves China into first-, second- and third-tier cities, with 100 per cent of the salary for employees in first-tier cities, 80 per cent for employees in second-tier cities and 60 per cent for employees in third-tier cities. Along with rapid economic growth, furthermore, the salary level has been increasing at a remarkable rate in China. It is estimated that the annual salary growth rate has been between 6 and 8 per cent in the country in recent years, much higher than in other parts of the world, and this trend is expected to continue in the foreseeable future. TNCs need to keep raising the salary of their Chinese employees in accordance with the rapid salary growth rate in the country.

The second element is the bonus. The bonus is the portion of a compensation package that is tied to performance, and it is used to provide an incentive for employees to meet certain goals. Although bonuses did not feature in compensation packages in China until recent years, they have now become increasingly popular and have been accepted by many companies in the country. They are most popular with TNCs, normally being used to encourage local employees to complete a particular job, such as a specified production or sales target. Sometimes they are also used to reward Chinese employees who propose creative ideas, such as new ways to cut costs of production, improve the quality of the output, make working conditions safer, increase efficiency in the workplace, etc. To an extent, bonus schemes help to attract local employees and keep them happy in the company.

The third element is stock options. A stock option is the right to purchase a specific number of shares of a company's stock at a specific price during a certain period of time. Some TNCs give stock options to all their employees, while others give them only to upper-level management. The attractiveness of stock options is dependent on the ups and downs of the stockmarket and on the performance of the company. If an employee gets stock options for 1000 shares in the company, for instance, he or she can buy these shares at some time in the future but at today's price. Managers who have received stock options thus have very strong incentives to work hard and stay in the company. Because of the foreign exchange restrictions in China, however, it is difficult for Chinese employees to own stocks listed overseas. TNCs operating in the country therefore have to get around these restrictions if they want to give their local employees stock options. This is why some TNCs have devised so-called 'shadow' or 'phantom' stock plans: under these plans, the companies issue their Chinese employees a letter in which the number and price of the stock options for a particular employee are clearly spelt out. The stocks are actually held by a professional broker overseas, not by the Chinese employees themselves. When the employees choose to cash in their stock options, the company or the broker makes the transactions for them and gives them the profits from the sale in Chinese currency. The stock option is a very effective retention tool, particularly when the stockmarket is performing strongly.

The fourth element is so-called 'golden handcuffs', also called deferred compensation plans. Golden handcuffs are very popular with TNCs operating in China, and are normally offered in the form of a contract-related gratuity. If a Chinese employee has signed a two-year contract with a TNC and does indeed work for that company for two years, for example, he or she would be given an extra year's salary at the end of the contract. Recently, some TNCs have begun offering a new version of golden handcuffs to young Chinese employees who would like to do an MBA degree at a prestigious overseas university: they promise to reimburse the tuition fees for these employees if they come back to work for the company after completing their degree. No matter which form they take, golden handcuffs, as the term indicates, are designed to provide incentives for talented local employees to remain in the company.

The fifth element is so-called 'iron handcuffs'. In contrast with golden hand-cuffs, iron handcuffs are punitive fines levied on employees who leave the company before their contract expires. If a Chinese employee leaves the company in these circumstances, he or she will have to pay back, for instance, the training costs, or the removal expenses, or whatever. All these conditions are clearly specified in the labour contract the employee signed with the TNC when he or she accepted the job offer. Clearly, the purpose of iron handcuffs is to deter employees from leaving the company. Although China's legal system is not firmly established and cannot fully guarantee enforcement of an iron handcuffs agreement between an employer and an employee, most Chinese employees working in TNCs are willing to abide by the terms and pay the penalties because they know very well that their future career will be at risk if they are sued in the courts for refusing to do so.

The sixth element is social and commercial benefits. Social benefits refer to contributions to government-run social insurance schemes, which currently cover housing, pensions, medical care, unemployment, accident and maternity care, etc. The contribution is split between the employer and the employee according to government-mandated percentages, and the amount paid out varies widely from one city to another. By contrast, commercial benefits refer to the benefits offered by an employer to an employee on a commercial basis, with no relation to government-run social insurance funds. A company may, for instance, offer employees the opportunity to borrow money to purchase a house or a car at below-market interest rates, or provide employees with finan-cial subsidies for childcare, a mobile phone or health club membership, or even give employees extra vacation time. These commercial benefits may be spread out over an extended period of time in order to provide further inducement to employees to remain in the company. Both social and commercial benefits are widely used by TNCs as means to retain Chinese employees.

Retention through training and career development

Even though a company may offer an attractive C&B package, employees may still leave if they cannot see opportunities for career development within the company. To retain a wanted employee, therefore, it is very important for a company to provide that employee with career development opportunities. But the problem faced by transnational corporations in China is that local employees, talented in some ways though they are, lack the kind of understand-ing of the corporate culture, basic knowledge, skills and experience needed for further advancement in the company. An effective tool for retaining talented

---

Box 9.2 In-house training at McKinsey (China)

McKinsey and Company, a US management consulting group, has now established more than eighty affiliates in over forty countries. It provides management consulting services not only for company presidents, senior executives and management boards but also for senior government officials and non-profit organizations. McKinsey began to move into China in the 1980s, and has established two branches there: one in Shanghai in 1993 and the other in Beijing in 1995.

To begin with, McKinsey mainly provided consulting services to TNCs operating in China, since domestic Chinese companies had not yet realized how valuable a consulting company could be to them. Gradually, McKinsey began to serve Chinese clients, including large state-owned enterprises, private companies and small high-tech companies. Now, more than 80 per cent of the clients of its Shanghai and Beijing offices are domestic Chinese companies. McKinsey became well known in China after it provided an excellent consulting service to assist the listing of China Petrochemical Corporation (Sinopec), a large state-owned enterprise, on the US stockmarket.

The consulting services that McKinsey offers cover a wide range of areas, including corporate development strategy, organization structure, business operations and other practical management issues. This kind of service is very demanding, and it requires service providers to have up-to-date professional and practical knowledge and skills. McKinsey established a special HRM system to look for qualified consultants with integrated skills to resolve practical problems for clients. Most of the new recruits have an MBA degree, and have substantial work experience.

It is very difficult, however, for McKinsey to find qualified local consulting staff in China, and it has had to make do with whomever it can find. In response to the shortage of local talent, McKinsey established a well-organized in-house training programme to train new recruits and retain them. Every week it runs an in-house training course. The training course focuses on the corporate culture, business concepts, case analysis methods and practical consulting skills that a McKinsey consultant must master in order to work well for the company. The training course adopts a one-on-one tutorial approach, with a less experienced staff member being coached by a more experienced one. Through the in-house training and team-working, not only can the knowledge base of the company be shared by all employees but also new recruits can gain the valuable knowledge, skills and experience that are essential for their career advancement in the company.[2]

Chinese employees is, therefore, to provide them with attractive training programmes so as to facilitate their career development in the company. TNCs operating in China offer many training programmes to local Chinese employees, including in-house training, outsourcing training, overseas training and local MBA training.

In-house training programmes have been developed by, and are conducted within, the company. In-house training is often used, as shown in the case of

McKinsey (see box 9.2), for training in the specific on-site skills needed in a company, and is often integrated into the daily operations in the company. In-house training is good at incorporating the TNC's policies, objectives and practices into the training programme, but it is very demanding and rather involved. It is not easy, for instance, for TNCs to find and retain qualified Chinese trainers for in-house training programmes. Due to the increasing demand for local talent in management, it is quite easy for qualified Chinese trainers to leave their jobs for management positions in order to make more money. Most TNCs either have to employ inexperienced local trainers or allocate an experienced expatriate trainer from the parent company to do the job. Butler (China), for example, sends professionals to China from its headquarters in the United States to conduct in-house training programmes on a regular basis. These expatriate professionals provide on-site training in finance, operations and systems processes.

Another difficulty that TNCs have encountered in connection with in-house training is the lack of an appropriate curriculum and materials. As in-house training normally targets skills specifically needed in a company, it is very hard for the company to find a ready-made curriculum and teaching materials from other companies and training providers. TNCs therefore have to develop their own curriculum and teaching materials (either in the Chinese language or in the company's native language) so that they incorporate local case studies that reflect local conditions, and then tailor the contents of the curriculum and materials to the practical needs of their companies. Developing the curriculum and teaching materials can be very costly and time-consuming, however.

The second training option is outsourcing training, which consists of the hiring of professional training firms to train employees. Outsourcing training is especially attractive because it enables a TNC to shift away from training and focus on its main business areas. To meet the demand for outsourcing training, many foreign professional training firms have moved into China. One case in point is MTI (Management Technologies, Inc.), a US professional training firm. MTI began its move into China in the late 1980s, and it has now established training offices in seven Chinese cities: Beijing, Tianjin, Qingdao, Changsha, Chengdu, Shenyang and Lanzhou. These offices provide training programmes for TNCs in China and large local companies alike, the programmes focusing on basic management skills and foreign-language skills. In recent years some local Chinese professional training companies have also emerged, and they provide the same kind of training service.

Nonetheless, there are some problems with outsourcing training. To begin with, outsourcing training is primarily used for training in general techniques such as team-building, communication and basic clerical skills, not for training in the knowledge and skills specifically needed in a company. It is, therefore, very difficult to incorporate a company's business policies, objectives and practices into the training programmes offered by professional training firms. Due to the intensifying competition in China, moreover, professional training firms are now forced to cut their prices at the expense of quality, and therefore find it difficult to provide satisfactory training services to their clients. If a TNC has multiple affiliates throughout China, furthermore, the cost of flying its staff to the training centres of professional training firms is very high. As a result, outsourcing training is popular mainly with smaller TNCs, which cannot afford to offer well-organized in-house training programmes themselves, and not with the larger companies.

A third training option is overseas training – the sending of employees on training programmes conducted overseas. Both in-house training and out-sourcing training are conducted within China and, therefore, are unable to provide trainees with a deep understanding of Western business culture in general and the parent company's corporate culture in particular. To overcome this shortcoming, many TNCs send the staff recruited in China to their corporate headquarters or regional centres to attend training courses, or send them on training programmes offered by an overseas university. It is overseas training that proves to be the most effective way of familiarizing Chinese trainees with the attitudes and habits that constitute Western business culture and practice, thus transforming them into senior-level managers of international calibre.

The great risk with overseas training, however, is that of losing valuable trainees after the training programme is over. Some Chinese trainees may choose either not to return to China after completing their training or to leave the company for a better-paid job offered by another company immediately after they return to the country. TNCs offering overseas training programmes need, therefore, to design these programmes carefully and devise after-training plans so as to retain their Chinese trainees. They may, for instance, help the trainees establish a clear vision as to how they can advance their careers within the company after training, or use bond and reward packages to prevent trainees from leaving the company. The experience of HSBC (Hongkong and Shanghai Banking Corporation), a very large international bank based in the United Kingdom, helps to dramatize this point. HSBC has established nine branches in China.[3] HSBC China sends its new local managers to its headquarter in the United Kingdom to attend ten weeks of training, with follow-up training in its regional centre in Hong Kong over a three-year period. To prevent these trainees from leaving, HSBC gives them bonuses and commercial benefits after they have completed the training programme and returned to China. As these overseas training programmes and C&B packages are very costly, however, they are offered only to senior Chinese managers or high-potential Chinese staff.

A fourth training option is to send local employees to MBA programmes run inside China. These Chinese employees can do an MBA degree on either a full-time or a part-time basis, and TNCs cover the tuition fees for them on the basis of a mutually agreed contract. This training option is normally less costly than overseas training, but it cannot offer the kind of immersion in Western business culture that overseas training can. Furthermore, MBA programmes offered in China are generally not up to international standards. The majority of teaching faculties in Chinese business schools do not speak English and have no background in Western education. Moreover, the teaching methods have not been updated; unlike MBA programmes in the West, for instance, those in China do not offer sufficient hands-on class assignments, internships with companies or joint research initiatives with companies. Nevertheless, foreign educational institutions have already begun to get involved with MBA education in China, and the quality of MBA programmes offered within the country is expected to improve in the future.[4]

Retention through intangibles

Although two companies may offer the same C&B package and the same training and career development opportunities, employees in one company may still leave for the other, which has much to do with so-called 'intangibles'. Although intangibles are difficult to define, they are primarily related to the ways by which employees and businesses are managed in a company. Management styles that make employees feel comfortable and contented increase the commitment of employees to the company and thus help to retain them, while management styles that make employees feel uncomfortable and unhappy disappoint employees and thus motivate them to leave.

In theory, there are many 'intangible' ways by which TNCs can increase their employees' commitment. A recent survey conducted by Watson Wyatt in China suggests that five factors are most closely linked to an employee's level of commitment to the company (Leininger, 2004). The level of commitment is found to be high if the company communicates clearly with employees about its business plans and objectives, and the steps and procedures to achieve these plans and objectives; if the company makes its employees feel that their work is meaningful, thereby giving them a sense of satisfaction and accomplishment from their work; if the company offers inspired leadership; if the company creates clear, objective performance-based reward programmes; and if the company provides a safe, healthy working environment.

A key to achieve retention through the use of intangibles is to understand Chinese culture and the Chinese way of thinking. For instance, Chinese employees value the relationship with their bosses rather more than employees in other countries do. As far as retention is concerned, therefore, Chinese employees tend to think that a good relationship with their boss is more important than a good C&B package or good training and career development opportunities. As one human resource manager in a large US company in China said in an interview, 'The personal relationship of the manager and employee is very important. The sense of loyalty is to the person – the company is nothing, it's a building. You need to move beyond work, to family. You have to invest some time in getting to know your employees' (Melvin, 2001, P. 7). It is reported that the reason most Chinese employees leave a company is because they lose confidence or interest in their boss. This highlights the fact that an understanding of Chinese culture and the Chinese way of thinking is integral to retention; this is discussed further in the section on expatriate training.

As shown in the above discussion, there are a variety of tools for retaining talented Chinese employees. These retention tools are closely related to each other, and should not be used in isolation; TNCs need to adopt a holistic approach to retention. No matter how hard TNCs may try, however, it is necessarily difficult, if not impossible, to make all Chinese employees equally happy and retain each and every one of them. TNCs therefore need to distinguish between different types of employees, and target those who are most talented and most needed in the company.

Managing expatriates

Despite the trend towards staffing localization, many transnational corporations in China continue to keep a number of expatriate managers, as expatriate managers still play a role that local Chinese managers cannot. TNCs consider an expatriate manager to be a representative of their corporate culture and management know-how, for instance, and thus take an expatriate manager as 'one of their own' in China. It is believed that expatriate managers can help transfer the corporate culture and management know-how from a parent company to its affiliates in China. Moreover, expatriate managers can help avoid the formation of 'little kingdoms' within the company in the staffing localization process, and therefore they play a key role in the integration of a parent company with its affiliates in China. Accordingly, it is essential for TNCs to fill some key management positions with expatriates. Given the high rate of expatriate failure, however, expatriate management is a daunting challenge for companies operating in China.

Expatriate failure

In the current literature, 'expatriate failure' is defined as the premature return of an expatriate manager to his or her home country on account of a failure to adapt to the host country. Cross-country evidence shows that the expatriate failure rate is very high. According to Jeffrey Shay and Tracey Bruce (1997), for example, the expatriate failure rate ranged from 16 per cent to 40 per cent for all American employees sent to developed countries, and rose to 70 per cent for all American employees sent to developing countries. Moreover, expatriate failure wrought huge damage on the parent companies. It has been estimated, for instance, that the average cost of an expatriate failure to a parent company is as high as three times the expatriate's annual salary plus reallocation expenses, running between $250,000 and $1 million (see Harvey, 1983, and Caudron, 1991).

As a matter of fact, the expatriate failure rate does not reflect the true degree of frustration experienced by expatriates in host countries. Expatriates may, for instance, perform poorly in their job even though they do not return early from their assignment. It was estimated that about 30 to 50 per cent of American expatriates stayed at their post but performed ineffectively or marginally effectively (Black, Mendenhal and Oddov, 1991). Strictly speaking, therefore, expatriate failure should include expatriate inefficiency as well, and should be defined as the premature return of an expatriate manager to his or her home country and/or the ineffective performance of an expatriate manager in his/her job due to a failure to adapt to the host country.

There are many reasons for expatriate failure, and the reasons vary in line with the nationality of the expatriates. According to a seminal study by Rosalie Tung (1982), for example, the top five reasons for the failure of American expatriates were, in order of importance, (1) the inability of the spouse to adjust, (2) the manager's own inability to adjust, (3) other family problems, (4) the manager's personal or emotional immaturity and (5) an inability to cope with wider overseas responsibility. By contrast, the top five reasons for the failure of Japanese expatriates were (1) an inability to cope with larger overseas responsibility, (2) difficulties with the new environment, (3) personal or emotional problems, (4) a lack of technical competence and (5) the inability of the spouse to adjust. As for European expatriates, the single most important reason for expatriate failure was the inability of the spouse to adjust to a new environment. Despite this variation between nationalities, recent cross-country studies have confirmed the three most fundamental reasons for expatriate failure as the inability of a spouse to adjust, the inability of the manager to adjust and other family problems. These three reasons together accounted for at least 60 per cent of all expatriate failures.

The empirical findings thus point to the importance of adjustment to the working and living environment in a host country on the part of expatriates and their families. As might be expected, the larger the cultural difference between the home country and the host country the greater the possibility of expatriate failure. It does not come as a surprise, therefore, that China is among the top countries where Western expatriates are most likely to suffer from failure. As shown in the case of an American expatriate in China (box 9.3), the huge cultural difference between the West and China poses a severe challenge to Western expatriate managers and their families in the country. Expatriate management should therefore focus on the careful selection of expatriates and a high level of preparation for their China mission.

Selecting expatriates

To reduce the expatriate failure rates, in the first place TNCs need to select the right candidates for expatriate positions and screen out inappropriate candidates. The reasons for expatriate failure discussed above shed light on how to select candidates for expatriate positions. As the main reasons boil down to an inability to adjust to the working and living environment overseas, the selection of candidates for expatriate positions should focus on the ability of these candidates to live and manage operations in different cultural settings overseas. Unfortunately, however, many TNCs have tended to select candidates for expatriate positions only on the basis of their performance within the parent company at home. A manager who performs well in a domestic setting may not necessarily have the potential to perform well in an overseas setting. In selecting expatriate candidates, therefore, TNCs should take into account the main reasons for expatriate failure, and use the relevant criteria accordingly. Four criteria have been found to be the most helpful in predicting the success or failure of expatriates, and thus they can be used in the selection of expatriates for China (Mendenhall and Oddov, 1985).

The first is self-orientation, which refers to attributes that strengthen expatriates' self-esteem, self-confidence and psychological health. Specifically,

Box 9.3 The story of an American expatriate

Silk Road Communications, a US consulting company, has reported the case of the experiences of an American expatriate and his family in China.[5] According to the reports, a large American manufacturing company in the automobile parts industry established a plant in China, and had to send an operations manager from its headquarters in Chicago to the plant. Through an informal procedure with no standard tests, the company selected Tom, an American national who used to work at the French and British affiliates of the company, for the China mission. Tom left for China, together with his family, without any training prior to their departure.

After his arrival, Tom encountered many difficulties and problems in the country. He knew nothing about either the Chinese language or culture, and he had to communicate with Chinese employees through a translator. Tom often attended meetings at which Chinese staff talked in Chinese, and he was completely at a loss. The Chinese staff, including the translator, did not show him respect. Thirty minutes' discussion at a meeting was, for instance, translated to him in only thirty seconds; he knew intuitively that more had been said and decided upon, but he had not been informed of the rest. As an operations manager, Tom felt like 'the awkward foreigner who was propped up like a figurehead with no substantive use, no real role to play'. One day Tom asked a Chinese employee, Mr Jong, to send him a report about an incident by Monday. Monday came, but the report did not appear on his desk. Tom went over to ask Jong about the report, who asked in reply if it was important. Tom felt he had lost face in the plant.

Tom's wife and children also experienced frustrations in China. The plant was located in a small suburban town in an industrial area, where foreigners were few. Whenever they went out shopping to the local markets they were surrounded by huge crowds of Chinese. Chinese women were particularly interested in, and friendly to, Tom's little daughter, who, with her big blue eyes, looked like a porcelain doll. Chinese women would often come close to the baby, pick her up and pinch her cheeks, which terrified her. There were no other expatriate families around, and the whole family, particularly Tom's wife, felt very lonely, as she had nothing to do, and stayed at home the whole day waiting for her husband to come home from work. She was disappointed and disillusioned.

After four months in China Tom and his family returned to the United States, to attend an intensive training course in Chinese culture and society for two weeks. Through the training Tom learnt a lot about how to work with Chinese. He realized, for instance, that the Chinese will only care about someone to the extent that that person cares about them. As a manager, he should show care for his Chinese employees and should be more interested in their well-being, and in so doing he would establish a good relationship with the Chinese employees and gain respect and face in the plant. Most importantly, Tom decided to start learning the Chinese language immediately on his return to China, not because he wanted to become an expert in the language but because he wanted to show his Chinese colleagues that he cared about the culture in which they live! Tom and his family returned to China in July 2002, and they have been well adjusted to life there ever since.

self-orientation's attributes include 'reinforcement substitution' – that is, the ability to replace activities that bring pleasure and happiness in the home country with similar activities in host countries. They also include 'stress reduction' – that is, the ability to deal with and reduce stress in different circumstances. Furthermore, the attributes include 'technical competence' – the ability and professional expertise needed for the overseas assignment. Candidates with strong self-orientation are, therefore, expected not only to be technically competent for overseas assignment but also able to adapt their interests and hobbies in the host countries so as to reduce stress.

The second criterion is other-orientation, which refers to attributes that enhance expatriates' ability to interact and communicate effectively with host-country nationals. Other-orientation's attributes include 'relationship development' – that is, the ability to develop and maintain long-term friendships with host-country nationals. Given the importance of *guanxi* in Chinese culture, as analysed in chapter 3, relationship development is more important in China than in many other parts of the world. Other-orientation's attributes also include 'willingness to communicate' – the ability and willingness to communicate with host-country nationals. Knowing the host-country language will, obviously enhance the ability to communicate with host-country nationals. It is always important for expatriate candidates to show an interest in learning the host-country language, and the Chinese are particularly keen to work with foreigners who are willing to learn Chinese.

The third criterion is perceptual ability, which consists of the ability to understand why people in other cultural settings behave the way they do. This ability helps expatriates predict how host-country nationals will behave towards them, and thus helps them reduce their level of uncertainty in interacting with nationals. Expatriates who lack this ability tend to see the behaviour of host-country nationals with a perceptual framework formed at home and evaluate the behaviour accordingly, which can often lead to conflicts with nationals. The argument goes, therefore, that well-adjusted expatriates with perceptual ability should be non-judgemental and non-evaluative in interpreting the behaviour of host-country nationals, and should make liberal or less rigid assessments as to why these nationals behave as they do.

The fourth is cultural toughness, by which is meant the ability to adjust to a particularly difficult cultural setting overseas. There are vast cultural differences between the countries of the world, and expatriates may consider some cultural settings as being tougher than others. Expatriates from the

United States may feel, for instance, that the cultural settings in Africa, South Asia and Middle East are much tougher than those in the United Kingdom, Australia and New Zealand, while expatriates from Japan may feel that the cultural settings in South Korea and China and other Asian countries that it has invaded in the past are much more demanding than those in other parts of the world because of the persistence of strong anti-Japanese sentiments. In selecting candidates for expatriate positions, therefore, attention should be given to evaluating their ability to handle especially tough cultural settings for their overseas posting.

The four criteria are closely related to each other, and should not be used in isolation. A variety of standard psychological tests can be used to assess the self-orientation, other-orientation and perceptual ability of a candidate in the selection process, while specifically designed comparative cultural analysis can be used to assess whether a candidate has the ability to adjust to a particularly tough cultural setting in which he or she is going to work. Unfortunately, to date very few TNCs have taken these psychological tests and cultural analyses seriously in selecting expatriates. It has been estimated, for example, that only some 10 per cent of Fortune 500 companies have asked candidates for expatriate positions to take psychological tests. The lack of an appropriate selection approach has doubtlessly contributed to the high expatriate failure rates illustrated above. To reduce such failure rates in China, therefore, it is incumbent upon TNCs to improve their selection processs for picking qualified expatriate candidates for their Chinese operations. In addition, they need to amend the general selection criteria discussed above to make them more suitable to the Chinese cultural setting. With regard to self-orientation, for example, attention should be paid to the ability to adjust to activities and hobbies that are popular in Chinese society. In assessing other-orientation, the focus should be on the ability of expatriate candidates to interact and communicate with Chinese, and their willingness to learn their language. In terms of perceptual ability, emphasis needs to be placed on the ability to empathize with the Chinese people. As for cultural toughness, the sensitivity of expatriate candidates to the particularities of Chinese culture has to be taken into consideration.

In reality, of course, it is very hard for TNCs to find expatriate candidates who are both qualified and willing to go to China, and they have to make do with whomever they can get. This shortage of appropriate candidates explains why strict selection procedures have not been widely used in choosing expatriates to go to China, and underlines just how important it is that the selected expatriates receive proper training.

Training expatriates

As with selecting expatriates, training them should also take into account the main reasons for expatriate failure. An inability on the part of both expatriate managers and their families to adjust to the host-country environment is the root cause for expatriate failure, so training programmes ought to involve the family members as well as the senior officials, and focus on strengthening their ability to work and live in the environment of the host country – China in our case. This kind of training can cover a wide range of areas, but definitely needs to include two of the most important components: cultural training and practical training.

Cultural training is intended to strengthen the ability of expatriate managers and their family to find out about Chinese culture, and help them understand why Chinese behave the way they do. The key elements of Chinese culture, such as the concepts of face, harmony and conflict avoidance, respect for age and seniority, *guanxi* and collectivism, should be included in the cultural training, as should practical approaches to dealing with them appropriately in workplace and social settings. The Chinese are very keen on keeping face, for instance, which expatriate managers should take into account in managing Chinese employees in the workplace. Some expatriate managers have been reported as often criticizing their Chinese subordinates in public, leading inevitably to conflicts with Chinese employees. As David Ahlstrom, Garry Bruton and Eunice Chan (2001, p. 63) note, '[Expatriate] managers must be careful not to reprove [Chinese] subordinates or colleagues publicly. If this is done in the presence of others, it can cause that person to lose face and may harm the internal management process. If a subordinate must be criticized, it is better to discreetly take him aside to explain the problem.' If expatriate managers do as Ahlstrom, Bruton and Chan suggest, they will not only achieve better results but also win respect from their Chinese employees. It should be noted that this approach does not necessarily apply to Chinese employees at all times. To a Chinese employee who does not care about face and makes mistakes intentionally and repeatedly, for example, reproving in public is appropriate and necessary. In the cultural training programme, therefore, expatriate managers need to absorb thoroughly the concept of face, and the different ways to deal with face-sensitive Chinese employees.

In addition, the Chinese place a great deal of emphasis on interpersonal relationships, and treasure a good relationship with their boss, colleagues and friends. Even in the workplace, as mentioned in the section on retention through intangibles, Chinese take the relationship with their boss much more seriously than Westerners. As noted by a Chinese female employee who has worked for several transnational corporations in China for years, 'Foreigners are very concerned about their work. Chinese people are more concerned about their relations with their boss and their colleagues. At work, foreigners only think about their job' (Melvin and Sylvester, 1997, p. 34). Expatriate managers should, therefore, try to understand this cultural difference, and pay more attention to people than work, talk to Chinese employees in a friendly fashion, take part with them in social activities organized by the company and visit them as friends from time to time. A people-oriented management style is most welcome in the Chinese cultural setting, and should be the focus of any cultural training programme.

Although it is important for expatriate managers to learn about Chinese culture, it is not advisable that expatriate managers should passively adapt to all Chinese cultural traditions. With the cultural tradition of respect for age and seniority, for instance, Chinese employees tend to be over-compliant and respond only to whatever their boss says; in other words, they do not take the initiative as actively or as often as their Western counterparts. While trying to understand the cultural roots of this over-compliant behaviour, expatriate managers should encourage Chinese employees to take the initiative at work and teach them how to do so. A further complication is that the collectivist orientation of Chinese culture emphasizes a group structure with appointed team leaders, and does not really encourage individuals in the group to take the initiative at work independently, let alone collaboratively. This boss-led collectivism is different from the kind of self-directed teamwork found in Western society, in which individual employees themselves are responsible for managing their team and for making decisions about their work. While trying to understand why Chinese employees are accustomed to boss-led teamwork, expatriate managers need to encourage them to learn about self-directed teamwork. Expatriate managers in Motorola (China), for example, have introduced Western-style teamwork in their operations, and 80 to 90 per cent of all their Chinese employees now work in self-directed teams. In cultural training programmes, therefore, expatriate managers need to learn that cultural adjustment is an interactive process that demands movement from both sides.

Another important aspect of cultural training is learning about the Chinese language. Language is the most effective tool of communication, and in a cross-cultural setting communication via the same language will necessarily have a great effect in enhancing mutual understanding between people with different cultural backgrounds. Evidence shows that expatriate managers who know the language achieve better results in China than those who do not. As shown in the story of Tom (see box 9.3), ignorance of the Chinese language can have a disastrous impact on the performance of an expatriate manager in China. In the cultural training programme, therefore, expatriate managers and their families should be taught the importance of learning Chinese. Although it may well be difficult for them to learn to speak the language fluently, it is important that they at least display a willingness to do so. On many occasions, even the use of just a few basic Chinese terms has helped expatriates work well with their local employees.

The other important component in any expatriate training programme is practical training, which refers to training in the basic knowledge of how to live in China. As shown with Tom's story, expatriate managers and their families can encounter many difficulties in their daily life in China. Practical training is designed to help them learn how to ease themselves into the day-to-day life of Chinese society. Expatriate managers and their families need, for instance, to learn what the Chinese normally do to relax in their spare time, and try to adjust their after-work activities and hobbies to Chinese practices. They need to learn about the Chinese education system, and find out where to send their children for schooling. They need to know the way the Chinese behave towards foreigners, and the appropriate approaches to dealing with it. They need to find out how the neighbourhood community works, and how neighbours communicate with each other. Most importantly, they need to find out how to get in touch with other expatriate managers and their families living in the same locality or in other parts of China. Expatriate communities can provide a support network of friends with a similar background, through which they can share information and experiences, and thereby help expatriate managers and their families to adapt to Chinese culture and society more quickly.

All these kinds of cultural training and practical training are essential to enable expatriate managers and their families to work and live productively and harmoniously in the Chinese cultural environment, and need to be implemented, whether it is before the expatriates leave for China or after they have arrived there. Despite the evident usefulness of this kind of training, however, most TNCs operating in China have provided little, if any. These untrained expatriate managers and their families have suffered frustrations both at the workplace and in society at large, as Tom's story demonstrates. In the end, they have to go through a training process in one way or another, sometimes at a high price.

Summary

Managing human resources in an international setting differs significantly from managing human resources at home, and confronts many new challenges. Entering the Chinese market, for instance, a TNC needs to learn how to recruit staff for its Chinese affiliates, how to retain talented locals and how to manage expatriates from the parent company. These issues are discussed in this chapter, with reference both to theoretical frameworks developed in the field of international business studies and to the practical experiences of TNCs operating in the country.

At first, TNCs adopted an ethnocentric staffing strategy in China, with all their employees being home-country nationals. In the face of intensified competition, however, they began to shift away from this policy and recruit locals for senior management positions. Staffing localization triggered a war for local talent, and TNCs had to make use of all available channels to look for qualified Chinese employees in the country.

TNCs also need to work hard to retain their talented Chinese recruits; otherwise, they will go elsewhere. While the standard retention tools, such as compensation and benefits packages and training and career development, are effective in the country, retention through intangibles is especially important in the Chinese cultural context. TNCs need to learn how to improve their management styles in order to increase the commitment of Chinese employees to the company. To that end, a thorough understanding of Chinese culture and the Chinese way of thinking is essential.

Despite the trend towards staffing localization, expatriate managers still have a role to play that cannot be played by local managers, and therefore they maintain a considerable presence in foreign affiliates in China. To reduce expatriate failure rates, TNCs need to be more careful in how they select candidates for expatriate positions in China, and it is imperative that they provide them and their families with the appropriate cultural and practical training, be it before their departure for China or after their arrival in the country.

FURTHER READING

Bruton, G. D., Ahlstrom, D., and Chan, E. S. 2000. 'Foreign firms in China: facing human resources challenges in a transitional economy'. *S. A. M. Advanced Management Journal* 65 (4): 4–36.

Gamble, J. 2000. 'Localizing management in foreign invested enterprises in China: practical, cultural, and strategic perspectives'. *International Journal of Human Resource Management* 11 (5): 883–903.

Leininger, J. 2004. 'The key to retention: committed employees'. *China Business Review* 31 (1): 16–39.

Shen, J., and Edwards, V. 2004. 'Recruitment and selection in Chinese MNEs'. *International Journal of Human Resource Management* 15 (5): 814–35.

Questions for discussion

1. Discuss the advantages and disadvantages of ethnocentric staffing, polycentric staffing and geocentric staffing.
2. Why did TNCs move away from ethnocentric staffing and begin to recruit locals for senior management positions in China? What are the main challenges faced by TNCs in staff localization? Relate your answer to the specific market conditions in China.
3. What are the main tools that have been used by TNCs in China to retain their talented local employees? What is meant by retention through intangibles, and how can local employees be retained through intangibles in the Chinese cultural context?
4. What are the main reasons for expatriate failure? What can TNCs do to reduce expatriate failure rates in China? What should TNCs focus on in selecting and training expatriates in the Chinese context?

NOTES

1. See Li (2000, p. 1).
2. For the details, see Song (2000).
3. HSBC's nine branches are located in Beijing, Shanghai, Tianjin, Guangzhou, Qingdao, Wuhan, Shenzhen, Xiamen and Dalian, respectively.
4. For example, the first joint business school, the China Europe International Business School (CEIBS), was established in Shanghai in 1994.
5. For the details of the case, see http://www.silkrc.com/Services/cases/toc_cases.htm.

The protection of intellectual property rights

Despite China's achievements in developing a comprehensive body of laws on intellectual property rights (IPR), effective IPR enforcement in China remains a serious problem . [. . .] These weaknesses mean that in the near term, foreign companies will continue to encounter trademark, copyright, patent, and trade-secret infringements in virtually every sector (Ann M. Weeks (2000, p. 28)).

The infringement of intellectual property rights is a very serious problem in China. Although the government has made great efforts to comply with the WTO regulations on intellectual property rights since accession in 2001, the enforcement of IPR laws and regulations remains ineffective in China even today. The protection of IPR is a daunting challenge to transnational corporations entering the Chinese market, particularly those with established brand names. In this chapter we discuss in section 1 the scale of the widespread IPR infringement in the country, and the reaction from the international community to the problem. In section 2 we discuss China's IPR regime, with a focus on the laws and regulations regarding IPR and the enforcement of these laws and regulations. In section 3 we analyse the shortcomings in the current Chinese IPR regime. In section 4 we discuss some practical measures that TNCs can take to protect their IPR in the face of the large-scale violation and ineffective IPR enforcement in the country.

Widespread infringement of IPR in China

Before China began its reform programme and opening up there was little IPR violation in the country. China was isolated from other parts of the world, and foreign brands were virtually unknown to the Chinese. Chinese firms were under public ownership, and had little incentive to make a profit by violating IPR; in fact, they had no incentive to make a profit at all. With the launch of the reform programme, however, foreign brands moved into China, and private firms and township and village enterprises (TVEs) emerged. These private firms and TVEs had strong incentives to make quick profits, which they could achieve through counterfeiting internationally famous brand names that were well received by Chinese customers. In the meantime, counterfeiters from Hong Kong, Macao and Taiwan began to move into China, bringing with them advanced counterfeiting technologies (Clark, 2000). The counterfeiters then made use of the advanced foreign technologies and the cheap Chinese labour force to produce high-quality counterfeits on a large scale at low price, making counterfeits very appealing to customers both in China and abroad.

Consequently, the infringement of intellectual property rights became increasingly common in the country, and counterfeits produced in China were sold in large quantities domestically and on international markets. Although it is very difficult to estimate the scale of the infringement, anecdotal evidence suggests that China ranks first in the world in IPR infringement. In terms of domestic sales of counterfeits, according to the Business Software Alliance (2003) the piracy rate of software was above 90 per cent in China from 1994 to 2002. According to a report written by the Development and Research Center (DRC) of China's State Council, the value of counterfeits amounted to $16 billion in the early 2000s, and 80 per cent of domestic and foreign firms were badly affected by counterfeiting (Trainer, 2002). In terms of exports of counterfeits, according to the US Customs Service China held the top spot in seized counterfeits in the United States in recent years, with the Chinese share in total seized counterfeits increasing year by year. In 2000, 2001, 2002, 2003 and 2004 China accounted for 33 per cent, 46 per cent, 49 per cent, 66 per cent and 67 per cent of the total counterfeits seized by the US Customs, respectively.[1] In Europe, according to the European Union, China also ranked first in seized counterfeits, accounting for 60 per cent of the total seized counterfeits in Europe in 2003. According to the International Anticounterfeiting Coalition (IACC), China was the top source of counterfeits exported to Japan in recent years, too (IACC, 2005). The US Trade Representative estimates that the overall level of IPR infringement in China has now reached '90 per cent or above for virtually every form of intellectual property' (United States Trade Representative, 2005, p. 3).

IPR infringement has done tremendous damage to TNCs, particularly those operating in China. According to William Lash, US Assistant Secretary of

Commerce, the total cost to foreign companies in China from the various forms of IPR infringement runs at about $20 to 25 billion annually (Kynge, 2003). According to the US Trade Representative (2005, p. 3), total 'US losses due to piracy of copyrighted materials alone range between $2.5 billion and $3.8 billion annually'. The international community, therefore, has urged China to strengthen its protection of IPR, and the United States and the WTO have played a key role in this respect.

The United States has negotiated with China on IPR since 1979, when the two countries signed an Agreement on Trade Relations. Article VI of the agreement requires China to implement patent, trademark and copyright protection in a way at least equivalent to that offered by the United States. Dissatisfied with the slow progress that China was making in promulgating laws and regulations on IPR, the United States threatened massive trade sanctions against China under section 301 of the US Trade Act 1974, which allows the US Trade Representative to identify countries with inadequate intellectual property protection and impose sanctions if necessary. Under this pressure, China signed a memorandum of understanding on IPR protection with the United States in 1992, narrowly avoiding an outright trade war between the two countries. Within two years, however, the United States was again frustrated by the rampant IPR violation in China. Tension between the two on IPR issues escalated and both sides threatened massive trade sanctions against each other. To avert the imminent trade war, a second MOU on IPR protection was signed in 1995, which urged China to 'improve the enforcement structure'.

The World Trade Organization has played an even more important role than the United States in urging China to strengthen its IPR protection, because it represents virtually all nations, being a multilateral trading body, rather than any single nation. From 1986 onwards China began to apply for WTO membership; in the negotiation process, the WTO required China to sign the Agreement on Trade-Related Aspects of Intellectual Property Rights (TRIPS) as a precondition for accession. TRIPS specifies various aspects of IPR protection, and sets the standard requirements for IPR protection in the member countries of the WTO (box 10.1). A study conducted by Keith E. Maskus (2002) for the World Bank on China's pre-WTO entry compliance with TRIPS identified twenty-two areas where the country fell short, suggesting that China needed to make substantial legislative changes to comply with the TRIPS norms. Under pressure from the WTO, China made efforts to improve its protection of IPR in order to comply with the TRIPS standards, and in 2001 signed the TRIPS Agreement and joined the WTO.

Box 10.1 The Agreement on Trade-Related Aspects of Intellectual Property Rights

TRIPS is the official document of the World Trade Organization on intellectual property rights, designed to unify IPR protection standards across member countries in order to resolve the problem of ineffective enforcement of intellectual property rights, which 'can encourage trade in counterfeit and pirated goods, thereby damaging the legitimate commercial interests of manufacturers who hold or have acquired those rights' (TRIPS, p. 1).

TRIPS consists of seventy-three articles, covering seven major areas of IPR: patents, copyrights and related rights, trademarks, industrial designs, the layout designs of integrated circuits, undisclosed information and geographical indications. TRIPS sets minimum standards for IPR protection in these seven areas, minimum standards for IPR enforcement in administrative and civil actions, and minimum standards for IPR enforcement in criminal actions and actions at international borders. These minimum standards are built on the existing international conventions on IPR.

In addition, TRIPS requires that a WTO member country should provide national and most favoured nation (MFN) treatment to the nationals of other WTO member countries in relation to IPR protection and enforcement. In order to ensure that IPR holders do not abuse the exclusive rights given to them, TRIPS sets a number of limitations and exceptions regarding IPR protection. TRIPS also specifies the procedures for consultation between governments in relation to IPR infringement disputes. Furthermore, TRIPS offers less developed countries a transitional period of five years during which they can bring their IPR legislation in conformity with the provisions of TRIPS; for least developed countries, the transitional period is eleven years.

TRIPS thus establishes a framework for IPR protection at the international level. All member countries in the WTO have to comply with the IPR standards specified in TRIPS. Any non-member countries that want to join the WTO have to sign the TRIPS Agreement, and promise to comply with it after accession.

It is argued that external pressure is a necessary, but not a sufficient, condition for establishing a sustainable IPR regime. In the light of the experience of other Asian countries in intellectual property protection, particularly Japan and South Korea, Warren H. Maruyama (1999) proposes a three-phase model for the development of a sustainable IPR regime. In the first phase, formal IPR laws and regulations are issued and improved following external pressure from the United States. In the second phase, a stopgap form of enforcement is strengthened following US pressure. In the third phase, thanks to the development of indigenous technologies, IPR agreements become self-sustaining and genuine rules of law begin to emerge following internal pressure from indigenous IPR holders. It seems that China has experienced the first two phases and is now moving towards the third phase, as evidenced by the emerging IPR lawsuits involving indigenous plaintiffs in China.[2] Unlike Japan and South Korea, however, where Western-style democratic institutions are long established, China has not made much progress towards setting up such institutions. Consequently, the transition to sustainable IPR protection may be something of a 'long march' for China, and TNCs need to find out how to protect their intellectual property in the context of the imperfect IPR regime there.

China's IPR regime

China did not have a proper legal framework, let alone an effective enforcement system, for IPR protection until the early 1980s, when its opening up to the outside world began in earnest. In the face of the widespread violation of intellectual property rights and growing pressure from the international community, the Chinese government then began to take positive action to strengthen IPR protection. There is no denying that China has made significant progress in establishing an effective IPR regime in the past two decades or so. Generally speaking, the current regime can essentially be broken down into legislation on IPR, the judicial enforcement of IPR and the administrative enforcement of IPR.

Legislation on IPR

After signing the China–US Agreement on Trade Relations in 1979, the government began to draft laws and regulations on intellectual property rights. In 1982 China promulgated its first IPR law – the Trademark Law. Since then China has passed numerous laws and regulations on IPR issues, as shown in table 10.1. Since 1999, in particular, China has undertaken a massive review of its IPR laws and regulations, amending the previous statutes and introducing new ones, in order to comply with the obligations associated with WTO entry. According to the White Paper on the Intellectual Property Rights Protection in China, '[A] total of 26 regulations and documents, which were not in accordance with the rules of WTO, were revised or cancelled' in 2003.[3]

Currently, China has a complete set of laws and regulations dealing with IPR. These laws and regulations cover almost all aspects of intellectual property rights and are basically in line with TRIPS under the WTO. There are still some shortcomings in Chinese IPR legislation, but the major problem is admitted to be in the enforcement of the laws and regulations. As the United

Table 10.1 Legislation on IPR in China

Legislation	Date
Trademark Law	1982, amended 1993 and 2001
Patent Law	1984, amended 2001
General Principles of Civil Law	1986
Copyright Law	1990, amended 2001
Regulations on Computer Software Protection	1991, amended 2002
Provisions on the Implementation of the International Copyright Treaty	1992
Provisions on Penalizing the Crimes of Counterfeiting Registered Trademarks	1993
Law on Prevention of Unfair Competition	1993
Decisions on Penalizing the Crimes of Infringing Copyright	1994
Regulations on IPR Border Protection	1997
Decisions on Safeguarding of Security on the Internet	2000
Implementing Regulations of the Patent Law	2001
Layout Designs of Integrated Circuits Protection Regulations (IC Regulations)	2001
Implementing Rules of the IC Regulations	2001
Regulations on Publications	2002
Regulations on Motion Pictures	2002
Regulations on Sound and Video Recordings	2002
Regulations on Administration of Imports or Exports of Technologies	2002
Rules on Registration of Technology Import or Export Contracts	2002
Rules on Technologies Prohibited or Restricted from Importation	2002
Rules on Technologies Prohibited or Restricted from Exportation	2002
Implementing Regulations of the Copyright Law	2002
Implementing Regulations of the Trademark Law	2002
Rules on the Determination and Protection of Well-Known Trademarks	2003
Measures on the Implementation of the Madrid Agreement on Trademark International Registration	2003
Measures on the Registration and Administration of Collective Trademarks and Certification Marks	2003
Measures on the Implementation of Administrative Penalties in Copyright Cases	2003
Regulation on the Customs Protection of IPR	2003
Judicial Interpretation	2004

States Trade Representative (2003, p. 3) has pointed out, 'China's WTO accession, and the concomitant entry into force of its intellectual property rights obligations, have resulted in improvements in China's statutory system for the protection of intellectual property. However, significant concerns remain, particularly with respect to enforcement of IPR.' The Chinese government also acknowledges the problem. Lianyuan Ma, deputy director of the State Intellectual Property Office of China, has stated clearly: 'China's intellectual property rights (statutory) system has basically met the standards required by the Agreement on Trade-Related Aspects of Intellectual Property Rights (TRIPS) . . . and China will shift from its previous focus on IPR legislation to law enforcement and supervision' (anonymous, 2002). The enforcement of IPR laws and regulations is not completely unrelated to the IPR legislative system, however, as is shown in section 3.

The enforcement of IPR laws and regulations is carried out through two routes or tracks in China: the judicial enforcement route and the administrative enforcement route. The victims of IPR infringement can bring the wrongdoers to justice through either route, or both. It is crucial for TNCs to know how the two enforcement routes work, and how to proceed to present an infringement case to the two sets of enforcement authorities in China.

Judicial enforcement of IPR

When an IPR infringement dispute arises the infringed party may launch a lawsuit against the infringing party at the special IPR tribunals of the courts in China. China's court structure consists of four tiers: the Basic People's Court at the district level, the Intermediate People's Court at the city and prefecture level, the Higher People's Court at the provincial level and the Supreme People's Court at the national level. As is in other large countries, such as the United States, IPR lawsuits are mainly handled at the local level in China. From 1993 onwards China began to set up special IPR tribunals in the Intermediate People's Courts and the Higher People's Courts in major cities and provinces. Therefore, the infringed party can bring a lawsuit against the infringer to the special IPR tribunal of the Intermediate People's Court, or the special IPR tribunal of the Higher People's Court, either where the infringer is domiciled or where the act of infringement took place.

According to Chinese laws and regulations, the judicial enforcement route applies only to serious cases of IPR infringement. Once a lawsuit has been handed to a special IPR tribunal, the case has to be dealt with seriously in accordance with strict judicial procedures (figure 10.1). As IPR cases are often

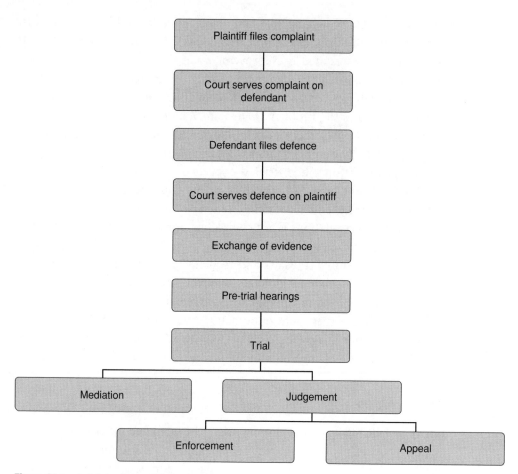

Figure 10.1   Judicial enforcement step by step
Source: Clark (2004).

rather involved, the special IPR tribunal normally requires a plaintiff to provide substantive evidence. To win a lawsuit, the infringed party needs to prepare the evidence very carefully beforehand, including evidence as to the identity of the infringer, evidence as to the infringement action and evidence as to the damage done by the infringement to the plaintiff. The painstaking and meticulous collection of evidence is absolutely essential if a plaintiff is to win an IPR infringement case through the judicial enforcement route.

As judicial enforcement takes time, the infringed party may request the special IPR tribunal to freeze the assets of the infringer before instituting legal proceedings if the situation is deemed to be an emergency, particularly when any delay in stopping the act of infringement may cause irreparable damage to the IPR holder. According to China's legislation, IPR infringers should bear civil liabilities, or criminal liabilities if the case is serious enough

Table 10.2 Administrative IPR enforcement authorities and their responsibilities

Administrative authority	IPR responsibility
The Trademark Office (under the State Administration of Industry and Commerce)	Trademark infringement disputes
The Intellectual Property Office	Patent infringement disputes
The Copyright Administration	Copyright infringement disputes
The Fair Trade Bureau (under the State Administration of Industry and Commerce)	Trade secret infringement disputes and other IPR issues covered by the Law to Counter Unfair Competition
Quality and Technical Supervision Bureau	Patent and trademark infringement disputes involving product quality and human health concerns
The General Administration of Customs	Issues related to exports/imports of fake products

to constitute a crime. The punishment may include a fine, detention or fixed-term of imprisonment of up to seven years.

Administrative enforcement of IPR

When an IPR infringement dispute arises, the infringed party may also bring the case to the administrative authorities at county level and above at the place of the infringer's domicile or where the infringing act took place. There are a number of administrative authorities dealing with IPR infringement issues, but six are most important: the Trademark Office, the Intellectual Property Office, the Copyright Administration, the Fair Trade Bureau, the Quality and Technical Supervision Bureau and the General Administration of Customs. Each of these administrative authorities is responsible for a specific type of IPR infringement, as shown in table 10.2.

To request these authorities to handle an infringement dispute, the infringed party needs to submit a written letter of request, proof of his/her intellectual property right and evidence of the infringement. The administrative authorities are required to make a decision on whether the case will be processed within a limited period of time.[4] The administrative authorities are empowered to investigate the case, and they also have the power to order the infringer to stop all the acts of infringement, compensate for all the losses and pay a fine. Furthermore, they also have the power to confiscate and destroy the infringing products and remove the equipment of infringement. The compensation varies from one case to another. The compensation for copyright infringement, for example, is calculated on the basis of the direct damages caused by the infringement and the expenses spent by the IPR owner on the case. The compensation for trademark and patent infringement is calculated on the basis of the profits earned by the infringer or the damage suffered by the infringed party.

If the interested parties are dissatisfied with the administrative punishment, they may take the case to the People's Court in the place where the administrative authorities are located within three months of receipt of the notification of the decision. If the interested parties do appeal to the People's Court and yet refuse to carry out the decision, the administrative authorities may apply to the People's Court for compulsory execution. Alternatively, the interested parties may bring the case to the administrative authorities at a higher level for reconsideration. The higher-level authorities are required to make a decision on whether or not to handle the case within ten days. The reconsideration should be made within two months. If the interested parties are not satisfied with the reconsideration, they may take the case to the People's Court in the place where the higher-level administrative authorities are located within fifteen days of receipt of the notification of decision. If the interested parties do appeal to the People's Court but refuse to comply with the decision, the higher-level authorities may request the People's Court for a compulsory execution order.

Shortcomings in China's IPR regime

China has now established a basic legislative and enforcement framework by which infringed IPR holders may seek protection and bring the infringers to justice. To be sure, this represents significant progress in the right direction. To a large extent, however, the enforcement of the IPR laws and regulations is ineffective, and IPR infringement remains widespread in China even today. This is attributed to the perceived shortcomings in the current IPR regime, which are highlighted below.

Ambiguity in the legislation

Although China has promulgated a complete set of laws and regulations on IPR that are basically in line with the TRIPS standards in terms of the IPR areas covered, there are some ambiguities in these laws and regulations in connection with specific aspects of IPR protection issues. These ambiguities may lead to confusion and difficulty in enforcing these laws and regulations. According to China's Trademark Law, for instance, the use of a trademark that is the same as, or similar to, a registered trademark is considered a trademark infringement. The question is, however: how do you measure similarity? The

Trademark Law does not specify the criteria by which similarity is measured, which makes it very difficult to enforce the law in practice, as shown in the case of Toyota's lawsuit against a Chinese car maker in 2002 (box 10.2).

Box 10.2 Toyota's lawsuit

Toyota Motor Corporation, the well-known Japanese car maker, moved into China immediately after China opened up to foreign investors, establishing a representative office in Beijing in 1980 that subsequently developed into Toyota's headquarters in China. Toyota also established, in cooperation with Chinese partners, including the First Automotive Works Corporation and Guangzhou Automotive Works Corporation, a number of joint ventures to produce automobiles and provide automobile services across China. Toyota has now become the largest Japanese investor in the Chinese automobile industry, and one of the most successful foreign car makers in the country.

To prevent the infringement of its intellectual property, Toyota registered 'Toyota', its Chinese equivalent and the logo associated therewith as its trademarks in China, in 1980, 1989 and 1990, respectively. Then, in the late 1990s, Toyota found that its trademarks were being violated by a Chinese car maker based in Zhejiang province – the Geely Group. The cars manufactured by the Geely Group were marked with a logo similar to that of Toyota, and were equipped with engines with the same label (TTME 8A-FE) as that of the engines manufactured by Toyota's joint venture in Tianjin. In addition, the Geely Group used the name 'Toyota' in advertisements for its products, such as 'powered by Toyota', 'with Toyota 8A-FE engine manufactured by Toyota', and 'with Toyota 8A-FE engine from Japan'.

In December 2002 Toyota filed a lawsuit against the Geely Group, and two car dealers based in Beijing selling Geely's vehicles, for trademark infringement. The main dispute in this case was over whether the defendant's logo really was similar to the plaintiff's logo. The plaintiff claimed that the two logos were similar in structure and colour, and that customers had confused Geely's logo with Toyota's. A survey commissioned by Toyota indicated that 179 out of 289 surveyed customers believed that the products of the defendant were those of the plaintiff, and that 84 out of 129 surveyed customers thought that there was some relationship between the products of the two car makers. Toyota demanded the three defendants pay RMB 14 million in compensation.

However, despite the apparent similarities between the two logos, Toyota's claim was rejected by an Intermediate People's Court in Beijing in November 2003. According to article 52 of the revised Trademark Law, trademark infringement occurs if there is 'use of a trademark that is the same as or similar to a registered trademark on the same or similar goods without the permission of the trademark registrant'. The test of similarity is not clearly defined in the legislation, however, which makes it very difficult for the court to convict the defendant.

This case shows clearly how the ambiguities in the laws and regulations can hinder IPR enforcement. As Randall Peerenboom points out, legislation in China is often worded as broad policy statements rather than clear and easily applicable provisions.[5] Further efforts should be made to clarify Chinese laws and regulations on the infringement of intellectual property rights.[6]

According to China's Criminal Code, furthermore, an IPR infringer may be sentenced to imprisonment for three years if the circumstances are deemed to be 'serious' or the sales are deemed 'relatively large', and imprisonment for seven years if the circumstances are deemed 'especially serious' or the sales are deemed 'huge'. There were no clear definitions of the meaning of 'relatively large' and 'serious' until 2001, when the Chinese government issued prosecution guidelines to explain the criminalization standards of IPR infringement. These guidelines impose some standards and even numerical thresholds for criminalizing IPR infringement, but these standards and thresholds are still somewhat misleading (Trainer, 2002). As discussed below, the legislative confusion contributes to the weak judicial enforcement of IPR in China. China needs to improve its legislation on IPR further to make it more detailed, specified and straightforward to enforce.

Weak judicial enforcement

The government has relied overwhelmingly on administrative IPR enforcement, and judicial IPR enforcement is very weak in China. It is estimated that only a tiny fraction of the IPR infringement cases are currently dealt with through the judicial enforcement route. According to the White Paper on IPR protection released by the government in 2005, Chinese administrative authorities dealt with 169,600 cases of trademark infringement in the period from 2001 to 2004, while the judicial authorities prosecuted only 2566 suspects for IPR infringement in the period from 2000 to 2004.[7] In 2004 the administrative authorities dealt with 51,851 cases of trademark infringement and 1455 cases of patent infringement, while the judicial authorities prosecuted just 638 suspects for all types of IPR infringement. It would appear that less than 1 per cent of IPR infringement cases are currently dealt with judicially in China. Judicial enforcement involves such criminal punishment as detention and imprisonment and carries, therefore, a greater deterrent effect on infringers than administrative enforcement, which involves at most monetary fines. Without strong judicial support, however, it is very difficult to enforce IPR effectively.

One reason for the weak judicial enforcement lies in the ambiguities and uncertainties in the legislation mentioned previously. According to the legislation, only 'serious' and 'especially serious' IPR infringement cases should be dealt with judicially. The Judicial Interpretation released in 2004 further imposes numerical standards to determine whether an IPR infringement case is serious enough to justify access to the judicial enforcement route. For trademark infringement, for instance, the threshold is approximately $6000 worth of counterfeit goods. There would arise, as pointed out in a report submitted by the International AntiCounterfeiting Coalition to the US Trade Representative, a question as to why $5999 worth of counterfeit goods does not qualify as a 'serious' infringement. The Chinese legislation cannot provide a reasonable explanation for this. This regulation actually serves to block the judicial enforcement route, in the sense that judicial officials are unwilling to accept a case unless IPR owners or the administrative authorities can prove that the numerical standards have been met. As most IPR infringers are smart enough to avoid being caught with the amount of counterfeits that meet the numerical standards for criminal prosecution, it is very difficult for IPR owners and the administrative authorities to collect the evidence needed to bring the infringers to courts. According to the IACC, China and Vietnam are the only countries in the world that impose numerical requirements for pursuing prosecution against trademark infringers, which 'simply create loopholes that provide safe harbors for counterfeiters' (IACC, 2005, pp. 17–18). To strengthen judicial enforcement, therefore, China needs to remove the numerical requirements for pursuing prosecution against IPR infringers and allow all IPR infringement cases to be handled through the judicial route.

As it happens, there are in fact financial incentives for the administrative authorities *not* to pass IPR infringement cases to the judicial authorities but to keep them on the administrative track. The administrative authorities are entitled, as mentioned previously, to impose a fine on IPR infringers, which is not paid to the infringed party but to the administrative authorities. The greater the number of IPR cases dealt with on the administrative track the more fines the administrative authorities can collect, and the more bonuses administrative officials can receive. This partly explains why the administrative authorities are reluctant to pass IPR infringement cases to judicial authorities. According to the US Trade Representative (2005), there has been a steady decline in the number of cases that the Chinese administrative authorities forwarded to the Ministry of Public Security for criminal investigation. There were eighty-six transfers in 2001, fifty-nine in 2002, forty-five in 2003 and only fourteen in the first half of 2004. In order to strengthen judicial enforcement, therefore, China needs to encourage the administrative authorities to move IPR infringement cases to the judicial authorities.

Weak judicial enforcement implies inadequate penalties for IPR infringement and, as a result, a lack of deterrence to IPR infringers. Most IPR infringers can avoid such severe criminal punishment as imprisonment, suffering, at most, a fine imposed by the administrative authorities. The current Chinese laws and regulations specify a maximum fine for IPR infringers, but do not establish a minimum fine. The maximum fine for trademark infringers, for instance, is 50 per cent of the illegal revenues or five times the illegal profits of the infringement operation. Given the large profit margin of infringement activities, the maximum fine is not sufficiently large to deter IPR infringers, who may simply regard these fines as the cost of doing business and resume their activities soon after the punishment.

Protectionism and corruption

Local protectionism and corruption are huge barriers in the battle against IPR infringement in China. The infringement of IPR often takes place under the protection of local government, in the form of inactivity when requests are received from infringed parties, lenient penalties, and tip-offs to IPR infringers just prior to raids by the local administrative and judicial authorities. Under this local government protection, many IPR infringers conduct their activities without any fear, in large premises with a fixed location, ignoring the laws and regulations on IPR passed by the central government and the protests of the international community, as shown in the case of the famous Silk Alley in Beijing (box 10.3).

Admittedly, there are economic reasons for the prevalence of local protectionism in China. As IPR infringement activities involved thousands of people in the production, wholesale and retail of counterfeits, local governments are worried that effective action against the infringement would increase unemployment and thus do damage to the local economy. As unemployment has already become a serious problem due to massive lay-offs in state-owned enterprises in China, local governments are not keen to worsen the situation by adopting an active policy against IPR infringement. In the meantime, the infringement activities, particularly those conducted openly in shops with a fixed location, generate considerable tax revenues for local governments, which provides an incentive for the local governments to protect such infringement. As the performance of local government officials is now assessed primarily by such economic indicators as employment and taxation, protecting IPR infringement appears to be an attractive option to local government officials.

In addition, large-scale corruption in local governments makes things worse. In some cases, corrupt local government officials even collude with IPR infringers. In fact, the tolerant attitude and lenient action taken by local governments facilitate the collusion between corrupt local officials and infringers. Without the collusion, it is very hard to imagine how billions of dollars of

---

Box 10.3 Silk Alley in Beijing

Silk Alley (Xiushuijie) was originally an open market located along a small alley in Jianguo Menwai Street in the Chaoyang district of Beijing, where most foreign embassies are located. The alley was less than one mile long and less than ten feet wide. As it was close to the embassies, hundreds of small Chinese vendors set up fixed stalls or shops there to sell various goods to foreigners, including jeans, silk pyjamas, silk scarves, outdoor jackets, shoes, children's clothing, tapestries, CDs, bags, hats, jewelleries and watches. In time, it became famous among foreign visitors to China for sales of cheap locally made goods, and drew crowds of up to 20,000 customers a day.

Many imitation products were also sold here, including counterfeits of such international brand names as Nike, Polo and Adidas. Attracted by the low price of these fakes, many foreign visitors, including those from Western countries that complained about counterfeiting, went there to buy the imitations. The market became so notorious for selling counterfeits that it appeared in a cartoon published in the *China Business Review* to illustrate the IPR infringement problem in China (Trainer, 2002). As the market contributed to the tax revenue of the local government, a blind eye was turned to the IPR infringement activities being carried on there. Under the protection of the local authorities, the market operated right under the gaze of the central Chinese government, despite protests from the international community.

The market was too crowded and shabby, however, which led to serious concerns over the danger of fire. In late 2004 the Chinese government made a decision to close the open Silk Alley market permanently, and replace it with a new indoor Silk Alley mall to be built next door to the old open market. The mall was designed as a five-storey building, with 1500 stalls, all to be rented out to small vendors on a monthly rate ranging from RMB 4000 to 40,000. The old open market was closed in early January 2005, and the new mall was opened two months later.

It is reported, however, that the local government completely relaxed IPR enforcement during the final days of the closure, giving the infringers an opportunity to sell their excess inventories of counterfeit goods.[8] In addition, the local government reportedly had no clear plans for enforcing IPR protection at the new Silk Alley mall, which led to fears that the new mall may simply become an indoor version of the old open market.[9] The local government appeared to be reluctant to accept the request from the brand owners for stricter lease provision to deter future tenants from selling counterfeits. This caught the attention of the IACC.[10] In fact, there are reports that imitations of famous international brands were spotted right on the opening day of the new Silk Alley mall![11]

---

counterfeits can possibly bypass the customs at local ports and be shipped all over the world.

Other problems

Some other problems with the current IPR regime in China also exist. One is the lack of transparency in the regime. It is reported that the Chinese government is unwilling to provide detailed information about IPR enforcement activities and IPR infringement damages. It is reported, furthermore, that the government still does not publish all the requisite IPR regulations, and does not make draft legislation available for public comment (Moga, 2002).[12]

Another problem is the lack of qualified enforcement officials. As intellectual property rights involve sophisticated technical issues, their protection requires government officials to have a certain level of knowledge and skill. In general, Chinese government officials, both on the judicial and administrative enforcement routes, and particularly those at local level, do not have the requisite knowledge and skill to fulfil complicated IPR protection tasks. The central government needs to provide training for them.

A third problem is the lack of coordination between the various government IPR enforcement authorities, there being so many of them that it is difficult to initiate coordinated actions against IPR infringement. This lack of coordination opens up opportunities for IPR infringers to break the monitoring of the enforcement authorities. The government has begun to take action to deal with the problem. In 2004, for instance, the State IPR Protection Work Team was set up, headed by a Vice-Premier of the State Council, to coordinate action against IPR infringement, and issued a document entitled Opinions on Increasing Work Contacts between Administrative Law Enforcement Organs, Public Security Organs and People's Procuratorates.[13] It will take time, however, for China to establish a well-coordinated IPR protection system at all governmental levels.

Tips for IPR protection in China

Given the shortcomings in China's IPR regime and the widespread IPR infringement, it is a daunting challenge for transnational corporations to protect their intellectual property rights. TNCs need to understand fully the difficulties they may encounter and learn how to protect their intellectual property rights in the Chinese context. Drawing on the experience of TNCs operating in the country, we offer some advice on practical measures for protecting IPR in China.

Zero-tolerance policy

To start with, some TNCs adopted a policy of tolerance towards IPR infringement activities. For fear that the publicity of IPR infringement cases would cause customers to distrust their brand names, resulting in declines in sales of their products, these TNCs kept silent and did not take action against counterfeiting. As Liang Yu, public relations manager of P&G (China), has admitted: 'The release of the news could have resulted in a rather negative effect on P&G. Once consumers know that P&G products on sale in the market are a mixture of genuine and fake merchandise, our product sales would decrease drastically' (Liu, 2000, p. 2). Consequently, these TNCs regarded IPR infringement as a highly sensitive issue and preferred not to mention it at all in public.

However, the tolerance policy actually encouraged IPR infringers, and had disastrous consequences. The infringers took advantage of the tolerance, considering it to be a fundamental weakness of IPR owners, and began to engage in infringement activities without any scruple. TNCs soon found that IPR infringement became outrageous and began to grow completely out of control. In the case of P&G, '[W]hat were formerly trickles of counterfeit products have gradually developed into deluges' (Liu, 2000, p. 2). The catastrophic cost of the tolerance policy taught TNCs a hard lesson; today more and more of them tend to adopt a zero-tolerance policy on IPR infringement and are resolutely opposed to any such infringement activities. The experience of TNCs in China indicates that appeasing IPR infringement does not serve the interests of the IPR owners, and that TNCs should virtually declare war on IPR infringement as soon as an act of infringement is detected.

Prevention first

In the face of the ineffective enforcement of IPR protection, TNCs need to try as hard as they can to prevent IPR infringement from happening in the first place. Once it has taken place, it is very costly to fight a battle against the IPR infringers and very difficult to win the battle in the current Chinese context. TNCs have realized this crucial point and begun to take preventative measures against possible infringements of their intellectual property rights.

Many measures can be taken to prevent IPR infringement, such as registering your IPR with the relevant Chinese authorities as soon as possible, modifying your product designs and developing new security features to make infringement more difficult, and pricing products reasonably to minimize the profits from infringement of your products. Entry mode selection is also important in the prevention of IPR infringement. As discussed in chapter 4, a wholly foreign-owned enterprise can better protect IPR than a joint venture. So far as it is possible, TNCs should establish a WFOE for production operations involving proprietary technology. If TNCs have no choice but to establish a joint venture in these circumstances (as required by China's industry entry policy), they should exercise due diligence in choosing a local partner, write the joint venture contract in a way that allows them to monitor and control the use of the proprietary technology and include confidentiality clauses in employment contracts when hiring staff so as to prevent individual employees from leaking trade secrets. In addition, it is important to restrict access to proprietary technology to key individuals in the joint venture.

IPR protection coalitions

In the current context of large-scale IPR infringement in China, it is difficult for a TNC to fight a battle against infringement activities alone. It is useful, therefore, for TNCs to form coalitions to take collective action against such infringement. In 2000, for example, some TNCs set up the Quality Brands Protection Committee (QBPC) in China to coordinate anti-counterfeiting activities. The QBPC was registered under the China Association of Enterprises with Foreign Investment (CAEFI), and is currently comprised of more than 100 large transnational corporations.[14]

The QBPC organizes various activities to improve the IPR regime in China in general and strengthen the protection of its members' IPR in particular. These activities include inviting government officials in charge of IPR enforcement to seminars, at which QBPC members show how to distinguish between genuine products and counterfeits, and offering awards to those government officials and authorities that have performed well in anti-counterfeiting actions. On 4 March 2003, for instance, the following awards were given to twenty-one government enforcement agencies at both the central and local levels: the award for special contribution to IPR protection, the award for outstanding contribution to protecting quality brands against fake and shoddy-quality products and the award for 'best cases' of IPR protection. The QBPC now plays an increasingly important role in the battle against counterfeiting, and TNCs need to consider joining IPR protection coalitions of this kind in China.

Selection of appropriate official enforcement route

TNCs have to rely mainly on the official enforcement routes to protect their intellectual property rights, even though these enforcement routes are not effective. Each of the two official routes for IPR enforcement has its own advantages and disadvantages, and it is very important for TNCs to be aware of these and choose the right enforcement route in the light of the particular circumstances they face.

The administrative enforcement route, for instance, is relatively prompt in terms of reaction time, but it does not have a strong deterrent effect. If it is important for TNCs to stop IPR infringement activities immediately in order to minimize their financial losses, they should take the administrative route. The judicial enforcement route, by contrast, is relatively slow in its reaction time, reflecting the need for the collection of hard evidence, but it does have a strong deterrent effect. If the IPR infringement activities are clearly discernible and evidence can be collected easily, TNCs may consider taking the judicial route. In practice, as shown in the case of P&G (box 10.4), most TNCs take the two IPR enforcement routes simultaneously, so as to take full advantage of both of them.

Whenever possible, TNCs ought to take the judicial enforcement route more often and more seriously than the administrative enforcement route, in order to achieve genuine long-term deterrent effects. The QBPC openly encourages its members to take the judicial enforcement route to protect their intellectual property rights, and has given most of its awards to the judicial rather than the administrative enforcement authorities.

Cooperation with the government

In many ways, improvements in IPR legislation and IPR enforcement have to come primarily from the Chinese government. In order to improve the present IPR regime and protect their own intellectual property rights, therefore, TNCs need to cooperate with the government, and this has now become a consensus position among TNCs operating in China. The QBPC has clearly stated, for instance, that the mission of QBPC is 'to work cooperatively with the Chinese central and local governments, local industry, and other organizations to make positive contributions to anti-counterfeiting efforts in the People's Republic of China'.[15] For this purpose, the QBPC has established a special subcommittee called the Government Cooperation Committee, specifically to engage in cooperation of all types with the government.

There are a number of ways in which TNCs can cooperate with the Chinese government. They may, for example, cultivate *guanxi* with top government officials to lobby for improvements in IPR legislation and the issuance of new laws and regulations on IPR protection. They may provide financial support for government enforcement activities and reward those who perform their duty well in monetary terms. They may also reward enforcement officials

Box 10.4 Anti-counterfeiting at Proctor and Gamble

Proctor and Gamble moved into China in 1988. As one of the largest producers and distributors of daily consumables in the world, P&G soon established its brand name in China and achieved impressive business success. Following this initial success, however, P&G began to find itself in trouble: counterfeit products were appearing in many parts of China. To start with, P&G did not move against the counterfeiting, fearing that the publicity surrounding the issue would adversely affect the sale of its products in the Chinese market. To the dismay of P&G, however, the tolerance policy actually encouraged infringers and worsened the situation; the counterfeiting of P&G products became increasingly rampant, resulting in a total loss of at least $150 million each year.

From 1993 onwards P&G began to change its approach from an appeasement policy to a zero-tolerance policy, and declared war on all counterfeiting activities. P&G cooperated closely with the Chinese government, and made full use of both the administrative and the judicial enforcement routes to bring the infringers to justice. Working in conjunction with the administrative authorities, it launched thousands of attacks and raids against the counterfeiters and confiscated millions of boxes of fake P&G products. In the meantime, it filed a number of lawsuits against counterfeiters in the courts, as a result of which several counterfeiters were sentenced to terms of imprisonment up to three years.

Apart from this cooperation with the Chinese authorities, P&G took the initiative in forming a coalition with other TNCs in the fight against counterfeiting. P&G played a key role in the establishment of the Quality Brands Protection Committee in 2000, and became one of the twenty-two founding members of the committee with voting powers. It also took independent action against counterfeiting, including the employment of international investigating firms to monitor and identify counterfeiting activities, and the establishment of a special task force named the 'counterfeiting crackdown corps' to coordinate anti-counterfeiting actions within P&G.

In consideration of the difficulties faced in the current situation in China, furthermore, P&G took a prevention first strategy in the fight against counterfeiting. One of the preventative measures undertaken was to design new security features that make it difficult for counterfeiters to produce imitation products and easy for customers to distinguish between the genuine and the fake articles. Another preventative measure was the careful specification of the terms of employment in employees' contracts to the effect that any involvement on their part in counterfeiting would be considered a breach of contract.

All these anti-counterfeiting activities cost P&G a huge amount of money: it has been estimated that P&G has to spend between $2 and 4 million annually. The move have generated very positive effects, however, and P&G has now become one of the most successful TNCs in China. Nonetheless, P&G remains aware that there are still many difficulties ahead, and that the battle against counterfeiting will be a protracted struggle.

in non-monetary terms, such as holding ceremonies to honour them for a successful raid, placing an appreciative letter for an enforcement effort in an IPR magazine or offering training programmes for government enforcement officials. In addition, they may send representatives to participate directly in raids organized by government agencies, to provide professional guidance on detecting infringement. Furthermore, they may launch public relations campaigns (including charitable works) to promote their image of long-term commitment to China, for government enforcement officials tend to respond more favourably to TNCs perceived as being 'friends of China' (Weeks, 2000, p. 31).

Although China has a centralized political structure, local governments now enjoy much greater autonomy than before, and almost all enforcement actions are taken by local governments. It is imperative that TNCs cooperate closely with local governments to ensure that IPR enforcement activities are carried out as effectively as possible. To that end, TNCs should patiently nurture good relationships with local government enforcement officials, and reward those who perform their duty well. Indeed, the QBPC has given the majority of its awards to local rather than central government enforcement agencies. Of the twenty-one awards given by the QBPC in 2003, for instance, seventeen were offered to local government enforcement agencies at the provincial, city and district levels, accounting for 81 per cent of the total. Given the prevalence of protectionism at the local level, however, TNCs need to cooperate with the central government to urge local governments to give up protectionism. In case the local protectionism is too well entrenched to be able to enforce IPR in the place where the TNCs are located, they should consider filing a lawsuit in other jurisdictions where the infringing activities (say, the sale of fake products) are alleged to have been committed. According to the Chinese Civil Procedure Law, the plaintiffs may bring a lawsuit either in the place of the infringer's domicile or where the infringing act has taken place.

Independent action

Given the shortcomings in the current IPR regime, TNCs cannot rely completely on the Chinese authorities for IPR protection. They may find it useful to take independent action against the infringement activities.

They may, for example, hire independent investigators. Some international independent investigative firms, such as Kroll Associates, Pinkerton's and Markvess, have moved into China and offer private monitoring and investigation services. TNCs can utilize these services to help identify infringers and collect evidence. Local Chinese investigating firms have also emerged, and they can offer monitoring and investigating services more effectively and at lower cost than the international companies (Weeks, 2000). If the scale of the

IPR infringement is too large to be handled by a single independent investigating firm, TNCs may engage the services of several independent investigative firms.

They may also train and use their own staff to monitor and investigate IPR infringement activities. TNCs are advised to teach all their staff, particularly local sales representatives, the importance of IPR protection and the skills to detect fake products. They should set up their own special task forces to monitor the production facilities and distribution networks they have established in China, so as to ensure that they are not used for infringement activities. The special task forces can also gather information on the infringement activities that occur more widely in the country, and identify the regions where the rates of counterfeiting are among the highest.

These external and in-house independent actions require financial support and coordination from the top leadership of a transnational corporation, however. The extent to which corporate resources are dedicated may well vary from one company to another, depending primarily on the financial strength of the various TNCs and the scale of the IPR infringement they have to suffer. If the infringement is large-scale, significant financial resources have to be devoted to the in-house and external independent investigation, and a senior director should be appointed to coordinate these independent activities.

Summary

Despite the efforts made by the government to comply with the TRIPS standards of the WTO, IPR enforcement is ineffective and infringement remains a serious problem in China. The ineffective IPR enforcement and widespread infringement are attributable to shortcomings in the present Chinese IPR regime, including ambiguities in legislation, weak judicial enforcement, protectionism and corruption, a lack of transparency, a lack of qualified enforcement officials and a lack of coordination between the government enforcement authorities. Protecting IPR in this imperfect environment is a daunting challenge for TNCs doing business in China, particularly those with proprietary technology and well-established brand names.

In the face of the ineffectual IPR enforcement and flourishing IPR infringement, TNCs need to take practical measures to protect their intellectual property rights. They should adopt a zero-tolerance policy, make proper arrangements to prevent IPR infringement, form protection coalitions to coordinate their actions against the infringement and carefully select which official enforcement route is most appropriate for them. They also need to cooperate closely with the Chinese government in this battle, while at the same time taking independent action to make up for the inadequacies in the official enforcement mechanisms.

FURTHER READING

Clark, D. 2004. 'Intellectual property litigation in China'. *China Business Review* 31 (6): 25–29.
Peerenboom, R. 2002. *China's Long March toward Rule of Law*. Cambridge: Cambridge University Press.
Trainer, T. P. 2002. 'The fight against trademark counterfeiting'. *China Business Review* 29 (6): 27–31.
Weeks, A. M. 2000. 'IPR protection and enforcement: a guide'. *China Business Review* 27 (6): 28–32.

Questions for discussion

1. Why is IPR infringement so widespread in China compared to other parts of the world?
2. What should the Chinese government do to strengthen IPR enforcement? Relate your argument to the experience of other countries around the world, particularly the experience of your own country.
3. In your opinion, how should transnational corporations protect their intellectual property rights in the face of the ineffective enforcement system and the large-scale IPR infringement in China?

NOTES

1. See also United States Trade Representative (2004, 2005).
2. In the nine IPR cases published on the website of the Supreme Court of China in February 2005, for instance, eight involve domestic plaintiffs.
3. White Paper on the Intellectual Property Rights Protection in China in 2003, issued by the State Intellectual Property Office on 3 June 2004. Available online of http://www.sipo.gov.cn/sipo_English/gftx_e/zscqbhbps_e/t20040603_29734.htm.
4. In patent infringement disputes, for instance, the administrative authorities have to make a decision within seven days.
5. Peerenboom (2002, p. 241).
6. Shi (2003).
7. The White Paper is entitled New Progress in China's Protection of Intellectual Property Rights, and was issued by the State Council Information Office on 28 April 2005. The English version of the full paper can be accessed at the website http://service.china.org.cn.

8. Simons (2005).
9. Lynch (2005).
10. See International AntiCounterfeiting Coalition: Special 301 Recommendations 2005, p. 15.
11. See http://www.chinatour.com/attraction/siushuidongjie.htm.
12. See also US Trade Representative (2005).
13. New Progress in China's Protection of Intellectual Property Rights.
14. In May 2005 there were 117 members of the QBPC: twenty-two voting members and ninety-five general members. The twenty-two voting members are BAT, Bosch, Colgate-Palmolive, Eli Lilly, General Motors, Gillette, Henkel, Hewlett-Packard, Intel, JT International, Johnson and Johnson, Koninklijke Philips, LVMH Fashion Group, La Chemise Lacoste, Mars, Microsoft, Nike, Nokia, Philip Morris, Proctor and Gamble, Sony and Zippo. The general members include such famous TNCs as Coca-Cola, Adidas, BP, BMW, Canon, Dell, Disney, Epson, Ford, Fujisawa, Hitachi, Heineken, Kodak, Mary Kay, Peugeot, Sanyo, Seiko, Siemens, Toshiba, Toyota, Unilever, Volkswagen and Yamaha, to mention only a few.
15. See the QBPC website: http://www.qbpc.org.cn/en/about/about/factsheet.

11 Corporate finance considerations

The government has already proposed measures to improve corporate governance and address the cost and priorities for enhancing a financial system appropriate for the potentially largest economy of the twenty-first century. It is important to acknowledge that the financial and governance arrangements that ultimately emerge in China will surely be unique. After all, the legacy of China's social, economic, and political systems is embedded in a history that has seen several waves of sweeping change since the People's Republic of China was founded in 1949 (Chris Gentle (2005, p. 69)).

Since China began to reform and open up in 1978, and particularly since WTO accession in 2001, China's financial system and corporate finance structure have undergone fundamental changes. However, they are still different from those in most other parts of the world in many respects, including taxation, banking services, the securities market, accounting and auditing. Transnational corporations need to understand the differences, and learn how to manage corporate finance in China. In this chapter we discuss some of the most important issues that TNCs have to take into account in corporate finance management in China. First we discuss China's taxation arrangement for foreign affiliates in section 1, and the banking services available to foreign affiliates in section 2. Then, in sections 3 and 4, we discuss Chinese securities market and accounting practices in relation to the operation of foreign affiliates, respectively. The final section summarizes.

Taxation

TNCs have to pay taxes in China, as they do in other parts of the world. The Chinese taxation system used to be very simple in the planning period, primarily because of the simplified ownership structure and the limited business activities at that time. Until 1978 China levied only thirteen categories of taxes nationwide, including an industry and commerce tax, an industry and commerce income tax, and an agriculture tax and tariff. Government revenues came mainly from the profits of state-owned enterprises, not from these taxes.[1] Along with the economic reform and opening up, ownership was diversified, foreign investors moved in and new types of business activity emerged. From 1979 onwards the government has implemented a series of taxation reforms to cope with these changes, and the taxation system has now become very complicated (box 11.1). At present China levies a total of twenty-nine categories of taxes, and some of these are applicable to foreign affiliates. Moreover, as discussed in chapter 2, China offers a number of preferential tax treatments to foreign investors. Faced with the complex taxation system, TNCs need to know what categories of taxes they have to pay, and what kinds of preferential tax treatment they enjoy.

Box 11.1 The reformed Chinese taxation system

China has been reforming its taxation system since 1979 to cope with the changes in the economic structure brought about by the rapid economic reform and opening up. The taxation reforms have focused on:

- applying income tax to state-owned enterprises to separate the taxes from the profits;
- applying income tax to foreign affiliates;
- adding new taxation categories, such as an individual income tax, value added tax, a resource tax and an urban construction tax; and
- reclassifying the existing tax categories.

China's present taxation system is the result of these reforms over the past two decades or so.

Currently, China has a total of twenty-nine categories of taxes: value added tax, consumption tax, business tax, customs duties, corporate income tax, foreign corporate income tax,[2] individual income tax, resource tax, urban and township land use tax, urban maintenance and construction tax, tax on farmland occupation, fixed-assets-investment orientation regulation tax (now suspended), land appreciation tax, vehicle acquisition tax, fuel tax (not yet levied), social security tax (not yet levied), property tax, urban real estate tax, inheritance tax (not yet levied), vehicle and vessel usage tax, vehicle and vessel usage licence tax, vessel tonnage tax, stamp duty, contract tax, security transaction tax (not yet levied), slaughter tax, banquet tax, agriculture tax and animal husbandry tax. These taxes have now become the main source of government revenue, accounting for 94 per cent of all revenue.

Value added tax is by far the most important contributor to tax revenue, accounting for more than 40 per cent of the total. The second largest contributor is business tax, accounting for 14 per cent, with the third largest contributor, enterprise income tax, accounting for a further 11 per cent. All the remaining categories of taxes each account for less than 10 per cent of total tax revenue – e.g., consumption tax (6 per cent), customs duties (5.7 per cent), individual income tax (5 per cent), stamp duty (4 per cent), urban maintenance and construction tax (2.7 per cent), foreign corporate income tax (2.5 per cent) and agriculture tax (2.3 per cent).

These taxes are either collected separately, by central government and local government, or the collection is shared between them. After the taxation separation reform of 1994, all taxes have been divided into three groups: (1) taxes as central government's fixed revenue, including consumption tax, vehicle acquisition tax, customs duties, vessel tonnage tax and value added tax collected by the Customs Bureau; (2) taxes as local government's fixed revenue, including urban and township land use tax, farmland occupation tax, fixed-assets-investment orientation regulation tax, land appreciation tax, house property tax, urban real estate tax, inheritance tax, vehicle and vessel usage tax, vehicle and vessel usage licence tax, contract tax, slaughter tax, banquet tax, agriculture tax and animal husbandry tax; and (3) taxes as revenue shared by central and local government, including value added tax (apart from that collected by the Customs Bureau), business tax, corporate income tax, foreign corporate income tax, individual income tax, resource tax, urban maintenance and construction tax, stamp duty, fuel tax and security transaction tax.[3]

Taxes applicable to foreign affiliates

According to the current regulations, the most important tax that foreign affiliates have to pay is foreign corporate income tax. The standard tax rate for foreign affiliates is 30 per cent, with an additional local rate of 3 per cent. In theory, in other words, foreign affiliates should pay a total of 33 per cent on their income from production and business operations and on their profits (dividends), interest, rentals, royalties and other income, derived from sources both inside and outside China, that are effectively connected with their establishments or ventures in China. In practice, as shown below, the rate of foreign corporate income tax is reduced by a large margin, thanks to the preferential tax treatments offered to foreign investors.

Apart from the foreign corporate income tax, foreign affiliates and expatriate managers are subject to sixteen additional categories of taxes: value added tax, business tax, customs duties, individual income tax, consumption tax, resource tax, land appreciation tax, vehicle acquisition tax, fuel tax, urban real estate tax, vehicle and vessel usage licence tax, vessel tonnage tax, stamp duty, contract tax, slaughter tax and agriculture tax. A detailed discussion of these taxes can be found elsewhere (Lo and Tian, 2005), and only the four most important are illustrated: value added tax, business tax, customs duties and individual income tax.

Value added tax is computed on the basis of output taxable, input taxable and the applicable taxation rate. There are currently three rates for normal value added taxpayers in China: a 0 per cent rate, a 13 per cent rate and a 17 per cent rate. The zero rating applies to exported goods. The 13 per cent rate applies to the following goods: agricultural products and animal husbandry products; edible vegetable oil and grains; tap water, heating, air-conditioning, hot water, coal gas, liquefied petroleum gas, natural gas, methane gas, and coal/charcoal products for household use; books, newspapers and magazines (excluding newspapers and magazines issued by postal and telecommunication departments); feeds, chemical fertilizers, agricultural chemicals, agricultural machinery and plastic film covering for farming; and dressing metal mineral products, dressing non-metal mineral products, and coal. The 17 per cent rate applies to crude oil, mine salt, goods other than those mentioned above and taxable services.

Business tax is computed on the basis of a company's turnover and the applicable taxation rate. Currently the following nine taxable items are subject to business tax: (1) a 3 per cent rate for communications and transportation, including transportation by land, water, air and pipeline, loading and unloading, and delivery; (2) a 3 per cent rate for the construction industry, including construction, installation, repair, decoration and other engineering work; (3) a 5 per cent rate for finance and insurance, including loans, financial leasing, the transfer of financial products, financial brokerage and other financial and insurance businesses; (4) a 3 per cent rate for post and telecommunications; (5) a 3 per cent rate for culture and sports; (6) a rate of between 5 per cent and 20 per cent for entertainment (except for nightclubs, venues for singing, dance halls, shooting, hunting, racing, games, golf, bowling and billiards, which are subject to a 20 per cent rate nationwide, the tax rate for all kinds of entertainment business is determined within the range specified in the taxation laws and regulations issued by the government of individual provinces and autonomous regions in the light of their particular local conditions); (7) a 5 per cent rate for the transfer of intangible assets, including the transfer of land use rights, patent rights, non-patent technologies, trademarks, copyrights and goodwill; (8) a 5 per cent rate for sales of immovable properties, including sales of buildings and other attachments to land; and (9) a 5 per cent rate for other service industries, including consultancy, hotels, catering, tourism, warehousing, leasing and advertising.

Customs duties are levied on commercial commodities or articles entering or leaving China's national boundaries or customs territories. Customs duties include an import tariff that is levied on imported goods, and an export tariff that is levied on exported goods. There are at present 7316 types of imported goods subject to tariff, and the average level of the import tariff is about 11 per cent. By contrast, tariffs are levied on only thirty-six types of exported goods, mainly raw materials in short supply domestically; the tariff rates range from

20 per cent to 50 per cent. Customs duties are computed on the basis of either the price or the quantity of the imported or exported goods, or a combination of the two. In line with China's accession to the WTO, customs duties are expected to fall over time.

Individual income tax is applicable to the income that individuals, residents and non-residents of China alike, derive from sources both inside and outside China. 'Resident' taxpayers are defined as Chinese citizens and foreign nationals residing in China; they have unlimited tax liabilities and have to pay individual income tax to the government on income from anywhere in the world. 'Non-resident' taxpayers are defined as those not residing in China; they have limited tax liabilities and have to pay individual income tax to the government only on income derived from sources inside China. Individual income tax is computed on the basis of a nine-grade progressive rating scale, with the lowest rate being 5 per cent and the highest 45 per cent; the more an individual earns the more he or she pays in individual income tax. As for expatriates, the following items are subject to tax concession: (1) housing allowance, food allowance, removal expenses and laundry fees received in non-cash forms or in the form of cash reimbursement; (2) travel allowance at reasonable levels; (3) the portion of home visit allowance, language course fees and children's education expenses deemed reasonable by the tax authorities; and (4) dividends and bonuses received from foreign affiliates. In addition, any foreign individuals who reside in China consecutively or accumulatively for no more than 90 days (or 183 days for those from countries that have signed tax agreements with China) in a tax year are exempted from individual income tax if their wage or salary is not paid or borne by their employers in China and is not borne by a resident establishment or permanent venue of their employers in China.

Preferential tax treatment

In order to attract foreign direct investment to China on the one hand, and to guide the FDI in the desired directions on the other, the government has introduced a range of tax incentives for foreign affiliates. These types of preferential tax treatment cover almost all the taxes applicable for foreign affiliates mentioned previously, and they are granted by either central government or local government. The preferential treatment offered by the central government covers mainly foreign corporate income tax, value added tax, business tax and customs duties, while that offered by local government varies from one locality to another. Using some examples, we illustrate the chief types of preferential tax treatment offered by the central government.

With regard to foreign corporate income tax, foreign affiliates in a production industry (such as machine building, electronics or textiles) are exempted from foreign corporate income tax for a period of no less than ten years in the first two years, and are granted a 15 per cent rate of foreign corporate income tax in the following three years. Foreign affiliates in energy, transportation and port construction, and integrated circuit manufacture enjoy a 15 per cent rate of foreign corporate income tax. In addition, export-oriented foreign affiliates utilizing advanced technology are eligible for either a 15 per cent or a 10 per cent (for those in Special Economic Zones) rate of foreign corporate income tax if the export value in the current year amounts to more than 70 per cent of total annual production and if the business's international payment position is in balance or in surplus. Furthermore, foreign affiliates located in Special Economic Zones, Economic and Technological Development Zones, Coastal Economic Open Zones, New and High-Tech Industry Development Zones and/or Bonded Zones enjoy a flat rate of foreign corporate income tax, ranging from 10 per cent to 24 per cent depending on where they are and what industries they invest in. Recently, foreign affiliates located in the western region have begun to enjoy some preferential foreign corporate income tax treatment as well (Lo and Tian, 2005).

As for value added tax, foreign affiliates are entitled to a full rebate on the purchase of domestically produced equipment within their investment amount if such equipment is listed in the catalogue of duty-free imports. In addition, foreign affiliates are exempted from value added tax on the equipment that they import from abroad for their own use.

With regard to business tax, the research and development centres established by foreign affiliates are exempt from business tax on their income. Foreign affiliates are exempted from business tax on their income derived from technology transfer, technology development, technology-related consultancy and technical services.

In terms of customs duties, foreign affiliates are exempt from import tariffs on the imported raw materials, auxiliary materials, parts, components, accessories and packaging materials that are used for the outward processing and assembly of final products or for the production of exported goods, and the exemption is calculated on the basis of the quantity of finished products actually processed, assembled and exported. In addition, foreign affiliates in both the 'encouraged category' and the 'restricted category', foreign R&D centres and foreign affiliates with advanced technology and export orientation are exempted from import tariffs and import-related taxes on imported equipment and supporting technologies, accessories and parts destined for their own use.

As shown above, China's taxation arrangements for foreign affiliates are highly complex. If local differences in taxation were taken into account, the complexity would become even more bewildering. As a result, business activities may have different tax consequences, and transnational corporations need to investigate and compare the tax cost when they choose from among the different business plans available. In striking a merger and acquisition deal in China, for instance, TNCs face a number of options, each of which involves different tax costs – as illustrated in box 11.2. Designing business activities carefully and with due regard to the Chinese taxation structure will help to minimize the tax cost. It is crucial, therefore, that TNCs have a clear understanding of the taxation structure to be able to tailor their business activities accordingly.

Box 11.2 The tax cost of merger and acquisition

There are, basically, four approaches to merger and acquisition: equity sales, asset sales, mergers, and spin-offs and split-ups. In the context of China's current taxation system, these approaches all have different tax consequences. TNCs that intend to strike an M&A deal in China need to compare the tax consequences of the four approaches carefully, and choose the approach that minimizes the tax cost of the deal.

Generally speaking, the tax cost of equity sales is lower than that of asset sales. With equity sales, what the acquirer needs to pay is the stamp duty and the tax on gains from the equity sale. With asset sales, in contrast, the acquirer has to pay not only the stamp duty and the tax on gains from the asset sale but also value added tax and business tax. Sales of tangible assets, for instance are normally subject to a 17 per cent rate of value added tax. Although the seller may pay the value added tax, the tax cost of the deal is often passed on to the acquirer in one way or another.

The merger approach does not incur any additional tax cost, because it is generally not taken to be a taxable event that gives rise to gains or losses. According to China's regulations, the merging enterprises should simply carry on as they did before the merger; that is, the assets and liabilities of the enterprises are carried over to the post-merger entity at their book value. In addition, any unexpired preferential tax treatment of the pre-merger enterprises is carried over to the post-merger entity.

Spin-offs and split-ups are also not regarded as taxable events in China, and therefore they do not incur additional tax cost either. The assets and liabilities of the original enterprise are carried over to the resulting enterprises at their book value. In contrast to mergers, however, any preferential tax treatment enjoyed by the original enterprise does not pass on to the resulting enterprises automatically; instead, the resulting enterprises have to qualify for the preferential treatment independently. If they do qualify, they can continue to enjoy the preferential treatment of the original enterprise for the remaining period of the unexpired preferential tax treatment.

As these M&A examples show, business activities may involve a variety of different tax consequences in China. TNCs need to exercise due diligence before making a decision on a business deal, and evaluate the feasibility of different options from a tax-efficient perspective. Because of the complexity of the Chinese taxation system, TNCs may need to consult with experienced advisers on the tax cost of a business deal.

Banking services

In managing their corporate finances, TNCs need to understand the Chinese banking system and the banking services available to them in China. Before 1978 China had a mono-banking system, and the People's Bank of China (PBOC), virtually the only bank in China, performed the mixed functions of a central bank and a commercial bank. Under the mono-banking system, interest rates, the money supply and the financial needs of the government and state-owned enterprises were all subject to central planning, and there was little room for financial intermediation. The PBOC was very much like the government cashier, exercising only very limited functions, such as issuing currency, taking deposits and lending on behalf of the government. It provided a large amount of loans to the state-owned enterprises and bailed out loss-making enterprises. Beginning in 1979 the government started to reform the banking system, and opened up the banking sector to foreign investors. As a result, the Chinese banking system is now very complex, and can be largely divided into domestic and foreign banking institutions.

Domestic banking institutions

Domestic banking institutions have been diversified since 1979 following a series of reforms. First, the Agricultural Bank of China (ABC), the Bank of China (BOC) and the Construction Bank of China (CBC) were established in 1979, and the Industrial and Commercial Bank of China (ICBC) followed in 1984. The four new banks began to take up the role of an independent state commercial bank, while the People's Bank of China retained its central bank function. Throughout the 1980s, however, the four newly established banks were still not really commercialized, and remained subject to the central government's policy instructions.

Then, in 1994, three policy banks – the State Development Bank of China (SDBC), the Agricultural Development Bank of China (ADBC) and the Import and Export Bank of China (IEBC) – were set up to separate policy banking and commercial banking in China's financial system. The three newly established policy banks began to take up the unprofitable 'policy lending', while the four aforementioned state commercial banks began to operate on a commercial basis. With the Central Banking Law and the Commercial Bank Law, both promulgated and enacted in 1995, China began to acquire a rudimentary legal framework for the supervision and functioning of its banking system.

Meanwhile, other commercial banks and financial institutions, both state-owned and non-state-owned, and national and regional, were also being set up, such as CITIC (China International Trust and Investment Corporation), the Industrial Bank, the Bank of Communications, the Everbright Bank, the Huaxia Bank, the Minsheng Bank, the Guangdong Development Bank, the Shenzhen Development Bank, the Merchants Bank, the Fujian Industrial Bank, the Shanghai Pudong Development Bank, the Yantai Housing Savings Bank, the Bengbu Housing Savings Bank and the Hainan Development Bank. China's banking system has become increasingly consumer-oriented, now offering almost all the financial services that are available in a market-based economy.

China currently has four state commercial banks, three policy banks, ten joint-equity commercial banks, 109 city commercial banks and numerous urban credit cooperatives, rural credit cooperatives, trust and investment corporations, finance companies and leasing companies. These banks engage mainly in Chinese-currency business, and only a few of them, such as the Bank of China and the Industrial and Commercial Bank of China, are authorized to engage in foreign-currency transactions. TNCs need to understand what kinds of banking services they can expect from domestic Chinese financial institutions.

Foreign banking institutions

As early as the 1980s some foreign financial institutions were allowed to set up regional branches or representative offices in China's Special Economic Zones. Shanghai was opened up to foreign banks in 1990. Then, in 1996, the PBOC issued the Administrative Measures on Representative Offices of Foreign Financial Institutions in China, and more and more Chinese cities were opened up to foreign banks and financial institutions thereafter. Currently there are more than 200 foreign banking institutions operating in China, principally in the large cities.

Foreign banking institutions are allowed to engage chiefly in foreign-currency business, including foreign-currency deposits, loans, bill discounting, investment, remittances, guarantees, import and export settlement, investigations of creditworthiness, consultancy and foreign currency trusts. In principle, they are not allowed to engage in Chinese-currency business unless they receive special approval from the PBOC. In 1996, for example, several foreign banks in Shanghai were granted licences to engage in Chinese-currency business on a limited basis. Later on, more and more foreign banks were granted such preferential treatment. At present the number of foreign banks allowed to carry out Chinese-currency transactions on a limited basis has reached twenty-five: nineteen in Shanghai and six in Shenzhen.

Given these restrictions on Chinese-currency business, foreign banks and financial institutions cannot function fully as providers of financial services in China. As such, therefore, the foreign institutions play only a very limited role in China today. Currently, their assets account for no more than about 2 per cent of the country's total financial assets and their foreign-currency loans account for only around 13 per cent of all foreign-currency loans. Their Chinese-currency assets amount to only about RMB 12 billion, their Chinese-currency loans stand at some RMB 8 billion and their Chinese-currency deposits amount to no more than around RMB 6 billion.

Following China's accession to the WTO, the restrictions on Chinese-currency business are being removed gradually, and foreign banks and financial institutions are therefore set to play an increasingly important role in the country's banking system. According to the WTO agreement, foreign financial institutions were at first allowed to provide Chinese-currency services to Chinese enterprises in a limited number of cities. Five years after accession – that is, by the end of 2006 – foreign financial institutions would be permitted to provide Chinese-currency services to all Chinese clients throughout the country. Intense competition for clients between Chinese and foreign financial institutions will arise in the years to come, giving TNCs more and better options to choose from in their banking services.

Problems with the current Chinese banking system

The Chinese banking sector remains primarily under state ownership, with the government owning more than 90 per cent of the sector's assets. Under government guidance, the state-owned banking institutions, policy banks and commercial banks alike, give priority to the state-owned enterprises in terms of service provision. As the majority of state-owned enterprises perform poorly, bad loans are a serious problem in the banking sector. It is estimated that the bad loan ratio in Chinese state-owned banks is at least as high as 25 per cent. As a result, the state-owned banks have become very inefficient, affecting the quality of service they are able to provide to customers, whether domestic or foreign.

In addition, the state-owned banks are poorly managed in comparison to the financial institutions in mature market economies. The banking regulations are complex and fragmented while banking services are restricted and limited, which cause difficulties for corporate finance management. The regional fragmentation of financial regulations, for instance, makes it very difficult for TNCs with multiple affiliates in China to manage cash flow within the company, and these TNCs often suffer from massively inefficient cash management structures because excess cash in one group entity could not be utilized by another. As experienced by Wal-Mart in China, a foreign 'company with joint ventures in several locations supplied by one supplier may have to make a separate payment from each venture to the supplier' (Huffman, 2003, p. 22). In the face of these difficulties, TNCs need to examine the available options carefully, such as corporate restructuring and entrusted loans or group entrusted loans, and adopt cost-efficient approaches to cash management. Many TNCs, including Wal-Mart, have chosen, for example, to set up a holding company with limited liability that can engage in direct investment activities across the country in order to consolidate cash management in their joint ventures in various parts of China.[4]

Furthermore, owing to the restrictive foreign exchange regime (discussed in chapter 2), TNCs may encounter difficulties in dealing with issues related to foreign exchange conversion, particularly when they want to bring the profits they earn from their Chinese operations back home. The bureaucracy in the government and the poor technology in the service sector make things worse. As Ted P. Huffman (2003, p. 22) points out, 'Business in China still depends heavily on a hard-copy paper flow of documentation, which adds cost, requires excess manpower, and creates opportunities for human error. The requirement for "chops" on official documents further complicates matters'. Faced with these difficulties, as shown in box 11.3, TNCs need to adopt cost-effective approaches to profit repatriation.

Box 11.3 The repatriation of profits from China

Under China's current foreign exchange regime, the Chinese currency is convertible freely on the current account, but not on the capital account. To bring the profits earned from their Chinese operations back home, TNCs have to go through a complex process to convert their profits from the Chinese currency to a foreign currency in the first place. The process involves a huge amount of paperwork, including the tax certificate, registered capital verification, official foreign exchange registration and a letter of approval from the board of directors. Banks in China will not process currency conversion and then profit repatriation until all the required documents are ready; but getting the paperwork done is not easy in China.

To get the tax certification, for instance, TNCs first have to undergo a certified accounting audit. Having little confidence in domestic Chinese accounting firms, large TNCs tend to employ foreign accounting firms to conduct the audit.[5] The annual audit is mandatory and should be completed by the end of April each year. Thereafter, TNCs need to file the audit documents with the local State Administration of Taxation (SAT) office, and will receive the tax certificate within several weeks if the filed documents meet the requirements. If SAT suspects accounting irregularities or illegal tax evasion, it will conducts its own audit, which will significantly delay the issuance of the tax certificate.

As the year-end audit mandates a full review of the business activities of an affiliate established by a TNC in China, it involves many government agencies and departments, including the Central Administration of Customs, the Ministry of Commerce, and the State Administration of Foreign Exchange (SAFE), in addition to SAT. Disputes with these government organizations may occur, potentially causing delays to the review process. TNCs are advised to plan carefully for the review beforehand, and anticipate possible problems that may arise in the process so as to be able to resolve them in a timely manner.

Furthermore, TNCs should establish good relationships with the local government bodies in charge of the review process, and maintain an open line of communication and information exchange with them. Reliable government contacts can help to clear up vague areas in government regulations and regional differences in requirements, and give advance warning of forthcoming campaigns and regulations that may affect the review and auditing process.

Learning from the experience of the Asian financial crisis, China is unlikely to relax its foreign exchange regime any time soon, and profit repatriation will remain a daunting challenge to TNCs operating in the country for the foreseeable future. Nevertheless, careful planning and good relationships with the local authorities will help minimize the complications when TNCs negotiate the convoluted repatriation process.

The securities market

Transnational corporations may want to finance their business activities through China's securities market, and therefore they will need to understand its workings in order to have the opportunity to make use of it in their business operations. The securities market was established in 1990, and it has now become one of the largest such markets in Asia, second only to that in Tokyo. China's securities market, despite many problems, now plays an important role in corporate financing, and has begun, albeit in a gradual way, to open up to foreign investors. In China there are currently 131 securities companies with 2900 branches, and twenty-one fund management companies running seventy-five securities investment funds. The highest authority for the securities market is the China Securities Regulatory Commission (CSRC), which was established in 1992.

At present there are four types of securities in China: state bonds, financial bonds, corporate bonds and stocks. State bonds are issued by the Ministry of Finance to finance government-supported construction projects. Financial bonds are issued by specialized banks and other financial institutions as a method of fund-raising. Corporate bonds and stocks are issued by companies, including joint-stock companies, as a means of corporate financing. As it is stocks that are of most interest to TNCs, we focus our discussion on the Chinese stockmarket.

There are two stock Exchanges in China: the Shanghai Stock Exchange and the Shenzhen Stock Exchange. The stockmarket was originally designed to offer opportunities for state-owned enterprises to raise capital, but it has been gradually opened up to non-state enterprises in recent years. To date, however, nearly 90 per cent of the companies listed on the two stock exchanges are still state-owned. Owing to the problems rooted in state ownership, the performance of the listed companies is not generally very impressive when compared to listed companies in mature market economies. Improving the efficiency of the listed companies has been a major concern of the Chinese government for many years.

According to the current laws and regulations, foreign affiliates are allowed to be listed on China's stockmarket. In reality, however, the application requirements are so demanding that it is extremely difficult for TNCs to get their affiliates listed. As it happens, the administration of the stockmarket has followed a restrictive 'internal' policy towards applications of foreign affiliates – a policy that is implicit but effective.

Along with the relaxation of the government restrictions on stock trading and M&A activity, nonetheless, TNCs can now purchase the shares of Chinese companies listed on the stockmarket. Two relatively recent cases involve Kodak and Newbridge Capital. In October 2003, as mentioned in chapter 5, Kodak succeeded in purchasing 20 per cent of the shares of Lucky Film, a local company listed on the Shanghai Stock Exchange. In early 2005 Newbridge Capital managed to purchase 18 per cent of the shares of Shenzhen Development Bank, a Chinese bank listed on the Shenzhen Stock Exchange. The government has relaxed the restrictions on the acquisition of listed Chinese companies and now allows TNCs to purchase controlling shares in them, as shown in box 11.4.

Box 11.4 The acquisition of listed companies in China

In 2002 the Chinese government relaxed the restrictions on mergers and acquisitions, and issued regulations allowing foreign investors to purchase controlling shares in companies listed on China's stockmarket. In theory, therefore, foreign investors can now take over a listed Chinese company. In reality, however, it is very difficult for them to do so, because of the complex approval procedures. In recent years there have been reports of some isolated cases of the acquisition of listed Chinese companies by foreign investors, but the foreign investors involved are actually not 'foreign' in the true sense.

In July 2003, for example, China Resource Enterprises (CRE), a company registered in Hong Kong, paid RMB 163.5 million to buy 51 per cent of the shares of Sichuan Jinhua, a Chinese textile company listed on the Shenzhen Stock Exchange. The deal was then reported as the first case of a listed Chinese company being acquired by a foreign company. CRE is not really a foreign company, however, but a subsidiary of China Resources National Corporation (CNRC), a state-owned conglomerate with interests in textiles, petrochemicals and property. In addition, the deal was a related-party transaction, as the seller of the Jinhua shares was CRE's parent company – CNRC!

A more recent case involved Brilliant Idea Investment Limited (BIIL), a company registered in the British Virgin Islands in February 2005. In April that year BIIL announced the purchase of 70 per cent of the shares of Shenzhen Property Development Group, a Chinese estate company listed on the Shenzhen Stock Exchange. In fact, BIIL is controlled by Kowloon Development Company Limited (KDCL), a company established in Hong Kong in 1962 and listed on the Hong Kong Stock Exchange in 1995. BIIL is, it would appear, a special-purpose vehicle established by KDCL specifically for the deal. The acquisition of SPDG by BIIL can hardly be classified as the acquisition of a listed Chinese company by a foreign company in the true sense, as the acquirer is actually based in Hong Kong.

Nevertheless, the door is now open for foreign investors to take over a local company listed on China's stockmarket through the purchase of a majority interest in that company. Along with further opening up of China to the outside world, it is expected that the acquisition of listed Chinese companies by foreign investors will become a reality before very long.

To date the acquisition in controlling shares in listed Chinese companies by 'foreign' investors, such as the cases mentioned in box 11.4, has all been achieved through peaceful negotiation and agreement, because hostile acquisition is hardly possible in the current regulatory environment. Nevertheless, the government has begun to allow foreign investors to purchase shares of Chinese companies listed on the stock market through open stock trading, thus opening, though only slightly, the door to hostile acquisition. Two significant steps have been taken in this regard: the B share scheme and the QFII scheme.

The B share scheme was designed to allow foreign investors to buy the stocks of a limited number of listed Chinese companies using foreign currency. When the Shanghai and Shenzhen Stock Exchanges were established, shares were at first made available only to Chinese investors and were traded only in Chinese currency. Then, in February 1992, a special class of shares began to be listed and traded on both exchanges: registered shares denominated in yuan and offered to foreign investors and investors from Hong Kong, Macao and Taiwan for purchase and sale using foreign currency. This special class of shares is referred to as B shares, to distinguish them from the A shares that are available only to Chinese investors and are traded only in Chinese currency. Not until 2001 could Chinese investors trade the B shares using foreign exchange. Although the B shares are all denominated in Chinese currency, B share transactions have to be settled in foreign currency: US dollars for stocks on the Shanghai Stock Exchange and Hong Kong dollars for stocks on the Shenzhen Stock Exchange. The price of these currency conversions is calculated on the basis of the official weighted average exchange rate in the preceding week.

To trade B shares, a foreign investor must first open a settlement account with either the Shanghai Securities Central Clearing and Registration Corporation (SSCCRC) or the Shenzhen Securities Clearing Company (SSCC). The account may be opened on behalf of the investor by his/her broker or custodian bank. Foreign investors can then invest in B shares during the initial offering period, or on the secondary market through open trading. In the primary market, investments can be made through the issuer's underwriters; for trading in the secondary market, orders must be placed through foreign or local brokers. Foreign brokers may establish links with local brokers in the execution and settlement of stock trading, and share commission with them. Alternatively, foreign brokers may apply for their own 'special' trading seats in the Shanghai and Shenzhen Stock Exchanges, and thus place trade orders directly into the trading system without going through local brokers.

The Chinese government has been very cautious about the B share market. By 2000 the number of B share companies listed on the Shanghai Stock Exchange had risen only to fifty-two, and on the Shenzhen Stock Exchange to fifty-six. Since then, moreover, the government has not approved the issuance of any new B share stock. As the B share market is so small, therefore, it provides very limited opportunities for foreign investors to purchase the shares of Chinese companies listed on the stockmarket. To an extent, the recently introduced Qualified Foreign Institutional Investor scheme helps to overcome this limitation.

The QFII scheme was designed to allow 'qualified' foreign institutional investors to purchase a limited amount of securities using Chinese currency, including the A shares of any Chinese companies listed on the stockmarket.[6]

Qualifying investors are those overseas fund management institutions, insurance companies, securities companies and other assets management institutions that have secured approval from the China Securities Regulatory Commission to invest in China's securities market and have received investment quotas from the State Administration of Foreign Exchange. QFIIs should mandate domestic commercial banks as custodians and domestic securities companies as brokers for their securities trading, and are required to comply with the laws, regulations and other relevant rules in China.

Both Chinese banks and foreign banks can apply to the People's Bank of China for a licence to execute custodian business for QFIIs if they: (1) have a dedicated custodian department; (2) have no less than RMB 8 billion paid-in capital; (3) have sufficient professionals who are familiar with custodian business; (4) have the ability to manage the entire assets of the fund safely; (5) have the necessary qualifications to conduct foreign exchange and RMB business; and (6) have not committed any breach of the foreign exchange regulations in the most recent three years. To date, nine banks have been granted such custodianship: the Industrial and Commercial Bank of China, the Bank of China, the Agricultural Bank of China, the Bank of Communications, China Construction bank, China Merchants Bank and the branches of Standard Chartered Bank, HSBC and Citibank in Shanghai.

To apply for QFII status, foreign institutional investors must meet one of the following basic requirements: (1) fund management institutions must have been in the fund business for at least five years and have managed $10 billion in assets in the last financial year; (2) insurance companies must have been in the insurance business for more than thirty years and have managed at least $10 billion in securities assets, with no less than $1 billion in paid-in capital, in the last financial year; (3) securities companies must have been in the securities business for more than thirty years and have managed at least $10 billion in securities assets, with no less than $1 billion in paid-in capital, in the last financial year; and (4) commercial banks must be in the world's top 100 in terms of total assets and have managed at least $10 billion in securities assets in the last financial years; (5) the requirement for trust firms and government-invested institutions will be determined by the Chinese government on an individual basis.

Upon approval, a qualified foreign institutional investor should open a yuan-denominated special account with its custodian bank, and apply to SAFE through its custodian bank for investment quotas. Then it needs to mandate a registered securities company to manage its investment. Under the QFII scheme, a qualified foreign institutional investor can invest in the following financial instruments: (1) all shares listed on China's stock exchanges;

(2) treasury bonds listed on China's stock exchanges; (3) convertible bonds and corporate bonds listed on China's stock exchanges; and (4) other products approved by the CSRC.

Apart from the basic legal regulations governing China's securities market, QFIIs have to follow some specific rules in securities trading: (1) the principals must be remitted into China and transfered directly into their special accounts within three months of the QFII licence being approved; (2) if the QFIIs are closed-end fund management companies, they cannot withdraw their money from China for three years after the remittance of the principals; (3) other QFIIs cannot withdraw their money from China for one year after the remittance of the principals; (4) the shares held by each QFII in a single listed company should not exceed 10 per cent of the total outstanding shares of that company; and (5) the total shares held by all QFIIs in a single listed company should not exceed 20 per cent of its total outstanding shares. It is expected that some of these restrictions will be removed as China further opens up to the outside world in the years to come.

By September 2006 forty foreign financial institutions had been granted QFII status, with the aggregate amount of their investment quotas totalling some $8 billion.[7] The first trade was made by UBS, in July 2003, with a purchase of shares in four companies listed on China's A share market. TNCs that want to purchase the shares of listed Chinese companies are now able to do so through these qualified foreign institutional investors.

Accounting

Since 1978 China has introduced measures to reform its accounting system, which is now converging with standard accounting practices in mature market economies. Nevertheless, significant differences remain with respect to these practices and the accounting institutional environment between China and mature market economies, which often make it difficult for TNCs to manage their corporate finance and enforce a standard code of accounting ethics in their Chinese operations. TNCs need to understand these differences and learn how to deal with the difficulties they cause.

The reformed Chinese accounting system

In the pre-reform period the aim of the accounting system was to help the Chinese government plan its economic activities and manage the various government funds, and it was therefore called the 'fund accounting system'. The fund accounting system provided information to the government about the implementation of state economic planning, and assisted in the state control of assets and funds. It offered limited assistance to enterprises in making economic decisions. In addition, all the accounting departments, institutions, associations and personnel were closely associated with the Chinese government at the central or the local level, and there were no independent accountants and independent accounting institutions at all. Furthermore, China's accounting system was completely closed to the outside world.

After the reform and opening up, more and more Chinese enterprises began to operate independently, foreign companies moved in and a stockmarket emerged. All these developments required fundamental changes in the accounting system. The reform of the system gained momentum in the 1990s, following the establishment of the Shanghai and Shenzhen Stock Exchanges and the acceleration of opening up after Deng Xiaoping's southern tour. A number of laws and regulations were issued to change 'the rules of the game' with regard to accounting practices in order to cope with the new developments. To meet the needs of TNCs operating in China, for instance, a separate set of regulations was formulated specifically for foreign affiliates, including the Accounting Regulations for Foreign Investment Enterprises of the PRC, issued in 1992. To meet the needs of stockmarket management, a separate set of regulations was compiled specifically for listed companies, including the Accounting Regulations for Selected Joint Stock Limited Companies, issued in 1991 and revised in 1998. To unify the accounting practice of business entities, moreover, the government promulgated the Accounting Law (1999), the Regulations on Financial Reporting of Enterprises (2000), the Accounting Systems for Business Enterprises (2001) and a number of specific accounting standards. These laws and regulations constitute the basic legal framework of the present Chinese accounting system.

As these newly issued laws and regulations draw heavily on regulations and practices in Western countries, the current accounting concepts and practices in China mirror, to an extent, those in the mature market economies, and are basically in line with international standards as specified in the International Accounting Standards (IAS), General Accepted Accounting Principles (GAAP) and Statements of Standard Accounting Practice (SSAP). In the meantime, a new auditing system has emerged, under which the purpose of auditing has changed from ascertaining a company's tax liabilities to ascertaining the truthfulness and fairness of a company's financial statements. Currently, most companies in China are subject to the annual audit carried out by certified public accounting firms registered in China (except for some state-owned enterprises in sensitive industries, which are explicitly exempted from auditing). To meet the demand for standard accounting and auditing, professional accounting firms have emerged in China and have moved in the direction of becoming independent providers of accounting and auditing services. In 1998, in fact, the State Council announced regulations that require certified public accountants to be independent from any government bureaus. Moreover, independent foreign accounting firms, such as the 'big four' – Deloitte and Touche, Ernst and Young, KPMG and PricewaterhouseCoopers – moved into China to offer accounting and auditing services to companies in the country, foreign and domestic alike.

Nevertheless, some differences remain between the Chinese accounting system and those in other parts of the world, particularly those in Western countries. In Western countries, for example, the setting of authoritative accounting standards is the responsibility of accounting societies, such as the International Accounting Standards Board, formally known as the International Accounting Standards Committee. In China, by contrast, the setting of authoritative accounting standards is the responsibility of the Ministry of Finance rather than accounting societies and institutions, such as the Accounting Society of China (ASC) or the Chinese Institute of Certified Public Accountants (CICPA). The ASC and the CICPA are responsible only for regulating, governing and monitoring the reform and development of the accounting profession in China. In addition, there are some detailed accounting regulations that are different from those in the West. In the Chinese regulations, for instance, the issue of employers' accounting for employees' post-retirement benefits is not addressed; the derecognition of financial assets is not specified; special-purpose entities are not specified; fair value is generally not recognized; and derivative instruments are not specified. More importantly, as discussed below, problems with China's institutional environment make it difficult for foreign affiliates to receive fair accounting and auditing services on the one hand, and comply with the ethical standards of international accounting practices on the other.

Problems with the institutional environment

There are many problems with the institutional environment in which accounting and auditing are carried out in China, but two in particular deserve attention. The first is the dependence of accounting and auditing on government organizations. Although domestic professional accounting firms have become more and more independent over the years, the practice of so-called 'hooking up' remains a barrier to accounting and auditing independence. The Chinese term for 'hooking up' is *gua kao*. *'Gua'* refers to going under the name of another person, while *'kao'* refers to relying on another person. In the context of accounting and auditing in China, 'hooking up' refers to an affiliated relationship between an accounting/auditing firm and its sponsoring organization. The sponsoring organization is normally one with a governmental background, such as a government agency or a government-run institute (see Dai, Lav and Yang, 2000).

The 'hooking up' relationship is rooted in the circumstances in which these professional accounting firms were originally established. At the beginning of the reform process the Chinese government required all newly established professional accounting firms to affiliate themselves with a government agency or a government-run institute. Although the government later encouraged these firms to become independent, it was difficult for them to do so then because the historical connections. As a result, most domestic professional accounting firms continue to have some government connection, and truly independent private accounting firms are rarely seen in China.

Under the 'hooking up' relationship, it is very difficult for these domestic accounting firms to perform their accounting and auditing duties independently, as they are under the influence of the 'hooked' organization. Some of the clients of these accounting firms are themselves directly or indirectly related to the 'hooked' organization because of complex ownership and control arrangements. Lacking independence, the firms often provide poor accounting and auditing services. This is partly because the 'hooked' organization frequently presses its affiliated accounting firms to employ retired or unqualified accountants who used to work in the organization, and partly because its affiliated accounting firms can hardly conduct unbiased accounting and auditing for clients that have close connections with the 'hooked' organization. As a result, fraud and other types of malpractice have become a serious issue in Chinese companies, including those listed on the stock exchanges. In the meantime, TNCs are in a disadvantageous position in seeking accounting and auditing services from these Chinese accounting firms, as normally they do not have any connections with the 'hooked' organization.

The second problem is corruption. As is widely acknowledged, corruption increased in China after the reform programme started, and has become widespread in recent years. Corrupt government officials who use public office for personal gain are now found in the Chinese government at all levels and in all deparments, including those that administer state-owned enterprises or government-run institutions. Bribery and embezzlement have become a customary way of doing business not only for the government but also for companies. There are numerous reports of cases of bribery and embezzlement involving high-ranking government officials or top corporate executives in the Chinese media these days. In most cases the corruption involves monetary transactions, and is assisted by personnel in the company's accounting department and in the accounting firms. The aforementioned 'hooking up' problem increases the chances that accountants will also be implicated in this corruption.

In a sense, the prevalence of *guanxi* contributes to the large-scale corruption in China. As analysed in chapter 3, *guanxi* consists of interpersonal relationships and connections that the Chinese use for the exchange of favours in personal or business transactions. Under its influence, *guanxi*-related considerations often outweigh ethics-related considerations in accounting and auditing practice. Accountants and financial managers sometimes, for instance, have to use *guanxi* to do business with business partners or government officials in a way that is in violation of their professional ethics. As Majidul Islam and Maureen Gowing (2003, p. 358) point out, 'When faced with the choice of complying with a code of ethics, or maintaining the important *guanxi* relationship and expediting business transactions, accountants and managers may opt for the latter course.' Many corruption cases, including those involved TNCs, would not have occurred if there were no *guanxi*-based business practice and therefore no need to promote sales through personal networks.

The problem of corruption and the involvement of accountants in corruption became so alarming that, in 2004, the Chinese government launched a nationwide 'Auditing Storm' campaign to check up on accounting misconduct in government agencies, institutions and enterprises. The Auditor General of the central government, Li Jinhua, was assigned to lead the campaign. According to the auditing report that he submitted to the National Congress, serious fraud and embezzlement of public funds were found in many government agencies and government-funded projects, and a staggering level of malpractice was found in the related accounting practices. Because of the excellent work he performed, Li Jinhua won the prize of Economic Figure of the Year in 2004.

Transnational corporations are not immune from the corrupted institutional environment in China. As corruption has become a routine way of doing business in China, some foreign affiliates in China try to achieve their business objectives through bribery or kickbacks. In the case of US-based Diagnostic Products Corporation discussed in Chapter 3, the bribery was apparently assisted by personnel in the accounting department of the affiliate

companies is still virtually impossible. TNCs need to think about how to make use of China's securities market in this context of this restrictive regime.

The Chinese accounting system has, essentially, been brought into line with international accounting and auditing standards, but it is still incumbent on TNCs to appraise themselves of the remaining differences between Chinese accounting practices and those in other parts of the world. More importantly, they need to pay attention to the problems in the institutional environment in which accounting is practised in China, including 'hooking up' and large-scale corruption, to avoid the possibility of becoming prey to persistent difficulties, or even criminal charges.

FURTHER READING

Dai, X., Lau, A. H., and Yang, J. 2000. 'Hooking-up: a unique feature of China public accounting firms'. *Managerial Finance* 26 (5): 21–30.

Fay, A. M., Zhang, H. K., and Roose, E. N. 2005. 'The tax cost of M&A'. *China Business Review* 32 (4): 50–3.

Gentle, C. 2005. 'China: keeping pace with the times'. *Journal of Risk Finance* 6 (1): 69–70.

Lo, V., and Tian, X. 2005. *Law and Investment in China: The Legal and Business Environments after the WTO Accession.* London: Routledge.

Questions for discussion

1. How does the Chinese taxation system, particularly the taxation applicable to foreign affiliates, differ from that in other parts of the world in general, and that in your home country in particular?
2. What do you learn about managing corporate finance in China from the cases of cash management and profit repatriation illustrated in this chapter?
3. How open is China's securities market to TNCs? In what ways can TNCs make use of the securities market in corporate financing and other business activities?
4. To what extent have Chinese accounting practices been brought into line with international accounting standards? Comment on the problems in the institutional environment surrounding accounting in China, and discuss how TNCs should deal with them.

NOTES

1. Taxes accounted for less than a half of the Chinese government's revenue in the pre-reform period.
2. In legal documents, this is officially called 'income tax on enterprises with foreign investment and foreign enterprises'.

3. It has still not been decided how the social security tax will be levied and shared.
4. See Cheung (2004) for a discussion of the options available.
5. See the next section for the details.
6. For the regulations and rules governing the QFII scheme, see the Provisional Rules on Administration of Domestic Securities Investment by Qualified Foreign Institutional Investors, issued by the CSRC and the PBOC on 5 November 2002.
7. The forty foreign financial institutions are Union Bank of Switzerland (UBS), Nomura Securities, Citigroup Global Markets, Morgan Stanley International, Goldman Sachs, HSBC, Deutsche Bank, ING Bank, JP Morgan Chase Bank, Credit Suisse First Boston (Hong Kong), Nikko Asset Management, Standard Chartered Bank Hong Kong, Hang Jeng Bank, Daiwa Securities SMBC, Merrill Lynch International, Lehman Brothers International (Europe), Bill & Melinda Gates Foundation, ABN AMRO Bank, Société Générate, Barelays Bank, BNP Paribas, Dresdner Bank, Fortis Bank, Power Corporation of Canada, CALYON, INVESCO Asset Management, Government of Singapore Investment Corporation, Goldman Sachs Asset Management International, Martin Currie Investment Management, Temasek Fullerton Alpha, AIG Global Investment, Dai-Ichi Mutual Life Insurance, DBS Bank, JF Asset Management, KBC Financial Products UK, Bank of Nova Scotia, La Compagnie Financière Edmond de Rothschild Banque, Yale University, AMP Capital Investors and Morgan Stanley Investment Management.
8. Agence France Presse, 11 April 2004.

References

Agarwal, S., and Ramaswami, S. N. 1992. 'Choice of foreign market entry mode: impact of ownership, location, and internalization factors'. *Journal of International Business Studies* 23: 1–27.

Ahlstrom, D., Bruton, G. D., and Chan, E. S. 2001. 'HRM of foreign firms in China: the challenge of managing host country personnel'. *Business Horizon* 44 (3): 59–68.

Alon, I. 2001. 'Interview: international franchising in China with Kodak'. *Thunderbird International Business Review* 43 (6): 737–54.

Anonymous. 2002. 'Nationwide checks set on intellectual property rights'. *China Daily* 27 April: 2.

　2005. 'Made in China'. *Technology Review* 108 (4): 24.

Arias, J. T. G. 1998. 'A relationship marketing approach to Guanxi'. *European Journal of Marketing* 32: 145–58.

Berlew, D. E. 1974. 'Leadership and organizational excitement'. *California Management Review* 17: 21–30.

Black, J. S., Mendenhall, M., and Oddov, G. 1991. 'Towards a comprehensive model of international adjustment'. *Academy of Management Review* 16 (2): 291–317.

Bransfild, S., and Schlueter, D. 2004. 'When joint ventures go bad'. *China Business Review* 31 (5): 24–8.

Bruton, G. D., Ahlstrom, D., and Chan, E. S. 2000. 'Foreign firms in China: facing human resources challenges in a transitional economy.' *S. A. M. Advanced Management Journal* 65 (4): 4–36.

Buckley, P. J., and Casson, M. C. 1998. 'Analyzing foreign market entry strategies: extending the internalization approach'. *Journal of International Business Studies* 29 (3): 539–62.

Buckley, P. J., Clegg, J., and Wang, C. 2002. 'The impact of inward FDI on the performance of Chinese manufacturing firms'. *Journal of International Business Studies* 33: 637–55.

Business Software Alliance. 2003. *Eighth Annual BSA Global Software Piracy Study. Trends in Software Piracy 1994–2002.* Available online at http//www.bsa.org/uk/search-results.cfm.

Caudron, S. 1991. 'Training ensures overseas success'. *Personnel Journal* December: 27–30.

Chan, R. Y. K., Cheng, L. T. W., and Szeto, R. W. F. 2002. 'The dynamics of *Guanxi* and ethics for Chinese executives'. *Journal of Business Ethics* 41 (4): 327–36.

Chen, M. 2004. 'Common culture, different styles'. *China Business Review* 31 (5): 53–8.

Chen, R. 2003. 'Price wars.' *China Business Review* 30 (5): 42–6.

Cheung, S. 2004. 'Cash management for foreign investors'. *China Business Review* 31 (2): 34–7.

Child, J., and Yan, Y. 2001. 'Investment and control in international joint ventures: the case of China'. In J. T. Li and P. N. Ghauri (eds.), *Managing International Business Ventures in China*. Amsterdam: Pergamon, 17–30.

Chu, W., and Anderson, E. 1992. 'Capturing ordinal properties of categorical dependent variables: a review with application to modes of foreign entry'. *International Journal of Research in Marketing* 9: 149–60.

Clark, D. 2000. 'IP rights protection will improve in China eventually'. *China Business Review* 27 (3): 30–4.

2004. 'Intellectual property litigation in China'. *China Business Review* 31 (6): 25–9.

Clarke, R. 1993. *Fundamentals of Negotiation*. Available online at http://www.anu.edu.au/people/Roger.Clarke/SOS/FundasNeg.html.

Clifford, M. L. 2003. 'Banking's Great Wall'. *Business Week*, 23 May.

Dai, X., Lau, A. H., and Yang, J. 2000. 'Hooking-up: A unique feature of China public accounting firms'. *Managerial Finance* 26 (5): 21–30.

Donaldson, T., and Dunfee, T. W., 1999. *Ties that Bind: A Social Contracts Approach to Business Ethics*. Cambridge, MA: Harvard Business School Press.

Dunfee, T. W., and Warren, D. E. 2001. 'Is *guanxi* ethical? A normative analysis of doing business in China'. *Journal of Business Ethics* 32 (3): 191–204.

Dunning, J. 1988. *Explaining International Production*. London: Unwin Hyman.

1993. *Multinational Enterprises and the Global Economy*. Boston: Addison-Wesley.

Economist Intelligence Unit. 2003. 'China industry: Kodak's new deal secures top market position'. *EIU Views Wire*, 12 November.

Fan, Y. 2002. '*Guanxi's* consequences: personal gains at social cost'. *Journal of Business Ethics* 38 (4): 371–80.

Fang, T. 1999. *Chinese Negotiating Style*. London: Sage.

2005. 'Chinese business style in three regions: an exploratory study of Beijing, Shanghai and Guangzhou'. In D. Brown and A. MacBean (eds.), *Challenges for China's Development*. London: Routledge, chap. 11.

Fay, A. M., Zhang, H. K., and Roose, E. N. 2005. 'The Tax Cost of M&A'. *China Business Review* 32 (4): 50–3.

Fisher, R., and Ury, W. 1981. *Getting to Yes*. London: Hutchinson.

Flagg, M. 2001. 'Coca-Cola adopts local-dinks strategy in asia'. *Wall Street Journal*, 30 July: 1.

Folta, P. H. 2005. 'Cooperative joint ventures: savvy foreign investors may wish to consider the benefits of this flexible investment structure'. *China Business Review* 32 (1): 18–23.

Gamble, J. 2000. 'Localizing management in foreign invested enterprises in China: practical, cultural, and strategic perspectives'. *International Journal of Human Resource Management* 11 (5): 883–903.

Gelb, C. 1997. 'Spicing up the Chinese market'. *China Business Review* 24 (4): 25–9.

2003. 'Investment pioneer: the first US–Chinese high-technology joint venture is alive and well'. *China Business Review* 30 (2): 70–4.

Gentle, C. 2005. 'China: keeping pace with the times'. *Journal of Risk Finance* 6 (1): 69–70.

Graham, J. L. 1986. 'The problem-solving approach to negotiations in industrial marketing.' *Journal of Business Research* 14 (6): 549–66.

1996. 'Vis-à-vis international business negotiations'. In P. N. Ghauri and J. C. Usunier (eds.), *International Business Negotiations*. Oxford: Pergamon, 69–90.

Graham, J. L., and Lam, N. M. 2003. 'The Chinese negotiation'. *Harvard Business Review* 81 (10): 82–91.

Hackley, C. A., and Dong, Q. W. 2001. 'American public relations networking encounters China's *Guanxi*'. *Public Relations Quarterly* 46 (2): 16–19.

Harvey, M. G. 1983. 'The multinational corporation's expatriate problem: an application of Murphy's Law'. *Business Horizon* 26 (1): 71–8.

Harwit, E. 1997. 'Guangzhou Peugeot: portrait of a commercial divorce'. *China Business Review* 24 (6): 10–11.

Hendon, D. W., Hendon, R. A., and Herbig, P. 1996. *Cross-Cultural Business Negotiations.* Westport, CT: Quorum.

Hill, C. W. L. 2003. *Global Business.* London: McGraw-Hill.

Hofstede, G. 1991. *Culture and Organizations: Software of the Mind.* London: McGraw-Hill.

Hofstede, G., and Usunier, J. C. 1996. 'Hofstede's dimensions of culture and their influence on international business negotiations'. In P. N. Ghauri and J. C. Usunier (eds.), *International Business Negotiations.* Oxford: Pergamon, 119–29.

Huang, G. T. 2004. 'The world's hottest computer lab'. *Technology Review* 107 (5): 32–42.

Huffman, T. P. 2003. 'The supply chain: Wal-Mart in China: challenges facing a foreign retailer's supply chain'. *China Business Review* 30 (5): 18–22.

Hulme, V. A. 2000. 'Seagram juices up the Three Gorges'. *China Business Review* 27 (5): 16–22.

2001. 'Mary Kay in China: more than makeup'. *China Business Review* 28 (1): 42–6.

IACC. 2005. *Submission of the International AntiCounterfeiting Coalition, Inc. to the United States Trade Representative: Special 301 Recommendations.* Washington, DC: International AntiCounterfeiting Coalition. Available online at http://www.iacc.org/resources/2005_USTR_Special_301.pdf.

Iklé, F. C. 1968. *How Nations Negotiate.* New York: Praeger.

Islam, M., and Gowing, M. 2003. 'Some empirical evidence of Chinese accounting system and business management practices from an ethical perspective'. *Journal of Business Ethics* 42 (4): 353–78.

Jagersma, P. K. 2002. 'Upfront best practice: building successful China alliances'. *Business Strategy Review* 13 (4): 3–6.

Krajewski, L. J., and Ritzman, L. P. 2002. *Operations Management: Strategy and Analysis.* New York: Prentice-Hall.

Kumar, V., and Subramaniam, V. 1997. 'A contingency framework for the mode of entry decision'. *Journal of World Business* 32 (1): 53–72.

Kynge, J. 2003. 'Beijing urged to act more firmly against intellectual property theft'. *Financial Times* 13 September: 9.

Lasserre, P. 2003. *Global Strategic Management.* New York: Palgrave Macmillan, chap. 4.

Leininger, J. 2004. 'The key to retention: committed employees'. *China Business Review* 31 (1): 16–39.

Levitt, T. 1983. 'The globalization of markets'. *Harvard Business Review* 61 (3): 92–102.

Li, J. T., Xin, K. R., Tsui, A., and Hambrick, D. C. 2001. 'Building effective international joint venture leadership teams in China'. In J. T. Li and P. N. Ghauri (eds.), *Managing International Business Ventures in China.* Amsterdam: Pergamon, 31–49.

Li, X., Liu, X., and Parker, D. 2001. 'Foreign direct investment and productivity spillovers in the Chinese manufacturing sector'. *Economic Systems* 25: 305–21.

Li, P. 2000. 'A foreign success story in China'. *China Economic Weekly* 16 June: 2.

Lin, X., and Germain, R. 1998. 'Sustaining satisfactory joint venture relationships: the role of conflict resolution strategy'. *Journal of International Business Studies* 29 (1): 179–96.

Liu, A., Li, S., and Gao, Y. 1999. 'Location, location, location'. *China Business Review* 26 (2): 20–5.

Liu, L. 2000. 'P&G launches massive war against counterfeiting in China'. *China Economic Weekly* 10 November: 3–6.

Liu, X., Parker, D., Vaidya, K., and Wei, Y. 2001. 'The impact of foreign direct investment on labour productivity in the Chinese electronics industry'. *International Business Review* 10: 421–39.

Lo, V., and Tian, X. 2005. *Law and Investment in China: The Legal and Business Environments after the WTO Accession*. London: Routledge.

Lovett, S., Simmons, L. C., and Kali, R. 1999. 'Guanxi versus the market: ethics and efficiency'. *Journal of International Business Studies* 30 (2): 231–47.

Luo, Y. D. 2000. *Guanxi and Business*. Singapore: World Scientific Publishing.

2001. 'Joint venture success in China: how should we select a good partner?' In J. T. Li and P. N. Ghauri (eds.), *Managing International Business Ventures in China*. Amsterdam: Pergamon, 108–30.

Lynch, David J. 2005. 'China closes market for pirated goods'. *USA Today*, 11 January.

Mansfield, E. 1981. 'How economists see R&D'. *Harvard Business Review* 59 (6): 98–106.

Maruyama, W. H. 1999. 'US–China IPR negotiations: trade, intellectual property, and the rule of law in a global economy'. In M. A. Cohen, A. E. Bang and S. J. Mitchell (eds.), *Chinese Intellectual Property Law and Practice*. London: Kluwer Law International, 45–66.

Maskus, K. E. 2002. *Intellectual Property Rights in the WTO Accession Package: Assessing China's Reforms*. Washington, DC: World Bank.

McCall, J. B., and Warrington, M. B. 1984: *Marketing by Agreement: A Cross-Cultural Approach to Business Negotiations*. Chichester: Wiley.

McComb, R. 1999. '2009: China's human resources odyssey'. *China Business Review* 26 (5): 30–3.

Melvin, S. 2000. 'Human resources take center stage'. *China Business Review* 27 (6): 38–49.

2001. 'Retaining Chinese employees'. *China Business Review* 28 (6): 30–6.

Melvin, S., and Sylvester, K. 1997. 'Shipping out'. *China Business Review* 24 (3): 30–4.

Mendenhall, M., and Oddov, G. 1985. 'The dimensions of expatriate acculturation: a review'. *Academy of Management Review* 10 (1): 39–47.

Miles, M. 2003. 'Negotiating with the Chinese: lessons from the field'. *Journal of Applied Behavioral Science* 39 (4): 452–72.

Miller, P. M. 2005. 'Super 8 in China: the US economy hotel chain offers China travelers a new lodging option'. *China Business Review* 32 (2): 24–44.

Ministry of Foreign Trade and Economic Co-operation. Various issues. *Almanac of China's Foreign Economic Relations and Trade*. Beijing: China's Prospect Publishing.

Moga, T. T. 2002. 'The TRIPS agreement and China'. *China Business Review* 29 (6): 12–17.

Monks, R. A. G., and Minow, N. 2001. *Corporate Governance*, 2nd edn. Oxford: Blackwell.

2004. *Corporate Governance*, 3rd edn. Oxford: Blackwell.

Morris, M., Williams, K. Y., Leung, K., Larrich, K. Mendoza, R., Bhatnagar, T., Li, D., Kondo, J., Luo, M., and Hu, J. 1998, 'Conflict management style: accounting for cross-national difference'. *Journal of International Business Studies* 29: 729–47.

Mun, K. C. 1990. 'The competition model of Sun Tzu's Art of War'. In H. Kuang (ed.), *Modern Marketing Management Encyclopedia*. Beijing: Economics and Management Press [in Chinese], 930–5.

Nalebuff, B. J., and Brandenburger, A. M. 1996. *Co-Opetition*. London: HarperCollins.

National Bureau of Statistics of China. Various issues. *China Statistical Yearbook*. Beijing: China Statistics Press.

Pan, Y., and Tse, D. K. 2000. 'The hierarchical model of market entry modes'. *Journal of International Business Studies* 31 (4): 535–54.

Park, S. H., and Luo, Y. D. 2001. '*Guanxi* and organizational dynamics: organizational networking in Chinese firms'. *Strategic Management Journal* 22 (5): 455–70.

Peerenboom, R. 2002. *China's Long March toward Rule of Law*. Cambridge: Cambridge University Press.

Peng, M. W. 2000. 'Controlling the foreign agent: how governments deal with multinationals in a transition economy'. *Management International Review* 40 (2): 141–65.

Pereira, A. A. 2004. 'The Suzhou Industrial Park experiment: the case of China–Singapore governmental collaboration'. *Journal of Contemporary China* 13 (38): 173–93.

Pfeffer, J., and Salancik, G. R. 1978. *The External Control of Organizations: A Resource Dependence Perspective*. New York: Harper and Row.

Pye, L. 1992. *Chinese Negotiating Style: Commercial Approaches and Cultural Principles*. New York: Quorum.

Raiffa, H. 1982. *The Art and Science of Negotiation*. Cambridge, MA: Harvard University Press.

Sanyal, R. N., and Guvenli, T. 2001. 'American firms in China: issues in managing operations'. *Multinational Business Review* 9 (2): 40–6.

Scarry, J. 1997. 'Making the consumer connection'. *China Business Review* 24 (4): 40–4.

Seligman, S. D. 1999. '*Guanxi*: grease for the wheels of China'. *China Business Review* 26 (5): 34–8.

Shay, J., and Bruce, T. 1997. 'Expatriate managers'. *Cornell Hotel and Restaurant Administration Quarterly* 38 (1). 30–5.

Shen, J., and Edwards, V. 2004. 'Recruitment and selection in Chinese MNEs'. *International Journal of Human Resource Management* 15 (5): 814–35.

Shi, Y. 2003. 'Trademark infringement and unfair competition case study: Toyota Motors vs. Zhejiang Geely'. *China Law and Practice* 3: 12–21.

Siebe, W. 1991. 'Game theory'. In V. A. Kremenyuk (ed.), *International Negotiation: Analysis, Approaches, Issues*. San Francisco: Jossey-Bass, 180–202.

Simons, C. 2003. 'Marketers woo China's real masses'. *Wall Street Journal* (Eastern edition), 29 August: 6.

2005. 'Faking it'. *South China Morning Post*, 10 January.

Song, X. 2000. 'McKinsey: hard to find good projects'. *China Economic Weekly* 4 August: 3–4.

Stiglitz, J. E. 2002. *Globalization and its Discontent*. London: Allen Lane.

Su, C. T., and Littlefield, J. E. 2001. 'Entering *Guanxi*: a business ethical dilemma in mainland China?'. *Journal of Business Ethics* 33 (3): 199–210.

Tang, J. 2005. *Managers and Mandarins in Contemporary China: The Building of an International Business Alliance*. London and New York: Routledge.

Tang, Q. 2003. 'Relationship mapping'. *China Business Review* 30 (4): 28–30.

Tian, X. 1996. 'China's open door policy in development perspective'. *Canadian Journal of Development Studies* 17 (1): 75–95.

1998. *Dynamics of Development in an Opening Economy: China since 1978*. New York: Nova Sciences.

Tian, X, Lin, S., and Lo, V. 2004. 'Foreign direct investment and economic performance in transition economies: evidence from Chinese provinces'. *Post-Communist Economies* 16 (4): 497–510.

Trainer, T. P. 2002. 'The fight against trademark counterfeiting'. *China Business Review* 29 (6): 27–31.

Tsang, E. W. K. 1998. 'Can *guanxi* be a source of sustained competitive advantage for doing business in China?'. *Academy of Management Executive* 12 (2): 64–74.

Tsui, A., and Farh, J. L. 1997. 'Where *Guanxi* matters: relational demography and *Guanxi* in the Chinese context'. *Work and Occupation* 24: 56–79.

Tung, R. L. 1982. 'Selection and training procedures of US, European, and Japanese multinationals'. *California Management Review* 25 (1): 57–71.

UNCTAD. 2005. *World Investment Report 2004*. New York: United Nations.

United States Trade Representative. 2003. *2003 Special 301 Report*. Washington, DC: Office of the United States Trade Representative.

2004. *2004 Special 301 Report*. Washington, DC: Office of the United States Trade Representative.

2005. *2005 Special 301 Report*. Washington, DC: Office of the United States Trade Representative.

Usunier, J. C. 1996. 'Cultural aspects of international business negotiations'. In P. N. Ghauri and J. C. Usunier (eds.), *International Business Negotiations*. Oxford: Pergamon, 93–108.

Von Clausewitz, C. 1984. *On War*. Princeton, NJ: Princeton University Press.

Von Zedtwitz, M. 2004. 'Managing foreign R&D laboratories in China'. *R&D Management* 34 (4): 439–52.

Walfish, D. 2001. 'P&G China lab has global role'. *Research Technology Management* 44 (5): 4–5.

Wall, J. A. 1990. 'Managers in the People's Republic of China'. *Academy of Management Executive* 4 (2): 19–32.

Wang, C., Lin, X., Chan, A., and Shi, Y. 2005. 'Conflict handling styles in international joint venture: a cross-cultural and cross-national comparison'. *Management International Review* 45 (1): 3–21.

Wang J. 2001. 'Wal-Mart's China march'. *China Economic Weekly* 6 April.

Weeks, A. M. 2000. 'IPR protection and enforcement: a guide'. *China Business Review* 27 (6): 28–32.

Weisert, D. 2001. 'Coca-Cola in China: quenching the thirst of a billion'. *China Business Review* 28 (4): 52–5.

Weiss, S. E. 1994a. 'Negotiating with the Romans – part 1'. *MIT Sloan Management Review* 35 (2): 51–61.

1994b. 'Negotiating with the Romans – part 2'. *MIT Sloan Management Review* 35 (3): 85–99.

Wheeler, E. L. 1988. *Stratagem and the Vocabulary of Military Trickery*. Leiden: E. J. Brill.

Williamson, P., and Zeng, M. 2004. 'Strategies for competing in a changed China'. *MIT Sloan Management Review* 45 (4): 85–91.

Woodard, K., and Wang, A. Q. 2005. 'Acquisitions in China: closing the deal'. *China Business Review* 32 (1): 13–17.

World Bank. 1997. World Development Report 1996: From Plan to Market. Washington, DC: World Bank.

Wu, A. 2003. 'Fashion house makes it 23 years in China'. *China Monthly Economic Review* 30 October.

Xin, K. R., and Pearce, J. L. 1996. '*Guanxi*: connections as substitutes for formal institutional support'. *Academy Management Journal* 39: 1641–58.

Yang, M. 1988. 'The gift economy and state power in China'. *Comparative Studies of Social History* 31: 25–54.

Yeung, I. Y., and Tung, R. L. 1996. 'Achieving business success in Confucian societies: the importance of *guanxi* (connections)'. *Organisational Dynamics* 25 (2): 54–65.

Yong, H. 2001. 'Carrefour faces restructuring order in China'. *China Economic Weekly* 16 March.

Index